# The Politics of Time

Henry J. Rutz, Editor

American Ethnological Society Monograph Series, Number 4
Donald L. Donham, Series Editor

**Library of Congress Cataloging-in-Publication Data**
The Politics of time / Henry J. Rutz, editor.
     p.     cm. — (American Ethnological Society monograph series ; no. 4)
    Includes bibliographical references.
    ISBN 0-913167-49-5
    1. Political anthropology.   2. Time—Social aspects.   I. Rutz, Henry
J.  II. Series.
GN492.2.P65    1992
306.2—dc20                                    92-5933
                                                       CIP

Copies may be ordered from:

American Anthropological Association
1703 New Hampshire Avenue, N.W.
Washington, D.C. 20009

# Contents

# Introduction

# 1

# The Idea of a Politics of Time

HENRY J. RUTZ

The unifying idea of this collection[1] is that time is an object of power relations. Contributors are concerned with different forms of objectification and, more especially, with contests of power that shape time as both concept and resource. There now exists a substantial literature on the anthropology of time.[2] Most of it, however, focuses on time concepts in disparate cultures or, alternatively, on the measurement of time. The emphasis has been on asking questions about what time is, how it is reckoned, or what standard is used to measure it. This collection, in contrast, emphasizes the multiplicity of times within single social formations, the potential for social conflict that arises from competing times, and the struggle or resistance that ensues when one group attempts to dominate the time of another in the interest of power.

With varying emphases, the recurrent theme of these essays is how control of time is *necessary* to the exercise of power. Paradoxically, however, the argument for necessity rests neither on the view that time is a universal coordinate of belief and action nor on the extreme view that time is purely a subjective phenomenon of individual experience.[2] These essays adopt the view, first, that there are different times according to particular cultural constructions placed upon a substratum of duration and sequence and, second, that the shape of time is forged in contests of social power. We can assert with confidence that power necessarily is "interested" in controlling time, but the relationship between power and time is contingent upon particular cultural and historical conditions. This collection is about contingent relations of power and time.

Contributors first encountered the problem that time poses for power in concrete fieldwork situations. Connections among the multiplicity of times encountered, their diverse objectifications, and the

constitution of power are made first in the compelling facts of ethnography.[4] Some of the essays concern fast-moving events or recent dramatic changes in different regions of the world. Contributors collectively discover the social reality of power among "the homeless" in
New York City, the struggles of immigrant Puerto Ricans with U.S.
federal and state agencies, the imminent failure of socialism in Romania, the fragile political conditions of the state of Israel, the political
crisis of resurgent cultural nationalism in Fiji, and the integration of
villages into regional bureaucracies as a result of the green revolution
in Sulawesi.

Diverse theoretical perspectives follow from, and are to be understood in terms of, the immediacy of the contributors' own experience
in societies where the reconstruction of time and the reconstitution of
power have become the temporal and political markers of the present.
A common thread that runs throughout the apparent diversity is a
shared belief that the study of time provides insights into understanding the exercise of power in social life. There should be little surprise,
then, that this collection largely eschews a general and abstract theory
of a politics of time in favor of a shared contextualized and relativized
exploration of the topic. The values of such studies, however, to the
comparative study of capitalist development, class formation, nationalism, ethnicity, and the encompassing tendency of bureaucracies is
apparent.

The remainder of this introductory essay paints with a broad
brush a collective political and temporal landscape that forms a backdrop to the crafted analyses found in specific essays. I look briefly at
the importance of a multiplicity of times before discussing a variety of
forms in which time can appear as an object of power. I conclude with
a discussion of political processes of appropriation, institutionalization, and legitimation that frame relations of time and power in this
collection.

## A Multiplicity of Times[5]

The key to a politics of *time* is the theorem that time is a social and
cultural construct. Two propositions follow from the view that time is
integral to the constitution of society and the social construction of
reality. The first is that *different* cultures construct different times. The
second is the probability that disparate times coexist in the *same* social
formation. Anthropologists have documented the relativity of concepts of time in different cultures, but they have been less assiduous
about observing a plurality of times within the same social formation.

From the perspective of this collection, there has been a failure to take the next step, which is to recognize that there is a plurality of cultural constructions in every society, and that "time belongs to the political economy of relations between individuals, classes, and nations" (Fabian 1983:x).

In this collection, the political economy of relations is a departure point for understanding the shape of time. Two different examples will illustrate the point. Verdery, in her essay, describes the seizure of daily routines or the uses of time that were the overriding interest of Ceausescu's centralized state. Reflecting these conditions, Verdery takes as given the centrality of labor time and its durative aspect as the shape of time in Romania. Paine, in contrast, finds that the legitimation of the state is the central issue of Israeli ideological debate, at the heart of which are competing "ontologies of time" that focus and limit the dialogue. For Paine, time is a text by which to read Israeli politics.

A problem related to that of a plurality of copresent times shaped by relations of power and inequality is that cultural concepts of time were presented as made of whole cloth from unchanging, or slowly changing, jural and normative codes that shaped the life of their adherents. One of the salutary developments in recent anthropological thought is the opening up of the culture concept to include interests and intentions in the invention of culture and tradition. Culture is commonly problematized, either as a text that requires interpretation or as practices that require reproduction. Agents and agencies are now in the foreground of cultural analysis. All of this renders more probable a politics of time in which agents place particular constructions on time, and time becomes objectified in "interested" and "intentional" ways. To illustrate, Urciuoli focuses on linguistic acts, specifically conversations between welfare agents and their female clients, to construct opposed notions of time in situations of structured inequality of power. In contrast, Bowen analyzes the problems of timing agricultural decisions when village calendars based on political cosmology are co-opted by a regional bureaucracy in whose hands the calendar is remade into a synoptic illusion (cf. Bourdieu 1977:97–108).

These essays collectively embrace the idea that time is neither objectively given as "real" time nor subjectively inaccessible to others as "lived" time, but rather is constructed as cultural object and internalized as a part of self. Most of the discussion of time in these essays is about such interstitial temporal phenomena as "timing" (Bowen), "now" as opposed to "later" (Rotenberg), "waiting" (Verdery and Gounis), "rest" (Rutz and Balkan), "seizing the moment," and other temporal notions that reflect particular constructions placed on duration and sequence in concrete relations of power and inequality. Eschewing worn-out temporal dualisms such as real vs. lived, linear vs. cyclical, abstract vs. concrete, or symbolic vs. material, these essays begin with the phenomenal reality of relations of power in their historical and cultural context and proceed to explore competing "interests" in a multiplicity of times.

## The Objectification of Time

If time is to be an object of power, then ideas about time and its significance must be objectified. I will refer to objectifications as technologies of time. From the perspective of a politics of time, clocks, calendars, schedules, normative codes (with notions such as "when," "how long," "before and after," etc.) and communicative acts are some of the ways in which the conceptualization and significance of time become objectified and thus accessible to control through relations of power.

The calendar is a technology of time that has proven to be among the most effective instruments for exercising power. To the Chinese, it was a heavenly clockwork that linked earth to sky and divine emperor to his people (Landes 1983:17–37). In the ancient Near East, kings and priesthoods challenged each other for control of empires using their respective calendars as instruments of power (Innis 1972). In a similar vein, the great religious communities of Judaism, Christianity, and Islam waged what Zerubavel (1985:27–43) refers to as the "seven day wars" over the temporal location of a sabbath day. In modern times, the secular and rational goals of the nation-state were advanced by particular technologies of time. The French revolution was followed by a thorough antimonarchical and anticlerical reform of the calendar. The same was true for the materialist production goals of the Russian revolution and the subsequent Soviet reform of the calendar to include more work days (Zerubavel 1981:82–95; 1985:28–43). Kabyle peasants have found that power has slipped from their hands into those of the Algerian government as oral practices surrounding the use of almanacs have been codified into a literate calendar (Bourdieu 1977:104). In this collection, Bowen analyzes the effective exercise of power by a regional development bureaucracy that must control the timing of agricultural decisions by means of co-opting and transforming village calendars. Rutz and Balkan describe the origins of Fijian time-discipline in the Methodist calendar and its significance for Fijian nationalism.

Historically, the calendar is an effective instrument of power in large-scale organizations that maintain continuity over relatively long periods, such as empires, religious communities and nations. In his essay, Rotenberg argues that most premodern calendars were temporal instruments controlled by tributary power and reflected elite ideologies of political cosmology. The modern secular calendar, of course, is a temporal instrument of the nation-state.[6]

If calendars are the instruments of temporal control of large populations on the scale of global societies, schedules are the weapons of temporal control within bureaucracies and formal organizations of all kinds. Schedules, by virtue of their routinization of short durations through endless repetitions (by the day or week), confine activity by delimiting goals. As instruments of ostensible efficiency at the level of the organization, schedules are implicated in power relations by virtue of the fact that some agent must construct and implement them, appropriating both the time of others and other times in the process. Schedules, it would appear, are major instruments deployed in the power to discipline and are instrumental in the power of surveillance.[7] Gounis's essay explores in depth the schedule as an instrument of administrative power in what he refers to as the "domestication" of homeless men living in shelters in New York City.

The time hidden in normative codes is more elusive than the rationalized and codified temporal relations of formal organizations, but for that very reason implicit and consensual codes are some of the most effective instruments of temporal control in relations of power. In Fijian villages of the interior, where calendars, clocks, and schedules have been known for a century, daily practices follow rhythms embedded in notions of kin reciprocity and social rank (Rutz 1984). Time is less a quantity than a quality, and less an attribute of the individual than of the group. Time is used "appropriately," not efficiently, and one's time is the property of others, not one's own, to be appropriated in the projects of others rather than allocated efficiently from the standpoint of a possessive individual. The more one shares time with others by sitting, talking, and drinking *kava*, the greater the mutual respect and love. One must be "released" by others from the temporal bonds that bring people together and hold them. The more unequal the social ranks of those gathered, the more deliberate the pace and tempo of the gathering, as if time were a measure of differential power.[8] In this collection, Urciuoli is particularly sensitive to some of the hidden temporal instruments of power and discovers them in the polysemism of communicative acts. Verdery achieves a similar result by means of a very different approach. At the outset, she reveals the temporal instruments of state power and then uses a whole variety of examples to show how the relentless control of time robs persons of cultural identity, social esteem, and a sense of self.

Societies exist in time, but in what time they exist is contested ground. Surely there is nothing new in this observation, as Pocock (1973) made clear in his general account of political strategies for depicting and controlling "tradition" from the standpoint of power relations in the present. Nevertheless, the construction of the "past" as a political problem has been taken up more recently by Appadurai (1981) and in this collection by Paine. Perhaps there is no society in which the legitimacy of the state rests more on the "inherent debatability of the past" than Israel. The objectification of the "past" in text and oral discourse links time to political ideology and both to the future of the state of Israel.

There remains the task of placing a multiplicity of times and their objectifications in the context of the organizations in which the control of time becomes institutionalized. A politics of time must take cognizance of the fact that relations of power that shape time are themselves shaped by different organizations.

In the course of discussing different social times and their technologies it was impossible to avoid introducing into the discussion the organizations in which power is exercised. Fernand Braudel (1958), for example, speaks of the long *duree,* a world-time that dominates a world system in which the central rhythms have to do with a shifting core and periphery. Anderson (1983) and Innis (1951) suspect that the characteristic time of modern nations is a notion of simultaneity that underpins a particular kind of imagined community to which there corresponds a present-mindedness (if not short-sightedness) in the conduct of affairs. Gurvitch (1963) assigns specific gradations of time to different levels of hierarchy in social structure. There exists a multiplicity of times *because* they are organized by and within a variety of social collectivities. The social time of one organized collectivity upsets the time of another, with the result that there arises a potential clash between social times and a struggle for domination. In the view of Innis (1972) and Bourdieu (1977), calendars are instruments of political hierarchization and centralization. Whatever the different times they represent and measure, calendars reflect the demands of political elites on the widest body politic—for example, empires, states, and other global societies such as religious communities. In contrast, Zerubavel (1979; 1981) treats the schedule as the dominant technology of time in mass democratic societies, where the varieties of lived time are shaped by administrative power in formal organizations.

In sum, the task of contributors to this volume is twofold: to show how and to what extent organizations realize their potential for exercising relations of power by means of the control of time while remaining mindful that few organizations succeed in encompassing the total duration and sequence of members' social practices, giving rise to conflict and contradiction over the need to control time in order to exercise power.

## Time and Power in Social Life

A *politics* of time is concerned with the *appropriation* of the time of others, the *institutionalization* of a dominant time, and the *legitimation* of power by means of the control of time. And above all, a politics of time is focused on the struggle for control and forms of resistance or acquiescence. The process of appropriation refers equally to seizures of embodied time, to symbolic manipulations of how time is apprehended or represented, and to direct control of the technologies of time. Appropriations of time must be institutionalized to be enduring. The routinization of control involves the "normalizing" of one kind of time as dominant over others, including mechanisms for its reproduction. Finally, a politics of time must be concerned to show not only how one or another of the multiplicity of times and its appropriate technology achieves dominance and is routinized, but it must also be concerned to show how an original appropriation and subsequent institutionalization come to be legitimate.

It is tempting to treat the three processes as a progressive sequence from seizure to routine to acceptance. The evidence, however, warrants no such conclusion. Which processes are realized from a set of possibilities, and in what order, must be determined empirically. These essays provide many examples of what happens when time is appropriated but not institutionalized, institutionalized but not legitimized, and so on. The essays are grouped for convenience of exposition into these three processes, but the reader should be aware that such analytical distinctions, while they clarify political moments, merge in the complexity of particular case studies.

An example of this merging occurs in the first chapter. Rotenberg, drawing on Eric Wolf's rendering of Marx's concept of a mode of production, makes a comparative contribution to a politics of time by exploring the strategic relationships underlying different modes of time and power in different modes of production—kin-ordered, tributary, and capitalist. Each mode of production, he argues, corresponds to a mode of power and time. Who controls time, how activities become routinized, how those in power legitimate their control of time, and how time is apprehended are questions for which answers can be sought within a systematic comparative framework.

Time is shaped by power in two ways. First, in the labor process, planners who control instruments of time control labor power. Second, representations of time become ideologies that legitimize the exercise of power. Rotenberg is concerned to locate the site of symbolic reproduction of time and power in the different modes. For example, in contrast to the kin-ordered mode, in which time is characterized by minimal planning and regulation and no fixed schedules, the tributary mode is characterized by ubiquitous calendars controlled from urban centers of a region. In the kin-ordered mode, there is a tendency for time to be institutionalized only in norms and social obligations, though individuals seem to be aware of (and wary of) control, judging by their frequent strategy of "exit" from burdens perceived to be onerous. Legitimation is not an issue. In contrast, a complex political cosmology of time is common in social formations structured by the tributary mode, where political elites seem preoccupied with the control of technologies of time in order to maintain their power. Consciousness of time is a mixture of the kin-ordered norms of social obligation and the genealogical depth of the dynastic family. Both of these modes contrast with the capitalist mode, in which buyers of labor control time and the site of symbolic reproduction is the workplace, where time is money.

## The Appropriation of Time

No purer cases exist as illustration of the appropriation of time in the interests of power than those in which the state, in the hands of a small elite backed by a strong military, is used as a direct instrument of time-discipline. Essays by Verdery and Rutz and Balkan describe both direct and indirect appropriations of time in the interest of state power. Appropriations of time, however, are not the exclusive domain of states, as Lovell makes clear in her study of the way in which street people in New York City must negotiate their own time in the interstices of capitalist time-discipline.

Verdery's sobering description of how Ceauşescu's regime seized control of the daily routines of the mass of Romanian citizens, and the consequences of this seizure for both the national political economy and the personal lives of citizens, serves as a sharp reminder that the purpose of power can be power, even when the ostensible purpose is to increase production. Borrowing the term "etatization" to describe the gradual expropriation of private control of time, Verdery shows how Ceauşescu's regime resulted—within the framework of the overall organization of a socialist planned economy—in a totalizing control of time over a whole society to a degree recorded only for more bounded and defined goal-oriented organizations such as prisons and asylums.

The ordinary uses of time became so atomized, with long empty periods of waiting between relatively brief moments of meaningful use, that people produced little of value. People also were demoralized and subdued as social beings. Verdery describes how state seizure of time destroyed lower-level initiative and planning, and more important, how it also had a direct impact on the "self" as this was constructed by the state in the image of a new socialist man. The seizure of time ultimately led to the erosion of those very relations of sociability that Romanians consider to be the *sine qua non* of what it means to be a person. We know from hindsight that the devaluation of time—in the production of things, the reproduction of persons, and the maintenance of the self—in time became implicated in an erosion of trust in the state and a loss of state power.

The appropriation of time by the state in Fiji was of another order. If less totalizing than the seizure of time in socialist Romania, it nevertheless was more traumatic in its instantaneous promulgation. The product of a political crisis, the seizure of time followed a successful military coup. Using the state as a direct instrument of power, the coup leader promulgated a decree that proscribed certain activities for all citizens one day every week—Sunday. And if its final causes can be located, as in Romania, in the systemic workings of political economy—in Fiji, a specific peripheral form of capitalist development and ethnic pluralist politics between Fijians and Indians—the proximate causes were motivated and intentional on the part of an actor on the historical stage. From beginning to end, the coup leader monopolized Sunday to shape his own vision of the legitimacy of the state.

Rutz and Balkan use the event of a seizure of time at the historical moment of radical political change to explore the specific shaping of time required by a particular constitution of the state. Using time-budget data, they show the tight fit between the time-discipline of Methodism and the Sunday practices of urban Fijians. The coup and decree, they argue, represent an anticapitalist and reactionary cultural pattern to the recent political history of Fiji.

The Sunday Decree is a discipline of time, real enough in its consequences for the economy and individual lives, but Rutz and Balkan assert that, in the case of Fiji, iterative practice of the decree serves as well an important symbolic function of power. The Sunday Decree is a trope, a rhetorical device enlisted in the larger political project of the coup leader to legitimate a usurpation of power. It is a metonym for basing the legitimacy of the new state on a religious fundamentalism at the core of which is the Sunday Observance.

Street people pose a different problem in the politics of time, one at the opposite pole of state seizures of time described by Verdery and

Rutz and Balkan. Those on the street appear to be "free" of the hegemonic control of capitalist time-discipline over the routines of those who work and have a home. As Lovell shows, however, their near-total exclusion from the dominant society and its rhythms poses a problem of how to include themselves in the spaces and times of others. Lovell's contribution to a politics of time is to show how the powerless and destitute negotiate inclusion in the daily rhythms of capitalist political economy by "seizing the moment."

Street people, she argues, develop practical notions of time as tactical weapons used to negotiate power relations with others around them in New York City. Marginalized by their exclusion from access to space, their tactics are understandably aimed at capturing public space or other minimal resources at the margin of survival. This is accomplished by "prolonging the duration conventionally accorded to the use of public space," by inverting their own rhythms to occupy the public spaces vacated by those whose rhythms fit capitalist work and leisure, by occupying the time of others to get their attention, and by spending long periods of time "now" in anticipation of help or to avoid trouble in the future.

The routines that result from these street practices are different from those of a dominant time and its apprehension in capitalist society. In contrast to the overscheduled, segmented, and rigid temporal order of life organized primarily around work in industrial society, street people's time consists of "large chunks of unallocated time" to be used to occupy the time and spaces "normally" occupied by workers during their leisure. And what is characterized as leisure in capitalist society is work in the rhythms of street life because it is aimed at the acquisition of productive resources for livelihood. What is crucial in the normalization of street time is the timing and sequencing of activities in order to seize the moment when a resource can be extracted. Thus do street people negotiate a way of life out of the initial condition of poverty and powerlessness.

## The Institutionalization of a Dominant Time

Capturing the process by which the time of one social collectivity not only is appropriated by another but becomes routinized and normalized is a major contribution to a politics of time. In this volume, several contributors focus on the institutionalization of time, the representation or practice of which already has been appropriated in a way that subjects people to a dominant time, placing them in relations of dependency. The essays by Urciuoli and Gounis show how "time is prime" in many relations of dependency, but each also shows the negotiation of alternative constructions of time and forms of mild resistance.

A political tactic of those already in positions of power is to "typify" the representations and behavior of others, in the process making them appear to be irrational, unreasonable, or just plain wrong. Urciuoli argues convincingly that time is a prime object by means of which officials in welfare agencies and educational bureaucracies in New York City deploy this tactic to subordinate their Puerto Rican clients.

Urciuoli shows how Puerto Rican client women, in their interaction with officials for the purpose of obtaining educational and welfare services, are made to feel that their time is inferior to what she terms a "Standard American Monochron." Drawing on Fabian's view that time is a carrier of significance, she examines a series of communicative acts between servers and clients to show how servers objectify their own bureaucratic routines in a way analogous to natural signs in language, recreating in the process the power relations that make their clients dependent upon them.

Urciuoli makes clear that the Standard American Monochron is more than a dominant kind of time. Its political significance derives from the metacommunicative function of conveying that it is a norm to define Puerto Rican representations and practices of time as deviant (i.e., morally inferior). Communicating the message that formally rational bureaucratic time is "natural" is a subtle but powerful way of mystifying the real issues in server-client relations—those which concern the ability of servers to deliver resources to clients in ways that nevertheless allow them to retain their control of time as a part of their definition of self. Urciuoli is skeptical that the larger class-based system can deliver on its promises to those in need of education and welfare.

Despite the delegitimizing efforts of servers in situations where Puerto Ricans are in relationships of dependency, Urciuoli offers evidence from her private interviews that Puerto Rican social time, grounded in the rhythms of extended kin relations and sociability, has resisted encroachment in significant areas of social life. The real inequalities of class and power that are recreated through communicative acts in agency offices are softened to a degree by the practice of a different time and the deeper significance it carries. But clearly there is a tension between times that surfaces in the frustrations and anxieties of Puerto Ricans who are made to feel "other" by being themselves.

If this collection concentrates on the politics of time, it does not neglect space. It is obvious that having a place—a home—has something to do with apprehending time and normalizing activity. What is more, to have a home of one's own is to control one's own time both in some sense and to some degree. One way in which to discover the significance of this dual proposition is to examine those who have no home. Gounis and Lovell do exactly that by telling us about people without homes in New York City. Gounis does so by focusing on the way in which the homeless are subjected to the time-discipline of shelters and submit to it; Lovell by focusing on the way in which street people, through their daily practices, manage to construct a "street time" they can call their own. These should not be viewed as contradictory positions on the same people but, rather, as different and complementary "moments" in the same political economy of the urban underclass that surfaces inside dominant capitalist rhythms.

The process of "shelterization"—which Gounis refers to as an attempt by authorities to circle the wagonless—gives men a temporary place to stay and provides services offered "at home" at the cost of overscheduling their time. There is the familiar problem of standardizing routines of inmates under the guise of institutional efficiency. But, for men who are subjected to this discipline, the most salient aspect of time they experience is "waiting," a form of inefficiency. From the standpoint of the shelter staff, the poverty and extreme social dependency of their clients places them in a category of persons whose time is worth nothing.

As Gounis shows, the whole process of shelterization inverts the value of most categories of time familiar to the capitalist world of work and workplaces that alternate with home and leisure. The shelter performs the material functions of home without its representations and practices. This situation leads to a negotiation of time and to distinctive rhythms of shelter life. In his description, Gounis observes in different ways an inversion in the meaning of categorical distinctions such as "public" and "private," "ever-availability and inaccessibility," or the discrepancy between shelter inmates' preoccupation with the category of "work" and the nonexistence of its possibility. In several vivid ethnographic descriptions of lived time in the shelter, Gounis makes those-with-a-home conscious of the fragile dependence of their own temporal experience on some very basic conditions of material existence.

Puerto Rican women and sheltered homeless men in New York City straddle an invisible but no less efficacious boundary between the threat of exclusion from the dominant rhythms of society and the promise of inclusion in them. Their dilemma might be captured in the dictum "to be educated is to be universalized, to be housed is to be normalized." With a provisional entrance ticket to normalized rhythms of the dominant society and the benefits conferred, the dilemma they face is to resist capture of their own rhythms while capturing those upon which their very survival may depend.

## Time and Legitimation

Of all the political processes that include time in relations of power, that of legitimation has held the most fascination for political philosophers and social scientists. Two contributors to this collection analyze the mutual shaping of time and legitimacy, each concerned with a different aspect of the problem. For Paine, the question is how time mediates ideological debate about the legitimacy of the state. For Bowen, the question is one of competing systems of legitimation when the time of one social collectivity is co-opted by another in the guise of efficiency and productivity.

The Israeli state and Jewish culture together arguably provide the richest—and most complex—materials imaginable for examining the materialization of time and power. In this volume, Paine looks at the way in which ideological debate over the legitimacy of the state of Israel is conducted among the Jewish population of Israel through the medium of time (and space). In an exposition of the language of time (and space) deployed by ultra-orthodox, labor Zionist, and orthodox Zionist elements, Paine shows how Jewish Israelis affirm or deny the eschatological significance of time in the constitution of the state.

Paine argues that the political culture of Jewish Israel is predicated on what he terms "ontologies of time" (and space), and that the question of legitimacy is inseparable from the ontology of time that frames it. He then shows how a dialectic of time is implicated in current political debates in Israel concerning whether or not the state of Israel is "legitimate." To help the reader through the complexities and intricacies of Israeli ideological conflict, Paine uses the metaphor of a pendulum that swings between the Law (a metaphor for a dialectic of time involving forgetting and remembering) and the Land (a dialectic of space involving exile and return) to generate the dialectic of time and space that frames debate. In unraveling this dialectic, Paine makes it clear that, to date, the ideologies of different segments of the Jewish community do not exhaust the possibilities of the dialectic of time. In fact, original contradictions make it likely that the question of legitimacy is as enduring to Israeli politics as that of the separation and balance of powers is to American political life.

In South Sulawesi, the timing of agricultural decisions has always been of central importance to villages because, as Bowen points out, the rainfall pattern is highly unpredictable. With the introduction of irrigation technologies accompanying the green revolution, however, the scale and importance of timing agricultural decisions took on a larger significance in the development plans of the country. Bowen describes the efforts of a regional agricultural development bureaucracy to increase state control of decisions that previously were in the hands of village agriculturalists.

Bowen argues that the ostensible goal of increasing economic efficiency masked the real issue of who was going to control timing and for what ends. What appeared to be a question of development economics soon became a struggle between regional coordination (and its economic advantages to the state) and local variation (and its socioeconomic advantages to villagers).

Further, the struggle was not primarily over coordination and routinization *per se*, but rather over the legitimacy of decision makers and their moral responsibility toward those who were affected by decisions. The struggle for legitimacy took the form of different calendars used to reckon timing, calendars that had different and opposed times. The villagers relied on local calendrical experts who interpreted almanacs, which were themselves sacred books predicated on multidimensional cosmological reckonings that indexed the movement of heavenly bodies to propitious and unpropitious days for various activities. Social and agricultural rhythms were intertwined. Enter the regional bureaucracy, with its formally rational goal of increasing the coordination of agricultural timing among villages by setting up a rotation schedule for planting and harvesting. At the core of the struggle was the issue of moral responsibility for decisions because, from the point of view of village time (and timing), a successful harvest was less a matter of economic planning than a prior determination of whether a government was honest, capable, and wise. In other words, absence of authoritative reckoning prevented a successful outcome no matter what rotation schedule was chosen.

## Conclusion

The most common cliché of our epoch is that "time is money," reflecting the dominant time-orientation of the capitalist world system and its relations of power. But, as I have tried to argue from several different points of reference, an anthropology of time might better be served by embracing the aphorism: "time is power." The wisdom of this assertion can be judged by the insights it generates into the complexity of the following cases.

## Notes

*Acknowledgments.* Erol Balkan, Donald Donham, Kostas Gounis, David Gray, Doris Rutz, Bonnie Urciuoli and three anonymous reviewers gave useful suggestions that I have incorporated in the final draft. This project would not have been completed were it not for the generous support of a Senior Faculty Fellowship from Hamilton College, the Fulbright Commission in Turkey, and the help of colleagues at Boğaziçi Üniversitesi.

1. The title of this volume is the same as that of an earlier article by Reid (1972), who was concerned that much of contemporary political and social science had assimilated uncritically into its own conceptual framework a time orientation that mimicked "machine cosmology." In his view, this led to a dangerous narrowing of our perception of possible futures. His solution was to suggest that phenomenological perspectives on time might be helpful in "developing our sensitivity to the plurality of time scales" (1972:459).

2. The comparative groundwork already had been laid by Nilsson (1920); for a classic study of time reckoning based on social structure and ecology, see Evans-Pritchard's study of the Nuer (1939; 1940) and Bohannon's (1953) study of the Tiv; for statements of symbolic representations of time, see Eliade (1959) and Leach (1961). For a study of the phenomenology of time, see Geertz's (1965) study of Bali. No general or critical review of the development of an anthropology of time has been written. For a thorough review of the development of a sociology of time, see Pronovost (1989).

3. The point is put best by Grene (quoted in Reid 1972:480) with reference to our own belief in chronology: "Chronology is a product of culture, which we rely on to set our alarm clocks, to meet classes, or fry chicken, or catch planes; but like clocks, classrooms, frying pans, and Boeings, it is an artifact which we use in order to move about *within* the richer framework of lived time. And lived time, is neither Cartesian-atomic nor Newtonian continuous . . . . it is not a measure but a medium."

4. For a spirited defense of this position with respect to field and intellectual products, see Lewis (1973).

5. The phrase is Gurvitch's (1963; 1964). He was among the first to formulate a relativization of time in political terms: ". . . each society, each social class, each particular group, each microsocial element—indeed every social activity . . . has a tendency to operate in a time proper to itself . . . no society, no social class, no structured group . . . can live *without trying to control these social times, which is quite a different thing from conceptualizing them and even more different from quantifying them*" (1963:174, italics mine).

6. Innis (1972) perceived clearly the connection between time, media of communication, and effective governance of space. More recently, Anderson (1983:17–40) has asserted that the modern nation-state is able to imagine itself in part because of a concept of simultaneity objectified in the novel and newspaper and made general by the spread of what he refers to as "print capitalism." In an earlier treatment of time and the prospects of the nation-state to govern itself, Innis (1951:88) expressed some skepticism about the ability of the nation-state to overcome its "obsession with the moment."

7. The politics of scheduling and the temporal discipline of the body in asylums and carcerals, respectively, have been explored in depth by Goffman (1961) and Foucault (1977).

8. Bourdieu (1963; 1977:165), after describing Kabyle submission to collective rhythms, asks "Why?" and argues that the practices themselves constitute symbolic power in existing relations among people of different sex and age.


# References Cited

Anderson, Benedict
    1983   Imagined Communities. New York: Verso.
Appadurai, Arjun
    1981   The Past as a Scarce Resource. Man 16:201–219.
Bohannon, Paul
    1953   Concepts of Time Among the Tiv of Nigeria. Southwestern Journal of Anthropology 9(3):251–262.
Bourdieu, Pierre
    1963   The Attitude of the Algerian Peasant toward Time. In Mediterranean Countrymen. Julian Pitt-Rivers, ed. Pp. 55–72. The Hague: Mouton.
    1977   Outline of a Theory of Practice. Cambridge: Cambridge University Press.
Braudel, Fernand
    1958   History and the Social Sciences: The Longue Duree. In On History. Sarah Matthews, trans. Pp. 25–54. Chicago: University of Chicago Press (1980).
Eliade, Mircea
    1959   The Sacred and the Profane. New York: Harcourt, Brace & World.
Evans-Pritchard, E. E.
    1939   Neur Time-reckoning. Africa 12:189–216.
    1940   The Nuer. Oxford: Oxford University Press.
Fabian, Johannes
    1983   Time and the Other. New York: Columbia University Press.
Foucault, Michel
    1977   Discipline and Punish. Alan Sheridan, trans. New York: Pantheon.
Geertz, Clifford
    1965   Person, Time and Conduct in Bali. New Haven: Southeast Asian Studies, Yale University.
Goffman, Erving
    1961   Asylums. Garden City, New York: Anchor Books.
Grene, Marjorie
    1967   Straus's Phenomenological Psychology. Review of Metaphysics 21:107ff.
Gurvitch, Georges
    1963   Social Structure and the Multiplicity of Times. In Sociological Theory, Values, and Sociocultural Change. Edward A. Tiryakian, ed. Pp. 171–184. New York: Free Press.
    1964   The Spectrum of Social Time. M. Korenbaum, ed. and translator. Dordrecht: D. Reidel.

Innis, Harold
   1951   A Plea for Time. *In* The Bias of Communication. Pp. 61–91. Toronto: University of Toronto Press.
   1972   Empire and Communications. Toronto: University of Toronto Press.
Leach, Edmund R.
   1961   Two Essays Concerning the Symbolic Representation of Time. *In* Rethinking Anthropology. Pp. 114–136. London: Athlone.
Lewis, I. M.
   1973   The Anthropologist's Muse. Welwyn Garden City, Hertfordshire: Broadwater Press Limited.
Nilsson, Martin P.
   1920   Primitive Time-reckoning. Lund: C. W. K. Gleerup.
Pocock, J. G. A.
   1973   Time, Institutions, and Action. *In* Politics, Language and Time. Pp. 233–272. New York: Atheneum.
Pronovost, Gilles
   1989   The Sociology of Time. Current Sociology 37(3):1–129.
Reid, Herbert
   1972   The Politics of Time: Conflicting Philosophical Perspectives and Trends. The Human Context 4:456–483.
Rutz, Henry J.
   1984   Material Affluence and Social Time in Village Fiji. *In* Affluence and Cultural Survival. Richard F. Salisbury and Elisabeth Tooker, eds. Pp. 105–118. Washington, D.C.: American Ethnological Society.
Zerubavel, Eviatar
   1979   Patterns of Time in Hospital Life. Chicago: University of Chicago Press.
   1981   Hidden Rhythms. Chicago: University of Chicago Press.
   1985   The Seven Day Circle: The History and Meaning of the Week. New York: Free Press.

# 2

# The Power to Time and the Time to Power

ROBERT ROTENBERG
*DePaul University*

As Philip Bock once observed, "power in the realm of social time means power to say, 'Do it now or else!' (1966:98)." Powerful actors in society can control the timing of social action as well as its direction. For many, this is all that one needs to say about the relationship between temporality and power. All expressions of this relationship become unique historical decisions that resist generalization. In this paper, I turn the question around to examine how the symbolic actions of social time map the institutional actions of the socially powerful.

My intention is to discuss the relations of power and temporality comparatively. All people experience some sort of constraints on the timing of activities that are beyond their control. Basic ecological or social structural constraints on activities usually present themselves as nonpolitical features of ordinary experience (Carlstein 1982). Such constraints affect the rankings or categories that may exist within the group in different ways, making some people more conscious of the constraints than others. All societies develop distinctions of some sort. Even if these distinctions involve codominant access to decision making over ordinary resources, there will necessarily be some sort of division of tasks, no matter how circumscribed or ritualized. It is in the experience of the people constrained from action that the social consciousness of time is born.

While everyone experiences the constraints of the environment through the diurnal or seasonal cycle, the constraints of social distinction are initially experienced by subordinated people. As distinctions and rankings proliferate with increasing social complexity, people give voice to their understandings of time. The position of the powerful is inextricably bound up with the symbolic and behavioral constraint that give order to the system of distinctions. Social power has a temporal as well as a spatial and a relational component. When the powerful are the timekeepers, time becomes symbolically elaborated through rituals that can control a greater number of activities. These compete for the limited time people can devote to any one of them. The experience of the schedule enters social consciousness. This is the power to time.

Institutionalized forms of temporality legitimate the authority of the power holders who hold office through the consciousness created by the temporal structures. This is the time to power. The coincidence of identity between power holder and temporal structure is not a given. In this complex ideological turn the creators of time, the powerful, become the progeny of time, legitimate authority. The producer of time is transformed into the product of time.

The organizational priorities set by power holders determine the importance given to these possible conjunctions in various societies. I will employ Eric Wolf's mode of production model to divide the range of social power into three types: kin-ordered, tributary and capitalist. This framework has the virtue of sorting out certain strategic relationships in production that are useful for discovering the organizational priorities of the power holders. More refined combination typologies and modeling of multiple relationships would result in more subtle and nuanced understandings. I am interested here in blocking out a general framework for understanding the relations of power and temporality, just as Wolf used the model to discover the strategic relationships between technology, economy and policies in world history. Like Wolf, I am less interested in the precision of the typologizing than I am the insights that the arrangements can expose. I do not presume pure types in history or society, nor am I arguing for a unilineal pattern of development in economic, political, or temporal institutions. The societies we encounter are mongrel hybrids of these various types. I want to address the contributions of these different arrangements to the political and temporal whole.

The three modes of production identified by Wolf refer to the patterns power holders use to mobilize the labor of others around specific legitimating appeals. In the kin-ordered mode, it is obligations of marriage and descent. In the tributary mode, it is political domination. In the capitalist mode, it is the market (1982). People involved in sustaining a mode of production forge legitimating ideologies. These ideologies must successfully link the distinctions of person, time, space, and occasion to the strategic relations that develop through kinship and politics (Sahlins 1976:211, 213). The following ethnographic examples are not merely different political economies, but also different social organizations that reproduce, and, in turn, are reproduced by, a structure of ideas about time.

## The Kin-Ordered Mode

In kin-ordered agricultural and pastoral communities, such as the Nuer and the Bemba, seasonal alternation in productive activities are merely the ecological half of a dual temporal constraint system. The seasonal alternations are economically significant. They mark the periods when surpluses in produce and labor are available. The other half of the constraint system is genealogical and kin-ordered systems; that is, "[the] fixed system having a constant number of steps between living persons and the founder of their clan "Evans-Pritchard 1939:213). The kin-ordered pattern is local, emphasizing those reciprocal obligations that bind family members to each other and to affines.

The strategic relationships in this mode are those that emerge from the obligations of exchange engendered by a system of marriage and descent. These systems favor some classifications of people to receive more than they give, and fate others to give more than they receive in return. This pattern of domination includes the control of people's time. But the degree of domination varies. Matrilineal systems involves a relative balance between these exchanges. Relationships that are the most likely to lead to imbalances, such as unequal obligations between affines and spouses, are mitigated by the separation of the husband from his group's resources during bride service. The ideology of descent through women insures greater independence of women within the marriage. When matrilocality preserves the separation of men from their mother's group throughout the life of the marriage, the result is a relatively weak system of domination. Men are more dependent on their wife's group and thus cannot fully dominate their wives. By the same token, daughters, who will stay in the homestead after marriage, are more dependent than sons, who will leave to join the homesteads of their wives.

We can take Audrey Richards's diaries of the daily activities of seven matrilocal groups in the Bemba village of Kasaka for twenty-three days during the wet season in September 1933 as evidence both of the distinctions that underlie the kin-ordered world and of the control of time embedded within them (Richards 1939). These diaries capture the pattern of everyday life when environmental constraints are weak.[1] They depict a complex organization of time in which multiple modes of production are operating under colonial conditions. This is not a pristine kin-ordered temporal organization. Many households had members, mostly young males, who were engaged in wage-earning positions at mission stations. These jobs took them out of the village for days and sometimes weeks. British colonial administration and the normalization of labor markets preceded Richards's research by only ten years. The rest of the village was engaged in wet season subsistence activities of gardening, gathering, hunting, and fishing. In the first few days of Richards's diary, seven women from the village were away at the chief's village performing tribute garden labor. The labor tribute is a vestige of the agricultural and military tribute labor demands imposed in the last century by regional elites during the struggle to control the ivory and slave trade in this area in the 1830s (Stevenson 1968:114). At the end of the month she documents, there is a village feast for which the women of each household must make beer. The feast lasts one day but requires two days to prepare and a day or two to recover from. While all three modes were present in the activities at Kasaka in 1933, the kin-ordered mode appears to govern day-to-day activities in the households.

The power to time is not immediately apparent in these diaries. People's schedules are not visibly controlled. There are few recurring patterns to Bemba activities. Even the most industrious of gardeners or hunters in the village never labored more than two days in a row. Bemba men appear to be free of the tyranny of routine. The preparation by women of millet porridge for the late afternoon meal is the only apparent repetition of activities in the wet season camps. The preparation of porridge and gathering of greens for the simplest of relishes is the responsibility of the senior wife/mother. She organizes her daughters' labor in the preparation of each meal.

Women may choose to prepare porridge whenever they like, but on two occasions they are obligated to do so. That is, there are two reciprocal obligations with the power to time women's meal preparation. The first is the delivery of meat to the household. For the majority of Kasaka homesteads, meat meals averaged two in 23 days. The meat may be a gift or the product of successful hunting. In either case, it is provided by men. In the diaries, it is clear that homesteads with dedicated hunters ate more meat than others. Also the headman's homestead received gifts of meat once or twice a week. Women are expected to drop other projects to prepare porridge when the meat arrives unexpectedly. These meals are only postponed if men are visiting other villages when meat arrives.

The second occasion with the power to time meal preparation coincides with the comings and goings of sons-in-law. During the period of bride service, the mother-in-law must provide her son-in-law with a full meal of millet porridge and relish every day he is resident in the homestead. This was originally intended to reciprocate for his work efforts. At the time of Richards's research, sons-in-law were difficult to come by. They often refused to contribute anything for their up-keep. Not feeding them would only make them angry, increasing the chances of an untidy divorce. Their presence forced the mother-in-law and her daughters to remain near the village. The sons-in-law may be in the village for weeks at a time, or enter and leave without warning. This effectively constrains the women from visiting other villages or engaging in other labor intensive activities.

Are the Bemba aware of a socially defined temporal structure over which they have no control? The answer is that they are not. Social obligations are powerful constraints on choice, but they are con-straints that people control. Both men and women seem to have op-tions to accept or avoid responsibilities. Men have productive respon-sibilities that are burdensome, but they need not engage in them everyday. Women are under far more specific obligations to produce meals when meat or sons-in-law are present. When the cooking re-sponsibilities become too onerous, women visit another village for a few days, abandoning their household to snack on sweet potatoes. When people lack this control over the timing of their activities, they are more likely to resent the constraints and give voice to their resent-ment. In the village of Kasaka in 1933, people complained of many things, but not having the time to do the things they wanted was not one of them.

Because of this lack of temporal structuring among the Bemba, the question of legitimating of power by features of time is not very mean-ingful. For example, male household heads schedule beer feasts dur-ing the wet season. Women prepare this beer, which must ferment for three days. Village headmen have a role in the setting of the dates for beer drinks, but only in their role as heads of households. Heads of households claim their positions through age set membership. Age sets were not determined by countable years but by the marriage and descent system. The power to call beer drinks was diffused through the households, since all households had at least one member in every age-set. This insured a high degree of consensus among the house-holds that the additional work of preparation would not become oner-ous.

When patrilineality and patrilocality characterize the relations be-tween families, strong patterns of temporal domination can result. The close proximity of men to their family resources, combined with an ideology that extolls descent through males, reduces the indepen-dence of women. Having completed the brideprice exchange with her father's group and removed the woman from her homestead, the husband has insured himself greater independence from interference from his affines. Wives and daughters in this system are more dependent on first their father's and then on their husband's group, and thus are more easily dominated. Daughters are valued for the brideprice they will bring, but sons represent the future of group.

Evans-Pritchard's analysis of the cattle-herding Nuer provides a type case of the patrilineal, patrilocal, kin-ordered systems (1939). A Nuer's activities were simultaneously constrained by the seasonal cycle of subsistence responsibilities and the person's identity in Nuer society. The temporal system becomes a mechanism for conceptualizing the relations between people. Evans-Pritchard holds that it is less a means of coordinating events than of coordinating relationships (1939:108). These are almost exclusively relationships between men as members of villages, of lineages, of age-sets, and of generations. The entire structure is projected onto the cattle, whose genealogies symbolically reflect the descent and marriage alliances of the lineage that owns them. Men have direct control over their wives through the brideprice in cattle they pay to the wife's father and brother, and over their daughters. As a man grows through the age-set system, he acquires a larger herd, until he can establish his own household, exchange cattle for a wife and begin his own family. Before, his activities are largely under the control of his father. Thus, cattle provide the power to time.

Rhythms of work are more regularized than among the Bemba.[2] Milking-time and cattle-time are the common elements of every Nuer's day regardless of the season. Except during the movements to dry season camps, there is always one common meal per day. It is prepared by the women of the homestead and eaten after the cattle return in the evening. Seasonal alternations shift productive activities from herding to gardening. Personal involvement in these activities varies from high degrees of choice among senior males to high degrees of constraint on the activities of young wives by their mothers-in-law.

The power to time is bound up in the concern for lineage genealogy and age-set progression. These are the instruments of male cooperation and solidarity. Just as these relationships are symbolized in the cattle, so too is the legitimacy of the men as power holders. There simply is no competing system, symbolic or material, to define a corresponding sphere of control for women and young people. Men acquire the power to time because they own cattle.

In the kin-ordered daily organization of activities, then, the presence or absence of kin with the power to make social demands on others is the single most powerful constraint on individual choice. In this form of temporality, productive activities are organized through commitments of network reciprocity, residence, marriage, and descent. These commitments survive through all successive transformations in the mode of production as the fundamental arrangement for allocating time to activities within households. Even in the sophisticated, time-conscious societies of advanced industrial capitalism, these same features reside in the organizations of households *after* they have met their commitments to external, public institutions.

## The Tributary Mode

Tributary states are regional organizations, often centralized around an urban center. These use military and bureaucratic structures to extract various forms of tribute (payments, taxes, sacrificial victims, etc.) from a captive peasantry. In these states, the peasants pay tribute from their productive work against their will or at least against their better judgment. Tributary states dominate people through a combination of violence and ideology. Wolf sees these states as developing along a continuum between decentralized, "feudal" forms and highly centralized, "despotic" forms. Each produces a class of nonproducing elites who coerce support from producers. The calendars that are ubiquitous in tributary states are objective instruments of coercion. Power holders appropriate the meaning of time, infuse it with political purpose and use it to raise their claims above all local claims to the labor or produce of subject peoples. External authority becomes the preeminent constraint on individual choice in daily activities.

In tributary states, the system of authority strives to undermine the diffuse, competing power of the marriage and descent obligations of the local kin-ordered world. Peasant producers must be convinced or coerced to generate a surplus for the state that kin would ordinarily divide among themselves. Physical coercion is an expensive mechanism for forcing the payment of taxes over the long term. Successful tributary states establish a more peaceful system in which peasant cultivators exchange tax payments for ceremonial and protective services (Fox 1977:41). Of these ceremonial services, calendrical rituals and calendrical divination are so common as to suggest a common strategy among tributary states. This widespread use is not so surprising when one considers that tributary states all face the same problems of legitimation and competition from local, kin-based authority. The calendar is the appropriation by the state of an already existing cyclical pattern of ordering time and space that is common to herding and gardening.

Tributary calendars develop a linkage between the seasonal cycle in productive activities and the cyclical consciousness of time. The calendar elevates the recurring pattern of activities to symbolic importance, while simultaneously undermining the importance of the kin-ordered system. Cyclicity, instead of lineality, defines the temporal consciousness of the tribute takers and the tribute payers. This principle becomes the basis for all temporal meaning: the answer to the question "Why now?"

Complete replacement of the kin-ordered notion of time by the tributary never occurs. Instead, the tributary offers itself as a refinement of the kin-ordered structures. The state calendar that explains the lineage of kings also provides an explanation for everyone's lineage. Instead of a fixed, constant number of lineal steps, the calendar generates a system of cycles. Depending on the confluence of these cycles, specific ancestors move closer to, or farther from, living persons. What was once a single, fixed sequence has become a field of cross-cutting and simultaneous cycles so complex that anyone who can interpret the present also can claim authority beyond the lineage.

The Highland Mayan Quiché-speaking community of Momostenango studied by Barbara Tedlock shows how the state calendar penetrates into the lives of the local community. Initiation into the status of *ajk'ij*, "daykeeper," is open to all members of a patrilineage who feel the spiritual calling, but people born on certain kinds of days in the 260-day sacred calendar are almost certain to enter the status. Once initiated, they perform calendrical rites for their household or lineage segment. Persons in a second stage hierarchy, known as *chuchkajawib*, "mother-fathers," undergo a second initiation and perform calendrical rites for lineages, clans, cantons, and the town itself. These rites include visiting various shrines on appointed days. There, they recite prayers to restore the proper relations between their lineage, and the ancestors and nature spirits believed to control all productive and reproductive activities. The daykeepers also interpret dreams and messages from the spirit world, whose meanings derive in part from the counting of the days of the calendar. Their dual role as spiritual intermediaries and mediumistic prognosticators elevates their social position. These roles are locally powerful because they provide access to spiritual resources that ordinary people do not have. One commands these resources by learning how to count the days of the old Mayan-system calendar and to identify which days are significant for various prayers, rituals and sacrifices.

It is as a diviner with the power to tell time that the services of a daykeeper are most often sought out. The kinds of questions that are most commonly put to the diviner concern "illness, accident, land dis-

putes, house building, inheritance, lost property, business transac-
tions, travel, marriage, adultery, quarrels, birth, death, dreams or
omens" (Tedlock 1982:153). The daykeeper divines by counting out
seeds (sortiledge) that stand for calendar days, interpreting the qualities inherent in these days according to an intimate knowledge of local
social structure, the personal history of the client and the current balance of forces in the client's social world. The temporal structure of the
calendar orders these levels of determinacy. The diviner converts
them into a single instrument for stipulating what kind of time it is
(Geertz 1973:393). In every divination, autochthonous, kin-based authority is weakened and supplanted by the calendrical mediation. In
the end, kin-generating fathers lose power to timekeeping "mother-
fathers!"

Even at this local level, we can observe the capacity of temporal
structures to empower authority, the time to power. There is a hierarchy of horological experts that corresponds to the larger social units
in the community. Becoming a daykeeper is the first step toward local
political power in one of the five corporate groups that dominate the
community affairs of Momostenango's hierarchy of priest-shamans.
Their movement up the hierarchy depends on their reputations as di-
viners. That, in turn, depends on how consistently they can satisfac-
torily combine their knowledge of the calendrical qualities with their
understanding of local social structure into a single explanatory pattern. Successful horometry leads to a successful political career.

In the power centers of Pre-Columbian Mesoamerica, a priest sha-
man hierarchy conducted the same calendrical rituals of day counting,
shrine sacrifices, and divination. Among the Mexica-Tenochca, legitimation of the state depended on timekeeping. The state authorities
had much to lose if the passage of time undermined their leading role,
exposed them to conquest or derailed the orderly succession to kingship within the royal lineage. Since these disorderly events had oc-
curred in the past, there was every reason to suspect that they will
occur in the future, if they were not already beginning to occur in the
present.[3]

It was crucial that timekeepers divine the direction of time itself
and counsel the king accordingly. Power holders themselves were not
timekeepers, but timekeepers were powerful and exercised their
power sometimes for or against specific persons in authority. Power
holders plotted and carried out conquests in consultation with the
timekeepers, courting disaster if they took action without prior consultation. This was truly the time to power.

The Mexica-Tenochca imagined the passage of time as a transformation from order to disorder, complete to incomplete, creation to de-

struction. Kay Read calls this worldview "continuing eschatologies
. . . a process in which many endings, from the daily to the cosmic
level, keep on occurring" (1989:5).[4] Person and time are codeterminate
in Mexica genetic notions. Living personalities are current transformations of their ancestral past. They are present-time variations on the
previously established themes of their families. Occasion and time relate to each other in the same fashion as person and time. Strong and
weak kings, military conquests, rebellion, imperial collapse and sustained periods of peace all represent the fruit of the seeds of transformation contained in the past. Motecuhzuma II, a strong king, combined in his person the potentialities of the ancestral Colhua line of
Aztlan Toltecs, the *teyolia* of Huitzilopochtli, the fearsome patron god
and the name of Montecuhzuma I, the most successful king in Mexica
history.[5] If everything was in a state of constant transformation toward
total destruction, so too was the Mexica state. Even the best-endowed
of kings could not withstand the force of time, when, according to a
cosmic schedule, its moment of final transformation arrived with the
Spanish. All occasions were timed to power, foreordained by myth
and scheduled by calendar.

The cyclical sequences of recurrent days produced by the Mesoamerican states are organizational features of those states and not
epiphenomena. They constitute the privileged loci for symbolic production within the tributary mode of organizing social work. As such,
tributary states cannot *not* produce calendars and the horometric reflex
in all spheres of activity.

## The Origin of Capitalist Schedules

The previous discussion has described the temporal understandings of kin-ordered and tributary modes of production as fully ma-
tured systems. There can only be speculation about how these understandings may have developed in the first place. The evidence is lost
to history. This is not the case with capitalist mode of production,
which developed relatively recently and within literate, record-keep-
ing cultures. This permits me to treat the understandings of time in
capitalism developmentally, describing its features as these became
instituted within the organization of the strategic relations common to
this mode.

In capitalist societies, it is not moments, occasions, or relations
that are ordered by time but categories of economically valued activities. Nonvalued activities, personal time, sleep, and housework are
unmarked, unremarkable, and conventionally invisible. As Edmund

Leach has pointed out, it is the production or consumption value of an activity that marks it for attention (Leach 1976:33–36). Productive activities become the figure against a ground of the unmarked and unscheduled needs of self and household. In this mode, the power to time is primarily held by work givers and their managers. The dimension of duration supplants those of sequence and recurrence as the significant aspect for the symbolic elaboration of time. The attention of the power holders shifts from the cosmic day to the cost per hour, and eventually, to the minute and second.

The transition from the tributary, repetitive sequence of meaningful days to the capitalist, repetitive sequence of meaningful activities took place in those small textile manufacturing centers in Italy and France between the 10th and the 13th centuries. The distinction between these ways of thinking about hours is easier to make in German than it is in English. The word *Horen* refers to the medieval idea of significant hours. These hours were not 60 minutes long but lasted the time it took to chant the office of that particular service.[6] There then followed a period that does not count, which lasted until it was time to chant the next named service. This system emphasizes exactness in the recurrence of the sequence of rituals and the relative unimportance of any competing activities. The word *Stunden,* on the other hand, refers to the idea of abstract hours in which every moment of the day lies within one of the 24 divisions of the day, each of equal, 60-minute duration. This system emphasizes openness and a capacity to fit any number of activities, ritual or secular, that need to be located within the day.

The central contradiction of industrial capitalism is the wage crisis. That is, over time and in all enterprises, the rate of profit falls and the cost of reproducing labor rises. When investors organized the first textile manufacturers, there were no precedents for dealing with this contradiction. Work-givers were surprised by how quickly their profits eroded and workers were surprised by how soon their standard of living dropped. The control of the pace and length of work became the battleground between the first large concentrations of wage-laborers and their employers to protect their stakes in the new mode of production. Employers began to increase the demand for productivity as profits fell. Workers began leaving the workshops when they felt the value of their wages matched the value of their labor time.

The period between 1324 and 1362 was particularly important for establishing the role of the state as mediator in these conflicts. In Arras in the early 1315, fullers' assistants demanded longer working days and higher rates to handle the increased weight and size of fabrics, as well as to compensate for currency devaluations. Philip the Fair intervened by issuing an ordinance authorizing night work (Lespinasse 1886:1). At Amiens in 1335, he granted an ordinance establishing time markers of the workday (Thierry 1850:456–457). Work would begin at the hour of Terce (9:00 A.M.). The factory owners agreed to recognize the midday hour of Sext as the work break but insisted that workers return after the break for more work. The break would last from the bells at Sext to those of Nones, three hours. The end of the afternoon work segment was signaled by the bells for Vespers at sundown. The name used for the midday break remained Nones. In this way, the canonical hour of Sext became known as the secular hour of *Nona* in Italy, *nonne* in France, *Nonzeit* in German and noon in English (Bilfinger 1969:59–90). An ordinance in 1395 fixed these hours for Paris (Lespinasse 1886:52).

The conflict over the length of the workday rather than the wage rate characterized the development of the capitalist mode through the early 15th century. Leaving the bells in the hands of the Church undermined control of production, both symbolically and literally. Factory owners soon bought their own bells to ring. Workers who did not obey the bell were fined. In Aire-sur-la-Lys in 1335 the governor authorized the town to erect its own bell tower to provide a neutral standard for telling time, while in Ghent in 1349 the city council was forced to permit workers to set their own hours in order to bring them back to work in what may be the first recorded industrial strike (Espinas and Pirenne 1906: part 1, 6; part 2, 471). These innovations were copied in various localities throughout the world as the capitalist mode diffused. Time had been successfully disengaged from the tributary and agricultural cycle to furnish a structure for everyday life, what Le Goff has called "a chronological net in which urban life was caught" (1980:48).

The definition of workday coincided with the slow but certain development of a single temporal system. This was not merely the diffusion of a single way of painting clock faces. It was the acceptance of the idea that a single method for naming time in all localities made the market principle itself more legitimate. If the market is a universal mechanism for measuring value, similar to the universal mechanisms for measuring space and time, then its legitimation lay in the claim for the existence of universality in the measurement of time and space. Previously, each town selected its own time measurement units from eight different regional systems. By choosing one system, the town linked itself to other centers with which it carried on trade. The unified time structure had important commercial implications. It determined the departure and arrival times of postal carriers with their price newsletters, bills of exchange, and bills of lading.[7] Standardized timekeeping, the length of the workday, and the increasing interest by states in regulating market activity all required a broadly accepted standard of temporal precision. This sparked investment in the development of ever more precise mechanical clocks (Landes 1983).

Early capitalists could be certain about the length of a journey, the period of a debt or the number of months until the next harvest, but not work time. In the workshops, relative inactivity alternated with frantic speed-ups. The latter phases of the capitalist transformation reorganized work into consistent periods of activity. International competition for markets in the 18th century elevated the pursuit of a disciplined national work force to the level of state ideology. E. P. Thompson has shown how this ideology imposed itself in England during the 18th and 19th centuries. Power holders in the state, the religious institutions and the print media worked with the factory owners to present a united viewpoint against what they called idleness and what was, in fact, worker control of work time. Acceptance of the work giver's power to time, known as "work discipline," was rewarded with wage incentives: the more disciplined the worker, the better the pay (1967:79–81).

Organizing the means of production involves planning more than the number of days in a row the workers will operate the factory. All aspects of the production process must be timed. Tasks proceed simultaneously, with many workers beginning and finishing tasks independently of each other. The owner or the manager, a specialized employee role first introduced in the latter half of the 19th century, must time these simultaneous actions so that backlogs and tie-ups do not occur as materials flow through the production process. One way to do this is to pay close attention to the duration of specific tasks and to establish a rate of work for each worker that insure the material necessary for all subsequent tasks will be available.[8] The power to time the activities of the workplace had finally reached its modern form. In answer to the question "Why now?," the worker in an enterprise must answer "Because the boss says so."

The issue of whether work givers, and ultimately, all power holders in capitalist society, hold authority because of the logic of the temporality they produce is a critical one. At first glance, capitalist societies appear to legitimate work givers through the principle of private disposal of private property, not through temporal metaphors.[9] Astrological columns in daily newspapers notwithstanding, no specific temporal patterns in capitalist societies determine personhood. The time structures that do exist are concerned almost exclusively with occurrence: locating activities in time. There is, however, an implicit connection between time and personhood through the mediation of the market. Time has a uniform, abstract value in capitalism that logically precludes some people's time from being more valuable than others. Nevertheless, the market assigns value to the time of different people based on the demand for scarce skills and knowledge. These wage differentials do legitimate the narrow differences between handworker and intellectual worker, as well as between worker and manager. The value of the person's time determines their personhood in the workplace. The more risk a worker is willing to take on, either in terms of skill preparation or fiduciary responsibility, the higher the wages. The higher the wages relative to other workers in the same organization, the greater the claim to authority to command other people's time. The wages determine a person's time to power.

The development of a uniquely capitalist temporal structure was initially the problem of the entrepreneurs and their representatives in local assemblies in free cities. As their power to influence social institutions grew, people outside capitalist enterprises found their lives organized around the demands of their work life. Even before the provincial factory owners moved their machines and their disciplined work forces to the centers of state power in the early 19th century, the structures of capitalist temporality were already in place. The circulation of people, goods and ideas that capitalism makes valuable is a faster moving transforming force than the industrial reorganization of work.

This is clearly seen in a publicist's account of the rhythm of everyday life in the commercial and administrative city of Vienna in 1792, that is, thirty years before the first boom in factory labor migration began to swell the suburbs of the metropolis. The day begins at 6:00 A.M., with servants hired from the provinces going to Church for early Mass. The farmers' markets open. The first customers are the cooks of the wealthy, followed by the wives and daughters of the lower classes. By ten o'clock these markets close. The coaches of the rich are never seen on the street before 9:00 A.M. but by 8:30 the three and half thousand clerks, secretaries, accountants, and office boys are at their desks. At 10:00 the streets are jammed again as these clerks make their way to the cafes for breakfast. The noble families attend Mass at noon, while this hour marks the beginning of the lunch break. The clerks go directly to the pubs because they must be back at work by 1:00 P.M. The managers visit their lovers or take a walk. They do not have to return until 2:00 P.M. The store owners and high government officials go home for a long lunch and nap. They do not return to their desks before 3:00 P.M. The streets are quiet in the early afternoon. They get noisy again around 6:00 as the offices and stores close for the day. After an evening spent in the theater or pubs or at home with the family, most people retire at 10:00 P.M., only to be awakened at midnight by the sound of noble carriages bringing the high-born home after a social evening.[10]

This is a clear instance of the emergence in the preindustrial city of a dominant public schedule against which private and domestic obligations are forced to compete. Employees began and ended their shifts at times believed by the office managers to be natural work hours: Terce to Sext and Nones to Vespers. How long the break between Sext and Nones lasted depended on class. The lower the level of education, income, and influence, the lower the wages and the shorter the lunch break. The truly powerful worked not at all, ate their meals when everyone else was working and socialized while others slept. It has all the elements of modern urban life: rush hours, shopping periods, collective mealtimes, specialized periods for recreation and rest, and clearly demarcated work periods reflecting the power of work givers to set the pace of work. More important, it was in place *before* the industrial revolution.

This population accepted the legitimacy of the public schedule. They did not resist or even imagine their lives in the city could be organized some other way. Aside from an ordinance that opened and closed the farmers' markets each day, this schedule lacked overt state intervention. Such intervention increases in the late 19th and 20th centuries, as the problems of circulation increase. By circulation, I mean the achievement of moving the large densities of people, goods, and information through space that the social investments in railroads, streetcars, subways, telegraph, and radio made possible. This was possible because the state invested in infrastructure on a scale that private investment could match. As David Harvey has argued, these investments had as much to do with realizing profits in an enterprise as did the rational management of workers and machines (1985:8–9). Accurate and reliable schedules assured efficient coordination in the movements of people, goods, and information. To accept a single, coordinated, public schedule of work shifts is the source of the greatest pressure for metropolitans. Once in place, this schedule is a powerful determining factor in limiting the variety and sequence of possible activities for households (Rotenberg 1989; 1992).

The existence of social relations that might compete with the commitment to work activities is precisely what the schedule aims to disarm. The face of social authority that implements the schedule is invisible. It provides no immediate target for political action or special pleading. The public schedule is anonymous, all pervasive and all powerful.

## Conclusion

These are examples of how people use power in the exercise of time. The institutional actions of power holders worked through the symbolic actions of social temporality to justify both the legitimacy of authority and that of the fundamental economic inequity between power holder and resource producer. Each mode of production requires a different temporal consciousness, different control techniques, plans and regulations, and ultimately, different legitimations within the developing structures of time. These are then seized upon by power holders and favored for symbolic elaboration by ideologues.

What holds the imagination here is the uncanny closeness between our consciousness of time and the political structures supporting a mode of production. For me, as for Durkheim in another time and another anthropological paradigm, "it is not my time that is thus arranged; it is time in general, such as it is objectively thought of by everyone in a civilization" (1915:23). What I offer here is an argument that the general time that is objectively thought of is itself the product, not of thought but of action, and specifically those actions through which the powerful divide the powerless from the products of their labor.

## Notes

1. Richards provides a brief, 14-day slice of life in a dry season camp, Kampamba. The differences are startling. For a number of reasons, the more difficult dry season subsistence activities, called by the Bemba "the starving season," require more arduous labor for many more days in a row than the wet season diary. Thus, the temporal behavior of Bemba villagers during these 23 days at Kasaka village in wet season may include the perception on their part that ecologically this is as close to vacation as they will ever get.

2. While his analysis of the distinction between ecological time (constraints imposed on activity by the subsistence possibilities of the natural environment), and structural time (constraints imposed on activity by genealogy and territorial identity) is well known, there is a marked absence of data on variations in daily activity in this work. Evans-Pritchard admits at one point that his observations on the matter of the personal experience of time "have been slight and that a fuller analysis is beyond our powers. We have merely indicated those aspects of the problem which are directly related to the descriptive modes of livelihood which have gone before and to the description of political institutions which follows" (1939:107).

3. Cyclical time becomes what Paul Ricoeur calls the "experience of nowness" (1985:14–19). This is an experience of time in which the memory of the past and the expectation of the future conjoins with the present. Persons and

events lose their temporal uniqueness. For example, a young man named for the memory of his lineal great grandfather participates in his ancestor's life (and has his actions interpreted through others' memories of that ancestor), just as he lays the groundwork for his memory among his descendants yet unborn.

4. Since these endings are continuous, they produce creation as well as destruction, but it is a creation produced by (ongoing) destruction and a destruction produced by (ongoing) creation. Thus, in the Aztec myth of the creation of the Fifth Age, the Age of Motion, the sun and moon were set in motion by the sacrificial (destructive) acts of the gods. At one point, the wind god Ehecatl sacrifices all the remaining gods to gain the power to blow the heavenly bodies into their motions, and produce the alternation of day and night that is the heart of Mesoamerican horometry (Read 1989:3).

5. Alfredo Lopez-Austin has shown that some elements of the composite soul in Mexica cosmology, such as the teyolia, remain intact (particulated), while other elements, such as the *tonalli*, shatter and disperse (1988:328–331).

6. The canonical hours that regulated monastic life among the tributary states of the European Middle Ages stemmed directly from the Roman *ordinatio horae*, but with some modifications. The monastic day was divided into seven periods of prayer, or offices, each announced with the ringing of bells and each assigned to a different part of the day. By the 15th century, these hours had been reduced to seven: Matins (daybreak), Prime (6:00 A.M.), Terce (9:00 A.M.). Sext (12:00 P.M.), Nones (3:00 P.M.), Vespers (sunset), and Compline (midnight).

7. These so-caled Courier Hours had been in existence in one form or another since the 18th century and provided an important degree of certainty that these all important, hand-carried instruments of commerce were moving across the land at a regular rate (Maurice and Maurice 1980:156). For example, under the Augsburg Courier Ordinance 1555, a merchant could be certain that a letter delivered to the post by 8 A.M. on Saturday would arrive in Venice at 8 P.M. on Tuesday, giving the Venice correspondent the entire night to reply and deliver the response by 8 A.M. Wednesday to the post for delivery in Augsburg by 8 P.M. on Saturday. The standardization of the names for clock time in both cities reduced the chance for errors and lost opportunity between correspondents. It also guaranteed that a bill of exchange posted on Saturday would not actually be presented for payment until three days later.

8. This was the forerunner of scientific management (Taylor 1947; Spriegel and Myers 1953), which dominated U.S. management strategies throughout the first half of the 20th century.

9. Some attempts at legitimation through temporality arise periodically. The best known of these is the Calvinist principle of election. It is a good example of predestination within a lineal time pattern. At birth, a person either receives or does not receive the deity's grace. This determines not only the events of his/her life, but also his/her ultimate ascension to heaven, or fall into hell. Wealth, private property, and the authority to decide the schedule of other people's lives as a work giver are all signs of God's grace on the Elect. Excepting Calvinism and marginal charismatic sects, the authority of capitalist power holders has rested solely on the acknowledgment by the capitalist state of the independence of private property.

10. This is from the 1923 edition of Johann Pezzl's 1792 volume of collected writings, *Skizze von Wien*. For a translation of the full text, cf. Rotenberg 1992.

## References Cited

Bilfinger, Gustav
    1969   Die Mittelalterlichen Horen und die Modernen Stunden: En Beitrag zur Kulturgeschichte. (Reprint of the 1892 edition.) Wiesbaden: Dr. Martin Sändig oHG.
Bock, Philip K.
    1966   Social Time and Institutional Conflict. Human Organization 25:96–102.
Carlstein, Tommy
    1982   Time Resources, Society and Ecology. Volume 1: Preindustrial Society. London: George Allen and Unwin.
Durkheim, Emile
    1915   The Elementary Forms of the Religious Life. New York: Free Press.
Espinas, G., and H. Pirenne
    1906   Recueil de documents relatifs à histoire de l'industrie drapière en Flandre. (Cited in Le Goff 1980:294)
Evans-Pritchard E. E.
    1939   Nuer Time Reckoning. Africa 12:189–216.
Fox, Richard G.
    1977   Urban Anthropology: Cities in their Cultural Settings. Englewood Cliffs, N.J.: Prentice-Hall.
Geertz, Clifford
    1973   The Interpretation of Culture. New York: Basic Books.
Harvey, David
    1985   Consciousness and Urban Experience. Baltimore: Johns Hopkins Press.
Landes, David
    1983   Revolution in Time: Clocks and the Making of the Modern World. Cambridge: Belknap Press.
Leach, Edmund
    1976   Culture and Communication: The Logic by Which Symbols are Connected. New York: Cambridge University Press.
Le Goff, Jacques
    1980   Time, Work and Culture in the Middle Ages. Chicago: University of Chicago Press.
Lespinasse, R. de
    1886   Les Métiers et corporations de Paris. Part 1. Cited in Le Goff 1980:294.
Lopez-Austin, Alfredo
    1988   The Human Body and Ideology: Concepts of the Ancient Nahuas. Thelma Ortiz de Montellano and Bernard Ortiz de Montellano, trans. Salt Lake City: University of Utah Press.
Maurice, Sigrid, and Klaus Maurice
    1980   Stundenangaben in Gemeinwesen des 16. and 17. Jahrhunderts. *In* Die Welt als Uhr: Deutsche Uhren und Automaten, 1550–1650. K. Maurice and O. Mayr, eds. Pp. 146–158. Munich: Bayerisches Nationalmuseum.

Pezzl, Johann
　　1923　Skizze von Wien. Gustav Gugitz and Anton Schlosser, eds. Graz: Lehkam Verlag.
Read, Kay
　　1989　Pipiltin/Macehualtin: Mexica-Tenochca Notions of Time and Kingship. Manuscript read at the 1989 meeting of the American Ethnological Society, Santa Fe.
Richards, Audrey
　　1939　Land, Labor and Diet in Northern Rhodesia. Oxford: Oxford University Press.
Ricoeur, Paul
　　1985　The History of Religions and the Phenomenology of Time Consciousness. *In* The History of Religions: Retrospect and Prospect. Joseph M. Kitagawa, ed. Pp. 13–31. New York: Macmillan.
Rotenberg, Robert
　　1989　Boundaries in Time: Macro-level Constraints on Micro-Level Allocations of Time to Consumption Activities. *In* The Social Economy of Consumption. Monographs in Economic Anthropology, Volume 6. Henry Rutz and Benjamin Orlove, eds. Pp. 149–176. Lanham, Maryland: University Press of America.
　　1992　Time and Order in Metropolitan Vienna. Washington, D.C.: Smithsonian Institution (forthcoming).
Sahlins, Marshall
　　1976　Culture and Practical Reason. Chicago: University of Chicago Press.
Spriegel, William R. and Clark E. Myers, eds.
　　1953　The Writing of the Gilbreths. Homewood, Illinois: R. D. Irwin.
Stevenson, Robert F.
　　1968　Population and Political Systems in Tropical Africa. New York: Columbia University Press.
Taylor, Frederick
　　1947　Scientific Management. New York: Harper.
Tedlock, Barbara
　　1982　Time and the Highland Maya. Albuquerque, NM: University of New Mexico Press.
Thierry, A.
　　1850　Recueil des monuments inédits de l'histoire du tiers etat. (Cited in Le Goff 1980:294).
Thompson, E. P.
　　1967　Time, Work-discipline, and Industrial Capitalism. Past and Present 38:56–97.
Wolf, Eric R.
　　1982　Europe and the People without History. Berkeley: University of California Press.

# 3

# The "Etatization" of Time in Ceauşescu's Romania

KATHERINE VERDERY
*Johns Hopkins University*

That the nature of time differs in different social orders has been a staple of anthropological analysis at least since Evans-Pritchard's work on the Nuer (1940) and Leach's classic paper on the symbolic representation of time (Leach 1961). Accordingly, anthropologists have catalogued the variant organizations of time in other cultures (e.g., Hallowell 1937, Hugh-Jones 1979, Munn 1986); they have also examined what happens when the bearers of nonwestern or noncapitalist temporalities confront the new organizations of time brought to them by capitalist commodity production (e.g., Burman 1981, Smith 1982). Such treatments of time as a social construction do not always make explicit, however, the political context within which time is experienced and the politics through which it is culturally "made." That is, to see time as culturally variable, with different conceptions of it functionally fitted to one or another social environment, is only part of the story. These conceptions themselves are forged through conflicts that involve, on one hand, social actors who seek to create or impose new temporal disciplines—either as elements of new productive arrangements or as the projects of revolutionary political regimes—and, on the other, the persons subjected to these transformative projects. In a word, the social construction of time must be seen as a political process.

The present paper explores temporal politics through an example in which regime policies created struggles over time, as people were subjected to and resisted new temporal organizations. The example is Romania of the 1980s, prior to the violent overthrow of Communist Party leader Nicolae Ceauşescu in December 1989.[1] Both directly, through policies expressly aimed at the marking of time, and indirectly, through policies aimed at solving other problems but implicating people's use of time, the Romanian Party leadership gradually expropriated Romanians of much of their control over time. I call this process "etatization," a term borrowed from Romanian writer Norman Manea (1989), who uses the word *etatizare* (literally, "the process of statizing") to describe the fate of people's private time in his native country. While some might wish to render this as "nationalization," I prefer the more cumbersome "etatization" because in Romania the "state" and the "nation" have not necessarily been isomorphic: the activities of the state-occupying regime have often been at odds with what some would see as the interests of other inhabitants—the nation or "people." While I will not make this distinction the basis of my argument,[2] one might phrase the struggle over time in Romania as, precisely, a struggle between "etatization" and "nationalization," that is, a struggle between the state and the people for claims upon time.

I concentrate here on the "etatization" part of this struggle: the ways in which the Romanian state seized time from the purposes many Romanians wanted to pursue. There are a number of means through which time can be seized—rituals, calendars, decrees (such as curfews), workday schedules, etc. My discussion focuses on the vehicle through which these devices organize time: the body, site of many possible uses of time, only some of which can be actualized. To phrase it differently, I treat time as a medium of activity that is lodged in and manifested through human bodies; that is, I emphasize not alternative *representations* of time but alternative *utilizations* of it. While acknowledging time's cultural element, I presuppose that there is an irreducible durative aspect in the passage of time no matter how it is constructed. Thus, at a given level of technology, an individual can accomplish only so much in the space between successive midnights. If political decisions force more activity onto individuals within this space without increasing their technical capacities, then certain purposes or projects will go unrealized, and this prospect may provoke resistance. While my premise may seem a failure to problematize time as a cultural construct, I hold that, to the contrary, struggles over time *are* what construct it culturally, producing and altering its meanings as groups contend over them.

To "mark time" in a particular way is to propose a particular use or deployment of bodies that subtracts them from other possible uses. Alternative deployments of bodies in time reveal for us the seizure of time by power, which I will illustrate with some ways in which the Romanian state seized time by compelling people's bodies into particular activities.[3] Bodies subjected to such seizure had a few options, in response. They could voluntarily acquiesce in it, acknowledging the state's right to make this claim and accepting the hegemonic order within which it was exercised. They could acquiesce in form only, compelled to do so by the way in which time was seized and alternative uses precluded, but not necessarily agreeing with the claim made on them. Or they could resist the seizure of time, seeking to withdraw themselves for purposes other than those proposed from above. Many Romanians in Ceauşescu's era chose the second and third options. Whenever possible, they preferred to use their bodies in time toward reproducing households and local relations rather than toward promoting the power of the Romanian state and its ruling Communist Party.

In my examples, I distinguish loosely between the fates of time-invested bodies in urban and in rural settings, without further specifying their class situation. Additionally, I consider how time is related to the sense of self. Because social senses of self are intricately bound up with temporal investments in certain kinds of activity, incursions upon these activities have consequences for how the self is conceived and experienced. Therefore, I also describe briefly how the state's seizure of time encroached upon people's self-conceptions.

## The Forms and Mechanisms of Etatization: Intention and Structure

For purposes of this volume, I organize my ideas in terms of the relation between structure and intention, viewing the etatization of time in Romania as the joint result of intentional projects of state-makers, unintended consequences of actions aimed at other problems, and structural properties of Romanian socialism as a social order *sui generis*. For my ethnographic examples to make sense, I should first characterize Romanian socialism in the decade of the 1980s, in terms of both the projects its leaders pursued and the inner logic of the social order itself, an inner logic only partly related to the leaders' intentional projects.[4] The tendencies I discuss antedated the 1980s but became especially visible then, as economic crisis sharpened their contours.

To a greater degree than in any other East European state, coercion combined with attempts at ideological persuasion were the basis of rule in Ceauşescu's Romania. This distinguished that regime from others in the region, in which material incentives generally played a greater role. The most extreme contrast in the bloc was between the virtual police state of Romania and relatively liberal Hungary, with its low level of police control and its high standard of living. Because the Ceauşescu leadership determined to reduce noxious "foreign interference" by repaying the foreign debt ahead of schedule, it imposed in-

creasingly severe austerity measures beginning in 1980. These included massive exports of foodstuffs and other necessities, and significant reductions of imported goods and fuel, to slow the drain of
hard currency. Expecting popular opposition, the regime intensified
its apparatus of surveillance and repression. Persons who raised a pro-
test were expelled or isolated by round-the-clock police watch; strikes
or riots were put down by force; increasing numbers of persons were
drawn into the net of collaboration, reporting to the secret police on
the activities of their friends and associates. Under these circumstances, resistance tended to take covert forms (cf. Scott 1985), such as
theft of public property, laxity in work discipline, and constant complaining within one's intimate circle.

The exercise of coercion accompanied concerted efforts to raise
popular consciousness in support of Party rule. Under Ceauşescu, ac-
tivists strove to create a "new socialist man," a clearly intentional project that involved wholly new ways of constituting the person. Some
of this, as I will show below, was to be accomplished through new
temporal markings. Another element of persuasion under Ceauşescu
involved overt nationalism, partially (though far from wholly) explain-
able as an explicit quest for legitimacy.[5] National heroes were exalted,
workers' energies were coaxed forth in the name of industrialization
as a national goal, national enemies were built up in more or less veiled
ways to mobilize the Romanian populace behind its Party's protective
front. Previously inculcated national sentiments made this a lively
field of activity, although not one of uniform agreement.

The intentions and projects of Romania's Communist Party leadership moved in sometimes coordinate, sometimes contradictory relation with a set of systemic tendencies that were not consciously
planned. These tendencies resulted from the overall organization of
socialism's political economy, with its collective rather than private
ownership of the means of production, its central allocations, and its
centralized management of productive activity. Basic to the workings
of firms within socialist economies were what Hungarian economist
Kornai (1980) calls "soft budget constraints": firms that did poorly
would be bailed out, and financial penalties for what capitalists would
see as "irrational" and "inefficient" behavior (excess inventory, over-
employment, overinvestment) were minimal. In consequence, socialist firms did not develop the internal disciplinary mechanisms more
often found in capitalist ones.[6] Because of this, and because central
plans usually inflated targets and productive capacities, firms learned
to hoard materials and labor. They overstated both their material requirements for production and their investment needs. Thus, these

systems had expansionist tendencies that were not just inherent in growth-oriented central plans but were also generated *from below*.

The result was, in Kornai's terms again, an *economy of shortage*. All producing units wanted more inputs than they could get. Hoarding made for unpredictable deliveries, which caused irregular production rhythms, with periods of slackness giving way to periods of frantic activity ("storming") when a delivery of materials finally enabled effort toward meeting production goals. Shortages were sometimes relative, as when sufficient quantities of materials and labor for a given level of output actually *existed*, but not where and when they were needed. Sometimes shortages were absolute, since relative shortage often resulted in lowered production, or—as in Romania—since items required for production or consumption were being exported.

Central decisions together with hierarchical interactions between planners and producing firms, then, resulted in "economies of shortage" that generated "scarcity" in Romania, a scarcity primarily of supplies rather than of demand (the scarcity central to capitalism).[7] Time was implicated in such scarcity in several ways, but particularly as the medium through which labor would act in production to make up for the nonoptimal distribution of the other productive resources. Once enough materials were brought together to produce something, the task of the authorities was to seize enough labor-time from workers to make up for earlier periods of shortage-enforced idleness. But precisely those periods of enforced idleness motivated the authorities to further seizures of time, for "idle" time might be deployed toward other objectives, and power might be served by interfering with them.

Two examples will show how the Romanian Party seized time in order to increase the production of goods within the system of shortage I have described. The examples come from the period 1984–88, a period in which relative shorage was greatly exacerbated by massive exports of foodstuffs and reduced imports of fuel. Thus, the "normal" systemic shortage was conjoined with explicit policies that worsened it.

One villager who commuted daily by train to an urban factory job complained to me of the irregularity of his work time. On some days he would hang around the factory doing very little, on others he would commute two hours to work only to be sent home owing to insufficient electricity; on still others he was required to work overtime, for which he was not paid. He would pay himself for the overtime by cutting work to help his mother plow, sow, weed, or harvest on the private plot they held as members of the collective farm. For such work, the mother would withdraw her labor-time from the collective, whose requirements she had filled by bailing and stacking hay during the winter months when her household economy could better tolerate her absence. Mother and son together produced enough food on their private plot to maintain four or five pigs, a number of sheep, and a good standard of living for their three-person household.

Beginning in about 1983, however, the state sought ways to move some of this "private" product into state warehouses rather than peasant cellars. At first, villagers were given a list of items and amounts— a pig, some chickens, 100 kg of potatoes, etc.—that they were required to contract to the state from their plot, in exchange for a minimal payment. When this proved inadequate, each rural family was told not just how much of various goods to *contract* but exactly how much of each to *plant* on the private plot. Upon delivery of the contracted amounts, the family would receive coupons entitling them to buy bread at the village store; without the coupon they could get no bread. Because private plots were too small to grow cereals, purchased bread was most villagers' only option. The new contract requirements therefore effectively seized the labor-time that had been given over to household production for household consumption; it added the products of that labor-time to the meager output of state and collective farms. In this way, the authorities recouped a portion of the enforced idleness of their factory worker, as well.

Comparable seizures of time were also found in village households whose adults all commuted to work in the city. Such commuter households were assigned a quota of agricultural production alongside their regular jobs; failure to meet the quota would mean confiscation of their private plot. Because the private plot guaranteeing them something to eat was the main reason these workers had not moved to the city altogether, the sanction was an effective one: without the plot, household consumption would suffer. To keep their plot, commuters now had to pay a substantial "tribute" in extra work. Both of these examples rest, of course, on the much earlier decision by the Party to collectivize land, enabling later seizures of the labor-time embodied in rural folk.

These examples show rural households compelled into the state's definition of their use of time. The source of compulsion in both instances was the state's leverage with respect to household consumption, which villagers wished to protect. To these specific instances one could add many other ways in which central planning, shortage, and export combined to reduce individuals' control over their schedules to a bare minimum. Zerubavel, in a discussion of scheduling control, observes that "every scheduling process implies a combination of personal and environmental elements, the proportion between which is very significant sociologically" (1976:91). Using the examples he adduces (from American society), over what sorts of items had Romanians lost scheduling control by the late 1980s?

Urban dwellers could generally choose the time when they would go to the bathroom, but their choice of when to flush or wash up was constrained by whether or not the public water supply had been turned off. Buckets of water stored in apartments might compensate, but not for bathing, which (if one wanted one's water hot) depended on having gas to heat the water. People could not choose the time when they would heat water or cook their meals, since the gas was generally turned off at precisely the times of normal use, so as to prevent excess consumption. Urban housewives often rose at 4:00 A.M. to cook, that being the only time they could light the stove. Unless one walked, no one could choose when to arrive at work, since public transportation was wholly unreliable (owing to measures to conserve use of gasoline), and the ration of gasoline for private cars was so derisory that cars did not provide an alternative for daily movement.

Although the natural environment usually controls when farmers must sow their crop, Romanian farmers were not permitted to plant by the timing optimal for nature; if tractors received no fuel allotment, there might be no planting until well into November or June. Village women lost control over when they would iron or do the laundry, for fuel conservation measures included turning off the electricity delivered to rural areas for large portions of each day—generally according to an unannounced schedule. Village women who commuted to urban jobs often found that there was no electricity when they returned home, and they were obliged to do the washing by hand. Electricity outages also prevented villagers from choosing when they would watch the two hours of television to which Romanian airtime had been reduced. The state infringed even upon the most intimate decisions concerning when to make love, for the official desire for (and shortage of) more numerous laboring bodies led to a pronatalist policy that prohibited all forms of contraception as well as abortion. This forced the "scheduling" of intimacy back onto the rhythms of nature.

To Zerubavel's strategic question, then, concerning who is authorized to schedule parts of the time of other people, we can reply that in Ceauşescu's Romania, national and local political authorities scheduled an extraordinary amount of others' time. Behind these appropriations of scheduling lay political decisions about how to manage austerity so as to repay the foreign debt. It is impossible to prove that an additional conscious intention was to deprive the populace of control over its schedules, but this was indeed an effect of the policies pursued.

Many of the seizures of time listed above were explicitly aimed at increasing production; yet these and other policies also had the effect, whether consciously intended or not, of producing not *goods for* the state but *subjection to* it. To clarify this I must introduce another structural element of Romania's redistributive economy. Redistribution, Wolf reminds us (1982:96–98), is less a type of society than a class of strategies implemented through various means. Redistributors must accumulate things to redistribute, which form their "funds of power." A redistributive system delivers power into the hands of those persons or bureaucratic segments that dispose of large pools of resources to allocate. From the highest levels of the planning apparatus on down, therefore, actors strive to bring as many resources as possible under their control.

In socialist redistribution, it was generally the Party and state apparatuses that disposed of the greatest means for redistribution. The practices of socialist bureaucrats thus tended to augment the resources under the global disposition of the apparatus of power, a tendency Fehér, Heller, and Márkus (1983:65) see as the basic "law of motion" of socialist societies. Particularly important, in their analysis, was that resources not fall out of central control into consumption but expand the basis of production for the apparatus. In other words, these systems accumulated *means of production,* above all (Campeanu 1988:116–117). Competitive processes within socialism's all-encompassing bureaucracy thus made *inputs* count more than production or outputs (Stark 1990:17). Inputs, however, might be both absolute and relative—relative, that is, to the resources commanded *by other actors.* To the extent that the resources of other actors could be incapacitated, the pool at the center would be enhanced. Jan Gross, from whom I draw this proposition, argues that Stalin's "spoiler state" produced its power by incapacitating those actual or potential loci of power that were independent of the state-sponsored organization. This regime's power came from ensuring that *no one else* could get things done or associate together for other purposes (Gross 1988:234).

This relative conception of power seems to me to illuminate a number of seizures of time in Ceauşescu's Romania. Their immediate "cause" was, again, a shortage economy strained to the utmost by austerity measures and exports; the effect was an astounding immobilization of bodies that stopped the time contained in them, rendered them impotent, and subtracted them from other activities by filling up their time with a few basic activities, such as essential provisioning and elementary movements to and from work. My examples show us how shortages of certain items were converted into a seizure of citizens' time, but rarely for producing goods that might *alleviate* shortage. These seizures instead produced incapacity, and therefore enhanced power.

The most obvious example, all too often signaled in the western press, was the immobilization of bodies in food lines. I see this as a state-imposed seizure of time because it was precisely the state-directed export of foodstuffs, alongside the state-supported crisis in agriculture, that raised to epic proportions in Romania a phenomenon also present in several other socialist countries. More generally, it was socialist policy to suppress the market mechanism (which, in western economies, eliminates lines by differentiating people's ability to pay). Urban in its habitat, the food line seized and flattened the time of all urbanites except those having access to special stores (the Party elite and secret police). Meat, eggs, flour, oil, butter, sugar, and bread were rationed in most Romanian cities; they arrived unreliably and required an interminable wait when they did. During the 1980s other food items, such as potatoes and vegetables, came to be in shorter supply than usual, as well. Depending on one's occupation, some of the time immobilized by provisioning might be subtracted from one's job—office clerks, for example, were notorious for being absent from their desks when food hit the local store—but people like schoolteachers or factory workers had to add onto already-long working days the two or three hours required to get something to eat.

In a brilliant discussion of socialism's queues (of which the food line is the prototype), Campeanu offers additional insights through which we can tie the immobilization of bodies in food lines to the en-hancement of central power (Campeanu MS).[8] Queues, he suggests, function as agents of accumulation. They do this, first, by reducing the opportunity for money to be spent; this forces accumulation on a pop-ulace that would spend but is not permitted to. Moreover, by rationing consumption, queues prevent resources from being drawn out of the central fund of use-values administered by the state, which (according to the argument above) would reduce the reserves that form the basis of its control. Queues thus maintain the center's fund of power. Sec-ond, Campeanu argues, queues serve the larger processes of central accumulation through the unequal exchange that is their essence. The state is entitled to buy labor at its nominal price, but labor must buy the goods necessary for its reproduction at their nominal prices *plus* "prices" attached to time spent in line and to good or bad luck (i.e., being served before supplies run out). Thus, the value of the labor force becomes paradoxically inferior to the value of the goods neces-sary to it, as waiting drives up the cost of consuming without affecting the price labor must be paid in the form of a wage. In other words, by making consumption too costly, queues enable a transfer of resources into accumulation. This forced accumulation is achieved by converting some of the "price" into waiting time (cf. Schwartz 1975:102)—that is, by disabling consumption as consumers' bodies are immobilized in lines.

Was there not some "cost" to the state, as well as to consumers, from immobilizing people in food lines? It must be remembered that socialist systems did not rest on the extraction of profits based in workers' labor-time (a process quintessentially rooted *in time*). "Time wasted," for a capitalist, is profit lost. In socialist systems, which accumulated not profits but means of production, "time wasted" did not have this same significance. Time spent standing in lines was not a cost to the socialist state. This same time spent in a general strike, however, would have been costly indeed, for it would have revealed basic disagreement with the Party's definition of "the general welfare" and would thereby have undermined that central pillar of the Party's legitimacy—its claim to special knowledge of how society should be managed (see Konrád and Szelényi 1979:48).

Still other seizures of time derived from official priorities in allocating fuel, already alluded to above. Some of the petroleum produced in or imported by Romania was exported for hard currency; beginning in 1984, this was facilitated by prohibiting the use of private cars for most of the winter. The remaining gasoline was preferentially allocated, first, to the chemical industry and other major industrial production; then to transporting goods destined for export; after that, to peak periods in agriculture; and only last to public transportation. Villagers who had to take a bus to town or to the train might wait for hours in the cold, or end by walking 6–8 km to the train station; residents of urban centers formed gigantic swarms at infrequently served bus stops; many urbanites preferred to walk long distances to work rather than be trampled in the melee. Vastly curtailed train schedules immobilized people for hours on end as they waited for connections. Trains were so crowded that most people had to stand, making it impossible to use the time to read or work (the more so as trains were unlighted after dark). No one has attempted to calculate the amount of time seized by the state-produced fuel shortage. Among friends with whom I discussed it, anywhere from one to four hours had been added on to the workday, hours that could be put to no other purpose (except, for some, to the exercise of walking).

The fuel shortage was converted into an additional "time tax" for residents of villages: it increased their labor. Labor-intensive agricultural production returned to replace mechanized agriculture, as tractors and harvesters were sidelined by insufficient fuel.[9] Tractor-drivers sought to conserve their tiny fuel allotments by making the furrow shallow rather than deep and by increasing the spaces between rows. This produced more weeds as well as an inferior crop yield. Exports of petroleum reduced production of herbicides, which meant that the bountiful weed harvest had to be weeded by hand. The greater demand for labor in villages was part of the motive for taxing commuters with farm-work, as mentioned above; added to the effects of reduced electricity upon the work of both urban and rural women, it greatly lengthened the working day for all.

While the austerity measures responsible for these conversions of shortage into a "time tax" were not entirely the state's "fault," the peremptoriness with which they were executed lends credence to the notion that power was constituting itself through the effects of austerity. An exchange in the correspondence column of an urban newspaper illustrates this nicely:

> [Query from a reader]: "For some time now, tickets are no longer being sold in advance for long-distance bus trips out of Iaşi. Why is this?"
>
> [Reply]: "As the Bus Company director informs us, new dispositions from the Ministry of Transport stipulate that tickets should not be sold in advance, and for this reason the bus ticket bureau has gone out of service."[10]

As an answer to the question, "why," the response leaves something to be desired, showing just how uninterested the authorities were in justifying the seizure of time. The distribution of time implied in the exchange was this: persons wanting to take a bus to another city would get up hours in advance of the scheduled departure (for one could never be sure how many others would be wanting to travel on the same day) and go stand in line before the booth that would open for ticket sales just prior to the departure hour. As usually happened in Romania, friends of the ticket-seller would have gotten tickets ahead, meaning that even those whose position in the line might lead them to think there were enough seats left for them could be disappointed, returning home empty-handed many hours later.

As this example shows particularly well, such seizures of time did more than simply immobilize bodies for hours, destroying their capacity for alternative uses of time. Also destroyed was all possibility for lower-level initiative and planning.[11] This was surely an advantage to those central planners for whom initiatives from below were always inconvenient; one cannot easily imagine such destruction of initiative, however, as the conscious motivation of the policy. The central appropriation of planning and initiative was furthered by a monopoly over knowledge that might have allowed people to use their time "rationally"—i.e., otherwise. Not knowing when the bus might come, when cars might be allowed to circulate again, when the exam for medical specializations would be given, or when food would appear in stores, bodies were transfixed, suspended in a void that obviated all projects and plans but the most flexible and spontaneous.

The above examples illustrate how a shortage of resources, especially fuel, was converted into a seizure of time that immobilized it for any other use. I would add to these an additional set of examples in which the "time tax" exacted of people came not from conversions of shortage but from the simple display of power, which was by that very fact further enhanced. In a modest form, this was what happened in most of the interminable Party or workplace meetings that occupied much time for persons in virtually every setting; since meetings also sometimes accomplished organizational business, however, I do not count them. I refer, rather, to displays such as the mobilization of bodies from schools and factories to line the route, chanting and waving, whenever Romanian President Ceauşescu took a trip or received a foreign guest. Delays in the hour of arrival seized more of the time of the waiting crowd. (It was not just Ceauşescu who was greeted by the appropriation of bodies and the time they contained: so also were other "important" figures, including even the writer of these lines, who as part of a group of Honored Guests helped to appropriate the entire afternoon of a welcoming committee of schoolchildren [see Verdery 1991a, Chapter 6]). Every year on August 23, Romania's national "independence" day, hundreds of thousands of people were massed as early as 6:00 A.M. for parades that actually began around 10:00 or 11:00. Because experience proved that parades could turn into riots, as of about 1987 these crowds were massed somewhat later, in closely guarded stadiums—to which, of course, they walked. There they witnessed precision drills, whose preparation had required many hours from those who performed them.

Here, then, is the ultimate "etatization" of time, seized by power for the celebration of itself. Tens of thousands of Romanians waited, daily, in contexts in which they could do nothing else: time that might have gone to counterhegemonic purposes had been expropriated.[12] Schwartz calls this "ritual waiting," whose cause is not scarcity in the time of someone being awaited. Ritual waiting serves, rather, to underscore the social distance between those who wait and whoever is responsible for the waiting (Schwartz 1975:39–41).

The various seizures of time in Romania were not distributed evenly across the landscape, for it was urbanites who waited the most: for transport, for food, for parades, for visiting dignitaries, for light, for hot water, for cooking gas. Villagers waited for buses and trains and light, but rarely for preorganized demonstrations, parades, or Honored Guests; their "time tax" came in the form of ever-greater claims upon their labor. The persons most removed from such encroachment were uncollectivized peasants living in the hills and not commuting to city jobs. Perhaps not surprisingly, these people were prime targets of Ceauşescu's infamous "settlement systematization" plan, which, by destroying their individual houses and settling them in apartment buildings, would bring them more fully under control, more vulnerable to seizure of their time.

What does all this suggest about the relation between intentionality and structure, and between "system logic" and contradiction, in the etatization of time? Without the possibility of interviewing high Party officials, one cannot say how many of the effects mentioned above were consciously planned *as such* by Party leaders. I find it difficult to believe, however, that the austerity program behind so much of the etatization of time was intended to produce subjection: it was intended first of all to pay off foreign creditors. That its consequences for subjection may have been perceived (and even desired) is very possible. Those consequences emerged, however, as *side*-effects of other policies carried out within a system governed by tendencies peculiar to it (the dynamics of a shortage economy based on centralized bureaucratic allocations).

This is nonetheless not to say that "system logic" is inexorable, and that the effects to which I have pointed were characteristic of socialism everywhere. Specific policies of specific leaderships made a difference, setting up contradictory tendencies and exacerbating them. So did the environmental conditions peculiar to one or another socialist country. The command structure of socialism in East Germany, for example, was similar to that of Romania; yet its proximity to West Germany required East German leaders to maintain a standard of living closer to that of the West, which, together with subtle investment flows from West Germans, resulted in productivity and consumption higher than Romania's. The "economic crisis" that so exacerbated Romania's shortage came in part from the leadership's desire to pay off the foreign debt, instead of rescheduling it as did leaders in Poland. Romania in the 1980s gives us an excellent example of the extremes to which political decisions could push the "logic" of socialism, producing a form of gridlock rather than processes analyzable as somehow functionally "rational."[13] This extreme case reveals potentials not generally evident, through which we can improve our grasp of sociopolitical processes under socialism and their relation to time.

## Spheres of Encroachment and Resistance

What was the Romanian state seizing time *from*? What activities was it incapacitating, whether by intention or by chance? To what other uses did people continue to put the reduced time left to them? To ask this question is also to ask where struggles against etatization were most evident—that is, where it issued in resistance to the state's encroachment. I will mention three areas particularly assaulted by the etatization of time: independent earnings, household consumption, and sociability. Each of these also constituted a focus of resistant deployment of time, resistances that—given the degree of coercion mobilized against them—were nearly invisible, but nonetheless real.[14]

The widespread shortages of virtually everything, coupled with cleverly disguised reductions of incomes in people's regular jobs, pushed everyone into secondary and often illegal forms of earning (particularly lucrative for the consumer services rationed by queues). For example, waiters or clerks in foodstores were in great demand as sources of food. They filched meat, potatoes, bread, and other items from their restaurants or shops, selling them at exorbitant prices to people who might have been so foolish as to invite an American, say, to dinner. (These practices naturally reduced the food available in shops and restaurants.) Gas station attendants, in exchange for a huge tip, some Kent cigarettes, or a kilogram of pork, would sometimes put extra gas into the tank. Ticket sellers at the railway station, if properly rewarded, might "find" tickets for crowded trains. People with cars hung around hotels to provide black market taxi service at twice the normal fare (demand for them was high, since the fuel allotments to regular taxis were so small that they were rarely to be found when needed). Drivers for the forestry service ripped off truckloads of wood to sell to peasant villagers and American anthropologists.

The sources of secondary income were legion, but the state's seizure of time pushed them in the direction of "hit-and-run" strategies requiring little time and few formal skills, rather than the moonlighting, spare-time sewing, extended housebuilding (see, e.g., Kenedi 1982), and other sources of skilled earning for which people no longer had enough time. It was difficult for a schoolteacher to find a few extra hours for tutoring after she had stood in several lines and walked to and from work, or for a secretary to take home the professor's manuscript to type for extra pay. In consequence, Romanians built up their unofficial earnings not as much from parallel *productive* endeavors as from *scavenging*.[15] The authorities did everything in their power to punish behaviors like those I have mentioned, for outside earnings not only diminished the state's revenues but also mitigated people's utter dependence on their state wage (Burawoy 1985:193), reducing the state's leverage over them.

Examples of outside earnings merge directly into the second locus of struggle between a time-seizing state and resistant households. The forms of the state's seizure of time encroached particularly on the consumption standards of households, whose members reacted by trying to seize some of it back in one way or another. Theft from the harvests of the collective farm was one prime instance. Another was ever-more-sophisticated ways of killing calves at birth or shortly thereafter; this relieved the villager of the obligation to sacrifice milk to the calf and to produce six months' worth of fodder for it, as the state insisted, and also (though this was not the first aim) afforded the household an illegal taste of veal. (The killing had to be sophisticated because all such deaths had to be vet-certified as "natural" if one were to avoid a heavy fine.)

The extent to which foodstuffs—repositories of the time and labor of village peasants and commuters—focused the struggle over time was brought home to me in October 1988, as I drove into the village of my 1984 fieldwork to pay a visit. Both early in the day when I arrived and late at night when I left, local authorities were out in the fields with those workers they had managed to round up for the potato and corn harvests, and the streets were crawling with policemen shining powerful flashlights on every vehicle that might divert corn or potatoes into some storehouse other than that of the collective farm. Whether on that night or on some other, numerous villagers would "recover" sacks of corn and potatoes from the collective farm, thereby recouping some of what they had been obligated to contract from their private plots. This enabled them and their urban relatives to eat better than they "ought" to. It also enabled a few other urbanites to avoid standing in food lines in October for the winter's supply of potatoes because—using the extra gas they had bribed from the gas-station attendant—they would drive their cars directly to a village and pay five times the market price to buy 40 kilograms of potatoes from some peasant. The practice naturally furthered urban food shortages and was one reason why policemen randomly stopped cars to spot-check for transport of food, which they would confiscate. Such events further illustrate my claim that the apparatus of coercion was central to Ceauşescu's regime and to its capacity to seize time.

In addition to the state's seizure of time from secondary earnings and from household consumption, state policies threatened a third area: sociability, or the reproduction of local social relations. It was one thing to struggle for the resources necessary to maintaining one's household; to find enough food to entertain friends and relatives, however, was something else. In urban centers the decrease in socializing (upon which many people remarked to me spontaneously) was the direct result of unavailable food and drink. In villages, somewhat better provisioned with these items, incursions on sociability came

from state attempts to mobilize village labor on Sundays and holidays
and from strict rationing of certain substances essential to providing
hospitality: sugar, butter and flour. Romanian villagers mark Christmas, Easter, Sundays, saints' days, and a variety of other occasions
with visiting sustained by cakes and wine or brandy (sugar is essential
to making all of these, butter and flour to making the cakes). The various seizures of villagers' time lengthened the hours that women had
to spend providing these items of hospitality; rationing lengthened
the time for procuring the ingredients; being mobilized to weed on
Sunday reduced the time for visiting; and exhaustion from the various
taxes on time often reduced villagers' interest in socializing. In both
urban and rural contexts, then, for different reasons, human connections were beginning to suffer from the etatization of time.

   This tendency was significant for a number of reasons, not least
the attenuation of social ties that might be mobilized in overt resistance to the regime. (The chaos during and after Ceauşescu's overthrow gave indirect witness to the social disorganization his rule had
produced.) I wish to focus, however, on the implications of attenuated
sociability for people's self-conceptions. This will enable me to discuss
more broadly the ways in which the appropriations of time inherent
in the state's projects were gradually eroding older conceptions of the
person. Through these examples we can see how attention to temporality reveals links between state power and the constitution of self.

## The State and the Self

   I understand the "self" as an ideological construct whereby individuals are situationally linked to their social environments through
normative statements setting them off *as* individuals from the world
around them; thus understood, individuals are the sites of many possible selves, anchored differently in different situations. The self has
been an object of intense interest for the organizations individuals inhabit, such as states and religions. Historically, the attempt to redefine
the self in ways suitable for one organization—such as the state—and
detrimental to another—such as the church—has been a locus of major social contention. Temporality can be deeply implicated in definitions and redefinitions of the self, as selves become defined or redefined in part through temporal patterns that mark them as persons of
a particular kind.

   For example, the periodicities of the major religions distinguish
different kinds of persons (see Ghani 1989). A person is marked as
Protestant by attending weekly church services on Sunday and by ob-

serving certain religious festivals, such as Christmas or Easter; a person is marked as Roman Catholic, in contrast, by attending Mass not only on Sundays (if not, indeed, daily) but also on the holy days of obligation (All Souls' Day, feast of the Immaculate Conception, the Assumption, etc.), more numerous than the holy days of Protestants. A person is marked as Orthodox by these rhythms of worship and also by the observance of myriad saints' days (which some Catholics also observe, but in smaller number). A person is marked as Muslim by multiple prayer rituals within each day, by religious festivals different from those of Christians, by special observance of Fridays rather than Sundays, and by the pilgrimage, which gives a distinctive rhythm to an Islamic life.[16] Jews, meanwhile, have long differed from both Christians and Muslims by special observance of Saturdays, as well as by a wholly different set of periodicities and sacred days (Zerubavel 1981:70–80).

In seeking to create the new socialist man, the Romanian state moved to establish new temporal punctuations that would alter the sense of personal identity tied to the ritual markings of the week, the year, and larger periods. In contrast with the religious rhythms just mentioned, the identity of the new socialist men was to be marked by *non*observance of a fixed holy day, his day(s) of leisure distributed at random across the week.[17] Party meetings scattered irregularly throughout the week also marked socialist man as *a*rhythmic, within short periodicities. Over longer ones, his annual cycle was to be punctuated not by religious festivals but by secular ones—e.g., New Year's, May Day, Women's Day (see also Binns 1979–80)—and, increasingly, by national ones—Romanian independence day, the 400th anniversary of the enthronement of this or that prince, the birthday of this or that Romanian hero. Many of these latter observances, however, unlike those of religious calendars, differed from one year to the next: this year the 200th anniversary of the enthronement of Prince X, next year the 400th anniversary of the birthday of hero Y. The arhythmia of these ritual temporalities echoed that of socialist production patterns, with their unpredictable alterations of slackness and "storming" to fill production quotas. If, as Zerubavel suggests (1981:12–30), one effect of temporal regularity is to create the background expectancies upon which our sense of the "normal" is erected, a possible consequence of socialism's arhythmia would have been to keep people permanently off balance, to undermine the sense of a "normal" order and to institute *uncertainty* as the rule.

The new periodicities aimed to supplant older ones that marked persons as Romanian Orthodox. This was met, however, by resistant self-conceptions, particularly over the suppression of religious holidays and, in the villages, over the Party's attempt to extract work on Sundays. Christmas was a major battleground, as factory directors announced that workers absent on Christmas day would not receive their annual bonus, while workers pulled strings to get formal medical statements that they had been absent for "illness." Peasants, harangued to present themselves for Sunday work, would hide if they saw their brigade-leader coming; or they would show up at the farm, having arranged to be called home for some "emergency" after half an hour. A similar tug-of-war took place between villagers and local Party officials whenever one of the many Orthodox saints-days fell on a normal workday. The Party defined this time as suitable for labor; villagers and the priest, by contrast, defined it as "dangerous," insisting that work done on such days would bear no fruit or even bring disaster. Behind these different interpretations lay something deeper, however: the definition of the self as secular member of a broad social(ist) collectivity, or as Romanian Orthodox member of a narrow household one.

In the context of variant self-conceptions, the erosion of sociability discussed above was very significant. Sociable gatherings would have cemented close solidary networks that might resist both the officially emphasized large-scale collectivism and the creeping atomization that regime policies produced. That is, sociability served to reproduce groupings intermediate between individuals and the social whole. The etatization of time prevented this, just as many other aspects of Party policy eroded the space intermediate between individuals and the state. In so doing, it incapacitated a major part of Romanians' conception of self, for in their view, to be Romanian—to be a person—is to offer hospitality.[18] If one does not have the wherewithal to do this, one is diminished as a human being. Some anecdotal evidence will support this claim. First, one hapless host upon whom a friend thrust me unannounced was complaining that it was impossible to entertain one's friends any more because one had nothing to offer them. To my matter-of-fact suggestion that maybe the food crisis would detach the idea of sociability from the offering of food, he stared at me open-mouthed, in shock. "Then we would be like Germans!" he said, "a people with a completely different nature!" This gentleman's self-conception was not unique; I encountered it often in my initial fieldwork in a German-Romanian village, where the offering of food was a principal indicator by which Romanians thought themselves distinct from Germans (see Verdery 1983:64–65). Second, like this man but in more exaggerated form, others upon whom I chanced without invitation presented their "paltry" offerings of food with a self-abasement I found unbearable.

Such instances brought home to me in a very direct way how shortages of food, the diminution of time that was associated with them, and the other "time taxes" that made provisioning so difficult had assaulted many people's self-image. The erosion of sociability meant more than the decline of a certain social order, marked by social observance of particular ritual occasions that reproduced solidarity among friends and family: it meant the erosion of their very conception of themselves as human beings.

Reports of friends suggested an additional assault on self-conception from the state's seizures of time. In one report, a friend had heard that eggs were to be distributed for unused ration coupons. Having a hungry 18-year-old son, she thought that by waiting at the store with a jar she might be able to get a few broken eggs without a ration card. She explained her idea to the clerk, who found one broken egg; after an hour another broken egg appeared. Another hour turned up no broken eggs, and customers had stopped coming. My friend approached the clerk in the now-empty store, suggesting that she simply break another couple of eggs and that would be the end of it. The suggestion evoked loud and anxious protests: what would happen if someone reported her, etc., etc. At length the clerk "found" one more broken egg, bringing the yield for two hours' waiting to three broken eggs. As my friend left the store, she burst into tears, feeling—in her words—utterly humiliated. The experience of humiliation, of a destruction of dignity, was common for those who had waited for hours to accomplish (or fail to accomplish) some basic task. Being immobilized for some meager return, during which time one could not do anything else one might find rewarding, was the ultimate experience of impotence. It created the power sought by the regime, as people were prevented from experiencing themselves as efficacious.

Such seizures of time were therefore crucial in the expropriation of initiative mentioned above; they were basic to producing subjects who would not see themselves as independent agents. They contributed to the "passive nature" by which many observers, including Romanians themselves, explained the lack of overt resistance to the Ceauşescu regime, as well as to the feeling many expressed to me that Communist rule was "ruining Romanians' character." The etatization of time shows how intricate—and how intricately temporal—were the links between sweeping state policies and people's sense of self, the latter being eroded by and defended from forces both intentional and systemic.

Finally, these links between the self and the etatization of time help us to understand better the regime's profound lack of legitimacy, amply illustrated in the manifestations of public hatred that accom-

panied the overthrow of Ceauşescu. These links become more percep-
tible if we define time in terms of bodies, as I have done in this paper.
By insinuating itself and its temporalities into people's projects and
impeding those projects through the medium of people's very bodies,
this regime reproduced every day people's alienation from it.[19] By
stripping individuals of the resources necessary to creating and artic-
ulating social selves, it confronted them repeatedly with their failures
of self-realization. As their bodies were forced to make histories not of
their choosing and their selves became increasingly fractured, they experienced daily the illegitimacy of the state to whose purposes their
bodies were bent.

Perhaps the contrasting trajectories of regime and social body
from which these alienations emerged helps to explain the contrast between two different expressions of time, which increasingly characterized the pronouncements of regime and citizens during the 1980s.
Pronouncements emanating from the top of society became more and
more messianic, invoking amid images of ever-greater grandeur the
radiant future whose perfect realization was just at hand; farmers and
factory workers, meanwhile, increasingly invoked the Apocalypse.[20]
For the Party leadership, time was in a process of culminating, of becoming *for all time*. For everyone else, however, time was running out.
In December 1989, it finally did—for the leadership, as well.

The above discussion suggests that the etatization of time in socialist Romania was quite a different matter from seizures of time at
one or another stage in the development of capitalism. Although some
of the time seized in Romania was put to the production of goods,
much of it went instead to displaying power, to producing subjection,
to *depriving* bodies of activity that might produce goods. Early capitalism seized the rhythms of the body and the working day, and it transformed them (Smith 1982; Thompson 1967); it stretched out into a linear progression of equivalent daily units what had once been the repetitive annual cycles of an agrarian order. The state in Ceauşescu's
Romania seized time differently. First, it generated an arhythmia of
unpunctuated and irregular now-frenetic, now-idle work, a spastically
unpredictable time that made all planning by average citizens impossible. Second, within this arhythmia, it flattened time out in an experience of endless waiting.[21] Campeanu expresses this admirably: "Becoming is replaced by unending repetition. Eviscerated of its substance, history itself becomes atemporal. Perpetual movement gives
way to perpetual immobility. . . . [H]istory . . . loses the quality of duration" (1986:22).[22]

"Capitalist" time must be rendered progressive and linear so that
it can be forever speeded up—as Harvey puts it, "the circulation of

capital makes time the fundamental dimension of human existence" (1985:37). Time in Ceauşescu's Romania, by contrast, stood still, the medium for producing not profits but subjection, for immobilizing persons in the Party's grip. The overthrow of this regime reopens Romania to the temporal movements of commodity production, consumption, time-based work discipline, and initiating selves.

## Notes

*Acknowledgments.* I am much indebted to Ashraf Ghani for extensive discussions that led me to frame this paper as I have and for suggesting many of its central ideas. Thanks also to Pavel Campeanu, Gail Kligman, and Henry Rutz for comments on an earlier version. Three research grants from IREX supported my fieldwork in 1984–85, 1987, and 1988, which provided the data I report here.

1. Because this is a paper about time and because in "real" time Romania is now a rather different society from the one described here, I will not use the "ethnographic present" but the past tense.

2. There is no room in this paper for extended definitions of terms. I would nonetheless distinguish between the concept that invokes those organizational structures which administer a polity, defend its territory, and maintain order (the "state," monopolized in the Romanian case by the Communist Party organization, until 1990) from the concept that refers to its ideal inhabitant, the "nation." Both are ideologically constructed "entities," but the discourses, the activities, and the personnel that construct and lead them are not identical. A "nation" often aspires to control its own "state" (particularly when it is subject to rule by persons of "other nations"); yet, achieving that condition does not mean that the two are permanently fused. Trouillot (1990) also makes an argument that separates the two notions.

3. The examples offered in this paper come from several different sites and time periods. In 1984–85 I conducted a year's field research that took me to the Transylvanian city of Cluj and to two villages in southcentral Transylvania; in 1987 and 1988 I returned for two summers, visiting both urban and rural locations and adding two other cities (Iaşi and Bucharest). All the examples I give here came from overheard conversations (rather than from interviewing expressly on these themes) in one or another of these times and places. Some examples draw as well on earlier fieldwork in 1973–74 and 1979–80 (see Verdery 1983).

4. A more detailed discussion of the points summarized here can be found in Verdery 1991a, chapter 2, and in Verdery 1991b.

5. See Verdery 1991a, chapter 3, for clarification of this point.

6. Kornai's own country led the departure from the model described here, with China and the Soviet Union later following Hungary's lead. Romania continued to be the classic example of a centralized economy of shortage, until the 1989 overthrow of Ceauşescu; hence, despite changes within particular socialist economies, the model I employ continued to be applicable there.

7. The dynamics outlined in these paragraphs explain why Schwartz and others are wrong to speak of the "wasted" labor of all those Soviet citizens standing in lines by the hour. Schwartz, citing a Soviet emigre, comments that the time Soviet citizens wasted annually in shopping for food in the late 1960s was 30 billion hours, or the equivalent of a year's work for 15 million people (Schwartz 1975:13). Many of those wasted hours would have been spent in idleness at factories, underutilized because of shortages of supply. In a capitalist economy, much of that same labor would be "wasted" in unemployment.

8. The manuscript referred to in this paragraph and cited in the bibliography was not available to me for page references. The summary I offer comes from a brief prospectus of the argument made in Campeanu's longer work.

9. Ceauşescu referred to these "new" forms in agriculture, improbably enough, as the "new agricultural revolution." Apropos the apparent reversal of technological progress in Romania, note the following joke—Q: What did we have before the candle? A: Electricity.

10. *Flacăra Iaşului* August 20, 1988, page 2.

11. Zygmunt Bauman (1987:64–67) sees the arrogation of the right to initiative and control over time as an element of the new structure of domination that marks the "modern world" more broadly; he would thus see in these socialist examples merely an intensification of processes at work everywhere, through the forms of the modern state.

12. "Expropriated" is, I think, a better word than something like "wasted," for people did not often report their experience of such immobilizations as a "waste of time." Sometimes they used the expression "*loss* of time," suggesting an experience of time as finite but not necessarily commodifiable or wastable. Those whose reaction was most likely to resemble my own (that time had been wasted) were some urban intellectuals.

13. This useful phrasing was suggested by a participant in the discussion following oral delivery of this paper at the 1989 AES meeting.

14. The question of why there was less overt resistance in Romania than in other Eastern European countries prior to December 1989 is one on which area specialists disagree. Some invoke "cowardice," some "Balkan traditions," and some a variety of structural variables. I side with the third of these. The degree of surveillance and repression, the successful squelching of opposition, the leadership's purging of disagreement within its own circles, and the destruction of independent organizational forms (church, voluntary organizations not tied to the Party, etc.) all gave no leverage to those who might have formed dissident movements from which other Romanians would have drawn encouragement. Also important was that western governments—particularly the United States—failed to take an interest in opposition to the rule of the applauded "maverick" Ceauşescu. All these factors enabled the Romanian Party leadership to act with an extreme arbitrariness that facilitated control over the population and kept it constantly off balance, to a greater degree than elsewhere. To observe that there was little overt resistance in Romania is not, of course, to say that the state under Ceauşescu was omnipotent. Covert resistance, sabotage, and withdrawal of effort and loyalty undermined regime projects throughout his rule.

15. I borrow this term from political scientist Kenneth Jowitt.

16. These examples come from Ghani 1989.

17. Although Sunday remained the "day of rest" in most factories, during the 1980s there were repeated incursions into this. Workers would be assigned a different day in the week as their "Sunday," making it impossible for them to attend church (for those who still wanted to) or, more subtly, to punctuate their week in identification with Christian norms.

18. Hospitality may be an important component of Hungarian ethnic identity in Romania, as well, though my experience of this group is limited. One example below comes from a family of Hungarians, behaving in this respect like my Romanian friends.

19. I owe this observation to Ashraf Ghani.

20. The observation noted in this paragraph is better called an impression, but I think it is a significant one.

21. Thom (1989) offers a fascinating discussion of linguistic aspects of this flattening of time. She observes that the prose style of Soviet-type socialism (called "Newspeak," in the book's English translation of the original *la langue de bois*) regularly sacrificed verbs to nouns. This fate befell above all those verbs that contain temporal referents or suggest temporal sequence. "Whenever possible, Newspeak avoids the precision of the verb and opts for a vague time-lessness, carefully evading narrative while stressing the movement that is immanent in all things" (1989:22). Additional aspects of the flattening of time, such as in Romanian historiography, are found in Verdery 1991a, Chapter 6.

22. The loss of the durative element in time is wonderfully captured in the following Romanian joke: "What do we celebrate on May 8, 1821? 100 years until the founding of the Romanian Communist Party."

## References Cited

Bauman, Zygmunt
  1987   Legislators and Interpreters: On Modernity, Post-Modernity and Intellectuals. Ithaca, NY: Cornell University Press.
Binns, C. A. P.
  1979–80   The Changing Face of Power: Revolution and Accommodation in the Development of the Soviet Ceremonial System. Man 14:585–606; 15:170–187.
Burawoy, Michael
  1985   The Politics of Production: Factory Regimes under Capitalism and Socialism. London: Verso.
Burman, R.
  1981   Time and Socioeconomic Change in Simbu. Man 16:251–267.
Campeanu, Pavel
  1986   The Origins of Stalinism: From Leninist Revolution to Stalinist Society. Armonk, NY: M. E. Sharpe.
  1988   The Genesis of the Stalinist Social Order. Armonk, NY: M. E. Sharpe.
  MS   A Sociology of Queues. Armonk, NY: M. E. Sharpe (translation in progress).

Evans-Pritchard, E. E.
  1940   The Nuer. Oxford: Clarendon Press.
Fehér, Ferenc, Agnes Heller, and György Márkus
  1983   Dictatorship over Needs: An Analysis of Soviet Societies. New York:
         Basil Blackwell.
Ghani, Ashraf
  1989   Consciousness of Conjuncture: Struggle over Seizure of Time, Af-
         ghanistan 1978–1988. Paper delivered at the 1989 Spring Meeting of the
         American Ethnological Society, Santa Fe.
Gross, Jan
  1988   Revolution from Abroad: The Soviet Conquest of Poland's Western
         Ukraine and Western Byelorussia. Princeton: Princeton University Press.
Hallowell, Irving
  1937   Temporal Orientation in Western Civilization. American Anthropol-
         ogist 39:647–670.
Harvey, David
  1985   The Urbanization of Capital. Baltimore: Johns Hopkins Press.
Hugh-Jones, Christine
  1979   From the Milk River: Spatial and Temporal Processes in Northwest
         Amazonia. Cambridge: Cambridge University Press.
Kenedi, Janos
  1982   Do It Yourself: Hungary's Hidden Economy. London: Pluto Press.
Konrád, George, and Ivan Szelényi
  1979   The Intellectuals on the Road to Class Power: A Sociological Study of
         the Role of the Intelligentsia in Socialism. New York: Harcourt, Brace, Jo-
         vanovich.
Kornai, Janos
  1980   Economics of Shortage. Amsterdam: North-Holland Publishing Co.
Leach, E. R.
  1961   Two Essays Concerning the Symbolic Representation of Time. In Re-
         thinking Anthropology. Pp. 114–136. London: Athlone Press.
Manea, Norman
  1989   România în trei fraze (cu comentariu). MS. (Published in 1990 in En-
         glish as Romania: Three Lines with Commentary. In Without Force or
         Lies: Voices from the Revolution of Central Europe in 1989–90. William
         M. Brinton and Alan Rinzler, eds. Pp. 305–334. San Francisco: Mercury
         House.)
Munn, Nancy
  1986   The Fame of Gawa. New York: Cambridge University Press.
Schwartz, Barry
  1975   Queuing and Waiting: Studies in the Social Organization of Access
         and Delay. Chicago: University of Chicago Press.
Scott, James C.
  1985   Weapons of the Weak: Everyday Forms of Peasant Resistance. New
         Haven: Yale University Press.
Smith, Michael French
  1982   Bloody Time and Bloody Scarcity: Capitalism, Authority, and the
         Transformation of Temporal Experience in a Papua New Guinea Village.
         American Ethnologist 9:503–518.
Stark, David
  1990   La valeur du travail et sa rétribution. Actes de la recherche en sci-
         ences sociales 85:3–20.

Thom, Françoise
1989   Newspeak: The Language of Soviet Communism *(La Langue de Bois).*
  London: Claridge Press.
Thompson, E. P.
1967   Time, Work-discipline, and Industrial Capitalism. Past and Present
  38:56–97.
Trouillot, Michel-Rolph
1990   Haiti, State Against Nation: The Origins and Legacy of Duvalierism.
  New York: Monthly Review Press.
Verdery, Katherine
1983   Transylvanian Villagers: Three Centuries of Political, Economic, and
  Ethnic Change. Berkeley: University of California Press.
1990   The Production and Defense of "the Romanian Nation," 1900 to
  World War II. *In* Nationalist Ideologies and the Production of National
  Cultures. Richard G. Fox, ed. Pp. 81–111. Washington, D.C.: American
  Anthropological Association.
1991a   National Ideology under Socialism: Identity and Cultural Politics in
  Ceauşescu's Romania. Berkeley: University of California Press.
1991b   Theorizing Socialism: A Prologue to the "Transition." American
  Ethnologist 18(3):419–439.
Wolf, Eric R.
1982   Europe and the People Without History. Berkeley: University of Cal-
  ifornia Press.
Zerubavel, Eviatar
1976   Time Tables and Scheduling. Sociological Inquiry 46:87–94.
1981   Hidden Rhythms: Schedules and Calendars in Social Life. Chicago:
  University of Chicago Press.

# 4

# Never on Sunday: Time-discipline and Fijian Nationalism

## HENRY J. RUTZ AND EROL M. BALKAN

> The reality is quite plain: the "end of the era of nationalism," so long prophesied, is not remotely in sight. Indeed, nation-ness is the most universally legitimate value in the political life of our time.
>
> —Benedict Anderson, *Imagined Communities*

> . . . the identity of the Fijians must encompass the *matanitu*, the *vanua* and the *lotu*, whose basic institution was the observance of Sunday.
>
> —Petition ("statement of faith") of Fijian Methodists to the President of the Republic of Fiji

> . . . dramatic political changes are often accompanied by equally radical changes in the social structuring of time.
>
> —Eviatar Zerubavel, *The Seven Day Circle*

## A Coup and a Decree

On the morning of 14th May, 1987, Lt. Colonel Sitiveni Rabuka, third in command of the Royal Fiji Military Forces, sat in Parliament and watched while soldiers loyal to his cause stormed into chambers and forced at gunpoint an end to seventeen years of democratic government in Fiji.

A week later, the Great Council of Chiefs convened at the Civic Centre in Suva, the capital and commercial center of the country, to speak with one voice against the principle of democracy, which the chiefs viewed as being in contradiction with the principles of a Fijian way of life. Their own conclusion was startling in its definitiveness: "While democracy preaches equality, in the Fijian system this is impossible" (*Fiji Times* May 25, 1987:3). At the closing of their deliberations, Lt. Colonel Rabuka stepped onto the balcony of the Centre to greet thousands of his admirers, proclaiming in Fijian, "We have won."

What he had won, he told the crowd, was the chiefs' support to change the constitution of the independent nation-state of Fiji in order to accommodate ". . . Fijian interests dear to their hearts . . . the chiefly system [*matanitu*], land [*vanua*], and religion [*lotu*]."

On 25th September, when political accommodations threatened his vision of the new state, Colonel Rabuka staged a second coup, bringing into being on 7th October the Republic of Fiji. One of his first acts was to invoke the Sunday Observance Decree (no. 20, 1987), which forbade the following activities on Sunday: agricultural work (except essential services in relation to domestic animals); commerce and trade for profit; the performance of professional services for a fee or levy; newspaper activity; the operation of public transport; and the use of private vehicles for activities other than transportation to church. The decree outlawed large social gatherings, ceremonies such as weddings, and meetings unrelated to religious worship. Operating hotels, cinemas, restaurants, nightclubs and related activities or businesses was forbidden. Sports events and family picnics were banned. The statement accompanying the decree declared that it "must be observed strictly" (*Fiji Times* Nov. 12, 1987:1). Penalty for failure to comply was a fine of up to one hundred dollars or a month in prison (*Nai Lalakai* Nov. 12, 1987:1).

This chapter is about the restructuring of time accompanying a radical political change. We use the occasion of a political crisis in Fiji to explore the thesis that time is an instrument of power. As an instrument of power, time is an object of control in the power struggles and political projects of different social collectivities. We are concerned in this chapter with two processes in the politics of time—appropriation and legitimation. We ask, first, what form political appropriation takes and how it shapes time. Second, we ask what particular time-discipline the decree instills and the extent to which that discipline is practiced among Fijians. And third, we ask about the struggle for control of different and opposed time-disciplines and their respective practices.[1]

## The Political Economy of a Bipolar Ethnic State

Neither coup nor decree makes sense without an overview of the structure of the political economy of independent Fiji. The competition for national power, framed by the 1970 Constitution, rested on racial politics.[2] Constituencies were either "communal" (i.e., racial) or "national," but in either case seats in the lower house were apportioned by race. An upper house, with appointees, was modeled on the British House of Lords.

There are two points to keep in mind for present purposes. First, the 1970 Constitution was an accommodation of political interests of the different races in Fiji, ensuring that orderly struggles for power would form along racial lines but would be softened by the requirement that each race would need to capture a number of seats from the opposite race to hold power (Nation 1978). Second, the political interests accommodated in the 1970 Constitution ensured that the contradictions and conflicts of an ethnically plural colonial society would be carried forward in the new state. These interests have been characterized as "paramountcy" for Fijians and "parity" for Indians (Lal 1986). Provisions guaranteed Fijians their own national administrative structure, ownership of their lands in perpetuity, and protection of their culture.[3] The parliamentary and electoral provisions gave Indians parity in political rights.

The coup in 1987 revealed what seventeen years of orderly power struggle under the guise of multiracial harmony had concealed: the paramount interest of Fijians was to control the state. Until then, the democratic competition for power was won by the Fijian-dominated Alliance Party, the party of the paramount chiefs. In April 1987, however, the Alliance Party was defeated at the polls by a coalition of the Indian-dominated National Federation Party and a newly formed Labour Party. The defeat, in the minds of most Fijians, called into question the paramountcy of Fijian interests guaranteed by the Constitution.

Racial politics in Fiji is fueled by racial economics. The European plantation and mercantilist capitalism of the colonial era carried over into the period of independence, during which time there has been a rapid expansion of financial, labor, and consumer goods markets stimulated by foreign investment. Financial capital remains primarily in the hands of overseas European investors, merchant capital is overwhelmingly in the hands of Indians, and Fijians own the land. Ownership of the means of production defines the basic lines of competition in the marketplace. The mainstay of the Fijian economy continues to be export-oriented sugar and tourism. Indian labor dominates the former, Fijian labor the latter. Indian labor in general is located in market-oriented agriculture or employment in the private sector, while Fijian labor is located primarily in subsistence/cash agriculture or public sector employment (Gounis and Rutz 1986).

The political economy of a bipolar ethnic state, then, structures struggles for national power along racial lines. Within the Fijian community, political identity—first during the colonial period and later during the period of independence—encompasses three basic elements that distinguish Fijians from Indians.

First, obedience to chiefs within a political hierarchy of chiefs and chiefdoms had been there from at least the time of Cession in 1874 and had become institutionalized early on as a form of British indirect rule and later in the party structure of electoral politics. The Great Council of Chiefs' assertion that the principle of democracy is in contradiction with the principles of "the Fijian way of life" needs to be placed in this context. Fijian political life continues to be powerfully structured around the obligations of mutual service and respect between chiefs and commoners, or what is termed "the chiefly system" (*vakaturaga*).

Second, Fijian ownership of 83% of the total land area of Fiji is the single most important interest that unites Fijians and distinguishes them from Indians. The reason is that Fijian land since the early colonial era was deemed inalienable and held in common by local descent groups (France 1969). The majority of Fijians today are landowners by virtue of their membership in a kin group. The "land" is metonymically "the Fijian people" and implies the heavy obligations of mutual support among kinsmen. In political terms, it refers to the interests of commoners in complementary opposition to the interests of chiefs. These relations, termed "customs of the land" (*vakavanua*), like those between chiefs and commoners, were institutionalized early on in native administration and later incorporated into the provisions of the constitution of the independent state. In the modern era, the "chiefs" are there to protect the "land" from encroachment by Indians.

Third, the element that most separates Fijians from Indians, the one that in the modern era has come to define them as a different *kind* of people from Indians, is Christianity, or, more commonly, the "church" (*lotu*). A major source of Fijian identity as a nation, Christianity, especially Methodism, is the oldest of colonial institutions and arguably the element that has most affected Fijian collective conscience. Until the 1987 coups, however, it had never been enlisted in the struggle for national power. Colonel Rabuka changed all that when he invoked "church" as the source of legitimacy for his appropriation of power, insisting that it be the foundation of the reconstituted state.[4]

## The Form of Political Appropriation and the Shaping of Time

The form of political appropriation is important for understanding the way in which the exercise of power shapes time. In the case of Fiji, we already have indicated that the coup was a seizure of the state itself as an instrument of power. The aim was to change the rules by which social collectivities competed for power. Colonel Rabuka initially seized power with a small band of loyal soldiers, but the army was quick to support him (recruitment to the Fiji Military Forces is 96% Fijian). He soon gathered the support of the Great Council of Chiefs and the vast majority of Fijians in both rural and urban areas. Resistance was weak, there being no organized and concerted reaction to match his own strength.

The political economy of Fiji and the evolution of Fijian identity within it are structural features affecting the form of appropriation of power, but the political project of Colonel Rabuka must be accorded its own weight. This is especially so if we are to understand the connections between the coup and the decree. He is a professional military man, but he also is a Methodist lay preacher who believes in a starkly fundamentalist Methodism that has more in common with the Old Testament than the New. His early religious training was reinforced by a tour of duty in the Middle East, where he came in contact with Biblical sites and teachings of the Old Testament, and where his early childhood upbringing predisposed him to pay attention to the Jewish themes of a promised land and a people held captive. Colonel Rabuka is responsible for appropriating power in the name of his own brand of religious fundamentalism, giving the state a new legitimacy grounded in his own vision of the Fijian nation, and shaping time in its image.

When Colonial Rabuka stood on the balcony of the Civic Centre and proclaimed victory in the name of "chiefs," "land," and "church," few would have predicted that Christianity was about to become the *dominant* legitimizing force of a new state premised on one particular vision of the Fijian nation. In ensuing months, however, he was quite candid in communicating his vision of the independent state of Fiji to citizens at home and interested parties abroad, and he proved capable of implementing most of it in the face of political opposition.

His vision was to appropriate power in the interest of a Fijian nation whose principle of legitimacy lay outside either the "tradition" of chiefdoms and dynastic families (Sahlins 1976; 1985) or a "Deed of Cession" and "Constitution." The legitimacy of "chiefs" and "land" had come to rest upon the events of British history and the legitimacy of the British Crown. In the months following the May coup, when politicians were seeking some accommodation, Colonel Rabuka never wavered in his assertion that Fiji become a Christian state. He stated repeatedly his belief that the Bible made clear that God chose Fiji for Fijians. "It is the land that God has given them," he declared (Dean and Ritova 1988:11), in effect untying Fijian ownership of land from its constitutional (and manmade) fetters. He cast the election of 11 April, in which the chiefs were defeated, in the language of prophecy and prefigurement, proclaiming that Fijians would be held captive by "an immigrant race that would ascend to a position of political power, to complete his control of Fiji" (Dean and Ritova 1988:11). He viewed the May 14 coup as "an act of God to save Fijians in their own land," in one stroke excusing himself from the scene and placing the origins of the Fijian nation outside (and above) history. The coup, he stated on another occasion, was "the greatest thing that happened to them [Fijians] since Christianity was brought to the islands in the 1830s" (Dean and Ritova 1988:90). In one verbal maneuver, he turned a usurpation of power into an act of redemption, devalued the most important events in the political history of Fiji (Cession in 1874 and Independence in 1970), and thereby subordinated a lower (secular) law to a higher (sacred) Law. He removed the origin of a Fijian nation, and of his own actions ("the coup is a mission that God has given me" [Dean and Ritova 1988:11]), to a time out of time.

Colonel Rabuka likened the plight of Fijians to that of the Israelites when they were exiled from a promised land. He quoted with approval the prayer at a gathering of militant Fijian nationalists which he had attended prior to the coup: "Save us and save our land. You saved the Israelites when their land was taken from them by foreigners. Dear God, please answer our prayer and do the same for us" (Dean and Rivota 1988:50). In Colonel Rabuka's rendering of the Fijian nation, Fijians were a chosen people in a promised land.

Colonel Rabuka also had religion in mind when, shortly after the second coup, he revoked the 1970 Constitution on 1 October but waited until 6 October to announce that 7 October would be the beginning of the new Republic of Fiji. This bit of numerology was explained thus: "In Hebrew belief, the sixth day is the day of agreement with their Lord. And the seventh signifies the completion of the work of the Lord (Dean and Ritova 1988:113) . . . [the Jewish date of October 6—Yom Kippur—] is the Day of Atonement, when we say to God, 'we have sinned, and we have not lived the past year according to your will. So, now, we pray that we may start afresh' " (Dean and Ritova 1988:119).

The Sunday Observance Decree takes its full significance as a temporal instrument of power from the specific form of political appropriation and legitimation of the state. The decree neither attempts to encompass all the routines of daily life—only those on Sunday—nor does it impose a specific schedule on Sunday routines. The decree proscribes categories of activity without prescribing specific practrices. Finally, the proscriptions are temporally bound but apply to *all* citizens. What is clear from the content of the decree is that it bans capitalist rhythms of work and leisure. Less clear is its intent, which appears only as linguistic qualifiers of bans on two activities: the use of private vehicles for activities *other than transportation to church* and large social gatherings *unrelated to religious worship*. Notwithstanding the relative absence of physical coercion, the lack of direct control of all aspects of individual routines by means of schedules, and the inability to impose precise mechanisms of punishment, the decree barely conceals the intent of its promulgator to instill in all the citizens of Fiji the time-discipline and practices of the Methodist Sunday Observance.

## Time-Discipline and the Cultural Roots of the Fijian Nation

The political value of the Sunday Observance, we argue, is that it has been woven into the fabric of a national identity, intertwined yet distinguishable from "chiefs" and "land." Our purpose is to show that the Sunday Observance is a kind of time-discipline that, when realized in practice, is a representation of the power of the Fijian nation as a legitimizing force in the creation of the state. We discuss two different connections between the decree and the coup. First, we sketch the cultural roots of the Fijian nation in the discipline of the Methodist week in order to connect "church" to "chiefs" and both to the emergence of a Fijian nation during the colonial era. Second, we describe the time-discipline of the Methodist Sunday Observance to show exactly what kind of time is to be practiced by all citizens on Sunday. We then look at the Sunday practices of urban Fijians prior to the coup to see to what extent the discipline is realized and poses a material problem for other races. This problem is then assessed by looking at the reactions of different segments of the population to restrictions imposed on their own variable discipline and practices.

### Methodist Time-Discipline and the Cultural Roots of Fijian Nationalism

Anderson (1983) has argued convincingly that modern nations are particular kinds of imagined communities of contemporaries, and that nationalism must be understood in terms of its cultural roots as well as in terms of fundamental changes in the modes of apprehending the world. Among the most important modes is that of time. The time peculiar to the modern nation, he argues, is a " 'homogeneous, empty time," in which simultaneity . . . is marked . . . by temporal coincidence, and measured by clock and calendar" (1983:30). Media of communication such as the novel and the newspaper are technical means for representing the time of the nation as a sociological entity, which consists of contemporaries who, while never meeting, nevertheless become connected. The nation as an imagined community is so powerful that people die for it. The first pan-Fijian collective pangs of national consciousness, we suggest, are to be found in the time-discipline of Methodism, which had effectively diffused by means of "print Methodism" among the many petty chiefdoms by the time of British cession of the islands in 1874. The connection between Methodist time-discipline and chiefly authority was institutionalized in the 19th century, but its invocation in the interests of modern nation-ness lay politically dormant until Colonel Rabuka's coup and decree.

There could be no two societies more different in their objective conditions of political economy than were England and Fiji in the early decades of the 19th century. Nevertheless, the "transforming power of Methodism" (Thompson 1965) in the civilizing improvement of the English working class bears uncanny resemblance to what was transpiring in Fiji around the same period. In Fiji as in England, Methodism was a new time-discipline affecting the temporal practices of ordinary people.

In English working-class districts, Methodists provided an organizational structure of lay preachers who held classes and ministers who delivered sermons, and of district meetings and an Annual Conference on the belief that a constant vigil was necessary to guard against "backsliding." A perpetual theme was the need to receive God's grace by continual atonement for sin. Methodism also was an assault on the traditional amusements of the poor. Workers were accustomed to use Sunday for a variety of feasts, fairs (for labor recruitment, among other purposes), and social visits. Such uses of time, some of them for work and livelihood as much as for drinking in the ale-houses and performing acts of "animal sexuality," were frowned upon as "spendthrift" by improving Methodists. These and other secular amusements were used in classes and sermons to illustrate a lack of discipline in everyday life.

The Sunday Observance, especially, reorganized work and leisure in terms of a higher meaning. Methodists were obliged to attend church thrice on Sunday, and to read only the Bible and Prayer Book (Thompson 1965:409). Other practices were zealously suppressed. In the Newcastle area, for example, where farmers obtained their harvest labor at fairs, there was a suppression of Sunday hirings in the summer (Thompson 1965:412). Sociability was curtailed: "Even the visiting of relatives on a normal Sabbath day could not be condoned, unless in cases of sudden sickness" (Thompson 1965:409). Thompson (1965:350) remarks that the political voice of Methodism fell uneasily between Dissent and Establishment, erring on the side of the latter: "Methodism hates democracy as much as it hates sin."

Fiji was a very different place from England, but perhaps less so from the point of view of missionaries, who could equate the bestial habits of the lower classes at the center of empire with the ludic habits of barbarians at the other end of the world. Objectively, there were chiefs and commoners in place of different classes. Public morals in Fijian chiefdoms were encoded in reciprocal kin obligations between clans and service to chiefs in exchange for peace, protection, and plenty. People lived in a thousand villages along the coasts and on the hillsides of the interior. Their livelihood derived from agriculture, not industry, and their social rhythms were consumption-oriented rather than driven by production and accumulation.

The Methodist missionaries who came to Fiji from England via Tonga beginning in 1835 were from humble origins and exuded the same missionary zeal chronicled by Thompson (1965:352) for their contemporaries in England. Methodist time-discipline was imminent. The first missionary, arriving on the shores of the island of Lakemba, records in his journal that six days after his arrival he observed his first Sabbath in Fiji, preaching to a crowd of several hundred who had gathered on the beach to sit patiently for three hours and listen to his sermon on atonement for sin, delivered in Tongan!

Methodist missionaries resolved early to connect atonement with time-discipline. Fijians' spiritual lives, "dark, vague and perplexing" (Thomas Williams 1858:215), inhabited by ancestors and deities, seemed to lack any sense of temporality. There was no calendar and, hence, no calendric festivals. Ceremonies of all sorts were abundant but seemed unmarked by any regular events in nature or culture. The "day" (*siga*) was reckoned as a unit of duration, but days passed without name or number to lend sequential order to lived time. There were temples, but priests made no regular supplications in them; instead, emergencies or fears dictated times of visitation and worship (Williams 1858:223). Temples remained in various states of disrepair until events such as war required the intercession of priests and the repair of the temples.

Like their contemporaries in England, missionaries in Fiji perceived the greatest need for discipline in social life. What was remarkable to them were the endlessly repetitive nameless days and the deliberate pace of social relations that admitted of little exactitude: "People went about their duties most deliberately, as every appearance of haste in such matters is supposed to detract from true dignity. A careful observance of established forms is deemed very essential" (Williams 1858:27–28).

Fijian culture was one of "much leisure" (Williams 1858:161). Among the most frequent activities were sleeping and eating, both of which were of long duration. There were, to missionary eyes, endless "vacant hours" filled with sport, dance, tricks, conversation and sociability. When the missionary Calvert spoke to the high chief Cakobau about enforcing the Sunday Observance, the chief made a speech in which he described the seriation of Fijian discipline thus: eat>sleep>bathe>eat>sleep>stroll.

Three decades later, the diffusion of Methodist time-discipline to all parts of Fiji, and its integration into the power relations of chiefs and commoners alike, was complete. The high chiefs, by adopting the new mode of religion, adopted a new mode of apprehending time. The Methodist week became the time-discipline of chiefly authority. Days were given names in a weekly cycle which revolved around "Sunday" (*siga tabu*, or "forbidden day"), a day devoted entirely to the atonement for sin. Sermons were delivered three or four times. There was a morning prayer meeting followed by chanting of the catechisms, then preaching; in the afternoon, more preaching. Days preceding Sunday were given names of tasks in the preparation for worship, such as "preparing firewood day" and "preparing water day." Any activities associated with work and traditional amusements were forbidden on Sunday.

The basic institution of the Methodist week was the Sunday Observance. The whole week, however, was suffused with a routine of classes and meetings which became a normal part of "the Fijian way of life." School for learning scriptures was held at daybreak for one-and-a-half hours. Reading and writing were taught to lay preachers every Tuesday and Friday. There were children's classes in the forenoon everyday except Saturday, followed by adult classes in the afternoon. On Wednesday there was a church leaders' meeting to assign the Lord's work for the following week. Saturday afternoon was reserved for a prayer meeting for all ages.

As in England, Methodism represented a rupture and fell ambiguously between dissent and establishment. At first, chiefs resisted missionary incursions on their power, especially the attempts by missionaries to curtail warfare. Despite chiefly bans on their activities, commoners began slowly to adopt the new discipline. In 1854, the high chief Cakobau embraced Methodism, and other high chiefs followed, creating the unity of religion and power that has persisted to the present time.

After 1854, the new time-discipline diffused rapidly throughout Fiji, along with "print Methodism." By 1850, the fledging Methodist press in Fiji had printed 56,000 copies of the Book of Genesis and thousands of prayer books, New Testaments, short sermons, teacher's manuals, and catechisms. The "truth" of the chiefs' power and authority became inextricably intertwined with scriptural language. In later years, Wesleyan Methodism would come to be known as "the religion of Cakobau," an apt phrase that described a single form of political legitimation. At independence, when Indians would achieve political parity and English would be designated the official language of the country, the motto on the new flag of the nation state would read, *in Fijian,* "Fear the Lord and Honor the Chiefs."

Methodist time-discipline and print Methodism were the first institutions to provide the technical means for the apprehension of a Fijian nation as an imagined community, the beginnings of a Fijian nationalism that became more self-consciously based on immemorial traditions of "chiefs," "land," and "church" as they became increasingly entangled in power struggles with other races during the colonial and independence period.

## The Methodist Sunday Observance at the Time of the Coup

Methodist time-discipline and its basic institution, the Sunday Observance, were reinforced by colonial administrative institutions and laws. In villages, Fijians continued the practices introduced by missionaries. In towns and cities, Sunday was a secular day of rest from wage labor as well as a symbolic day of rest within the Judeo-Christian tradition. For Fijians, Sunday retained its symbolic character as a day of atonement for sins and also as a day of celebration of the Resurrection of Christ. A peculiar structure of feeling (Raymond Williams 1973) that can be characterized as somber joy sets Sunday off emotionally from other days.

The tempo of Sunday is deliberate, a feeling that derives, in part, from the relatively long duration of a few activities. Sunday feels different because it draws a circle around the immediate members of a household or close kin. There is a withdrawal into the house away from public view. The intent of the day is to seek redemption through atonement. Quietude and soft-spoken conversation is punctuated by longer than usual periods of silence. As a day of celebration, warmer than normal feelings attach to the gathering of men around the kava bowl after the morning service before they return home to the midday meal, which is more commensal and elaborate than on other days, when the main meal is simpler fare taken in the evening.

The Sunday Observance is a discipline of practices, proscribing some while prescribing others (Figure 1). Work activities other than minimal housekeeping, childcare, and some cooking are not condoned. Secular amusements of all kinds—movies, discos, sports, restaurants, taverns, etc.—are frowned upon. Time-discipline centers on church attendance in the late morning and afternoon for adults and children. The duration of each service is normally an hour-and-a-half in the morning and two hours in the afternoon.

**Figure 1**
**Classification of Sunday Practices**

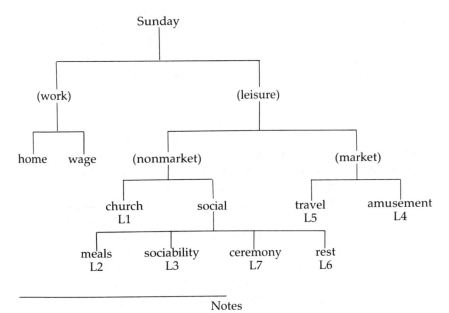

---

Notes

1. "Leisure" category is defined formally, i.e., as all activities not directly related to "wage work" and "home production" (see Balkan and Rutz n.d.).
2. Practices of "meals," "sociability," and "rest" are subject to the disciplines
of "chiefs," "land," and "church"; "travel" and "amusement" are subject to
the discipline of "market."

Activity Code

| | *Classification* | *Activity* |
|---|---|---|
| L1 | Church | attending church or church meeting |
| L2 | Meals | breakfast, lunch, dinner |
| L3 | Sociability | drinking kava and storytelling in own or an-other's house, "hanging around" |
| L4 | Amusement | playing cards in own or another's house, sports training, playing a sport, spectator at a sport event, movies, drinking beer, danc-ing, eating out at a restaurant, playing video games at an amusement center, playing bingo, attending a fund-raising |
| L5 | Travel | waiting for bus or taxi, travelling by bus, taxi, or on foot |
| L6 | Rest | lying down in own house during daylight hours, reading, listening to music |
| L7 | Ceremony | collective rituals related to life cycle events |

The remainder of the day is stipulated. After the morning church service, while men gather for kava, women return home with children to finish preparing the mid-day meal. The Sunday meal is a time of commensality, which includes food sharing of dishes passed among neighbors or very close kinsmen. Fijians normally rest after meals and at various times of the day. Sunday rest differs in at least two respects. The duration is much longer—often the whole afternoon—and rest has symbolic, not secular, meaning. It is a time for prayer, reading the Bible, or listening to sermons or choir music on the radio. The connotation of rest is communing with God, not reproducing labor power. Sunday afternoon is a quiet time when people will feel free to close their doors and shut their curtains, one of the rare occasions in Fijian social life when any strong expression is given to privacy. If children play outside, they are enjoined to do so quietly.

Afternoon is separated from evening by another church service, followed by a light meal, often of leftovers from the mid-day meal. Once again, the evening is different from the normal weekday evening, which consists of sociability with members of other households that can extend late into the night. The period of quietude continues as family members converse, listen to the radio, or perhaps read the Bible before retiring earlier than normal.

The Sunday Observance is the time-discipline Colonel Rabuka intended for all the people of Fiji when he promulgated his decree following the coup. The decree enfolds in a time-discipline a reactive cultural pattern that subserves capitalist development to the rhythms of Fijian culture.[5] It is anticapitalist and anti-Indian, which often means the same thing from the Fijian point of view.[6] By promulgating the decree, Colonel Rabuka served the aim of his coup, which was to establish the interests of the Fijian nation as the ruling interests of the sovereign independent state of Fiji.

## Sunday Practices of Urban and Working Middle-Class Fijians

Iterative practices, like chants, serve the symbolic function of empowering the meaning they enact. In this sense, the Sunday Observance Decree best serves the aims of the coup when its time-discipline is realized in Sunday practices. Otherwise, the negation of one time-discipline and the affirmation of another remains in the realm of ideological struggle.

Fijian villagers might be expected to support Colonel Rabuka's promulgation of the decree among other races and urban dwellers, whom they come increasingly to see as persons with privileged access to market labor and leisure. But what about urban Fijians, who sell their labor and purchase most of their consumption on the market (Rutz 1989)? What reaction could Colonel Rabuka expect from urban Fijians to a decree that banned secular amusements on Sunday?[7] Time-budget data can tell us the extent to which urban Fijian Sunday practices were disciplined by the Methodist Sunday Observance prior to the coup.[8]

Fijians have become increasingly conscious of the historical conjuncture of what they perceive to be their own cultural forms and practices and how these conflict with market-discipline. Colonel Rabuka himself wondered whether those who follow one discipline can have "respect" for another.[9] Prior to the decree, movie houses had established their right to open on Sunday. And the market has steadily encroached on Methodist discipline, mainly due to an expanding international tourist industry whose rhythms ignore temporal boundaries to the week. The tourist industry has lobbied successfully for duty-free stores and restaurants to remain open on Sunday, and for tourist hotels to sell alcoholic beverages.

The interplay of different time-disciplines can be discerned in measured social practices. "Wage work" is virtually absent among urban Fijians on Sunday (Table 1). "Home production" is practiced, but the tasks are limited primarily to cooking and childcare, which fall primarily on women in the partriarchal Fijian household. Urban Fijian Sunday practices, then, must be categorized as predominantly ones of "leisure." No other day of the week has this pattern. The reason is that, despite the inroads of market-discipline on the lives of urban Fijians, the discipline of the Sunday Observance dominates Sunday

**Table 1**
**Durative Practices on Sunday**
(average minutes per person and percentage of total)

| | Urban Fijians (N = 110 adults) | | | | | | |
|---|---|---|---|---|---|---|---|
| | Working Class (n = 45) | | | | Middle Class (n = 65) | | |
| | Men (n = 26) | | Women (n = 19) | | Men (n = 30) | | Women (n = 35) |
| | min | % | min | % | min | % | min | % |
| Wage | 0.00 | 0.0 | 0.00 | 0.0 | 90.00 | 6.2 | 24.60 | 1.7 |
| Home | 126.50 | 8.8 | 214.50 | 14.9 | 151.80 | 10.5 | 252.80 | 17.5 |
| Leisure | 783.30 | 54.4 | 619.70 | 43.0 | 723.30 | 50.2 | 683.00 | 47.4 |
| Sleep | 530.20 | 36.8 | 605.80 | 42.1 | 474.80 | 33.1 | 479.60 | 33.4 |
| Total | 1440.00 | 100.0 | 1440.00 | 100.0 | 1440.00 | 100.0 | 1440.00 | 100.0 |

practices with the sequence: church attendance>meals
>sociability>rest. Its discipline excludes and punishes market leisure
(Figure 1).

Notwithstanding a general dominance of church-discipline, secular amusements are not wholly absent from Sunday practices. Methodists have been unable, until the decree, to enlist government in their
cause to the extent of banning all forms of "work" (Table 1) and "market leisure" (Table 2). The primary struggle for dominance is between
the disciplines of "church" and "market." The struggle is most apparent in different practices by members of different social classes.

These practices can be summarized as follows. Overall, the discipline of "chiefs" and "land" has been weakened by that of "market," which can be seen in the practices of the middle class, whose
members have more income and opportunities to allocate time to
"market" leisure at the expense of "sociability" and "rest." But Sunday practices, prior to the coup, continued to be subordinated to the
discipline of "church." With respect to church-discipline, however,
neither class is homogeneous. Each has members who are churchgoers and nonchurchgoers. Prior to the coup, churchgoers outnum-
bered nonchurchgoers by more than two to one. Among nonchurchgoers—a distinct minority—practices had shifted markedly, to the
point where market-discipline had established a beachhead for secular
amusements.

Churchgoers, who are the overwhelming majority, embrace
church-discipline and resist all but the most modest attempts by the
market to seize control of Sunday time. This is apparent, first, in the

**Table 2**
**Duration of Sunday Leisure Practices**
(average minutes per person and percentage of total)

|            | Working Class | | | | Middle Class | | | |
|            | Men | | Women | | Men | | Women | |
|            | min | % | min | % | min | % | min | % |
|------------|-----|---|-----|---|-----|---|-----|---|
| L1 Church    | 223.85 | 30.4 | 233.16 | 33.2 | 193.67 | 28.2 | 204.29 | 31.1 |
| L2 Meals     | 113.46 | 15.4 | 116.58 | 16.6 | 120.00 | 17.5 | 125.57 | 19.1 |
| L3 Sociable  | 161.15 | 21.9 | 69.47 | 9.9 | 79.00 | 11.5 | 78.00 | 11.9 |
| L4 Amusement | 82.50 | 11.2 | 45.26 | 6.4 | 115.33 | 16.8 | 65.71 | 10.0 |
| L5 Travel    | 10.38 | 1.4 | 11.32 | 1.6 | 20.33 | 2.9 | 25.14 | 3.8 |
| L6 Rest      | 137.50 | 18.7 | 181.32 | 30.3 | 110.00 | 16.0 | 116.00 | 17.7 |
| L7 Ceremony  | 6.92 | 1.0 | 12.63 | 2.0 | 48.00 | 7.1 | 41.14 | 6.4 |
| Total        |        |       |        |       |        |       |        |       |
|              | 735.77 | 100.0 | 669.74 | 100.0 | 686.33 | 100.0 | 655.86 | 100.0 |

practices of different social classes, and second, in the short duration of "market" leisure.

Market-discipline can be said to have gained a toehold on the Sunday practices of both working-class and middle-class Fijians (Table 2). While the routine of church-discipline dominates the practices of both classes (the sequence "church")"sociability")"meal")"rest"—activities that together comprise not less than three-quarters of the duration of "leisure"), secular amusements occupy a period of the day, for men more than for women, and for middle-class more than for working-class men. The distinction by gender conforms to the discipline of "chiefs," whereas class differences are disciplined by the "market." The incursion of secular amusements in the routine of middle-class men is now an average duration of about two hours. Even this much has been resisted strongly by the voices of patriarchal authority.

Among a minority of both working-class and middle-class Fijians, this toehold of market-discipline has become a beachhead (Table 3). A third do not attend church at all, raising the prospect of radically different Sunday practices that could effect a total transformation of the meaning of Sunday leisure. The duration of "market" leisure increases significantly, nearly doubling for men of both classes. But there is a divergence in experience of the market. Working-class men and women have taken from "church" to increase primarily their secular "rest," while middle-class men and women have taken from "church" to increase their secular amusement.

**Table 3**
**Duration of Sunday Leisure of Nonchurchgoers**
(average minutes per person and percentage of total)

|  |  | Nonchurchgoers ($n = 36$) | | | | | | | |
|---|---|---|---|---|---|---|---|---|---|
|  |  | *Working Class* ($n = 19$) | | | | *Middle Class* ($n = 17$) | | | |
|  |  | Men ($n = 10$) | | Women ($n = 9$) | | Men ($n = 8$) | | Women ($n = 9$) | |
|  |  | min | % | min | % | min | % | min | % |
| L1 | Church | 0.00 | 0.0 | 0.00 | 0.0 | 0.00 | 0.0 | 0.00 | 0.0 |
| L2 | Meals | 105.00 | 15.7 | 128.33 | 21.3 | 78.75 | 12.0 | 85.63 | 13.4 |
| L3 | Sociable | 188.33 | 28.3 | 103.33 | 17.1 | 33.75 | 5.2 | 121.25 | 19.0 |
| L4 | Amusement | 129.44 | 19.4 | 45.56 | 7.6 | 205.00 | 31.3 | 117.50 | 18.5 |
| L5 | Travel | 11.11 | 1.7 | 6.11 | 1.0 | 6.25 | 1.0 | 27.50 | 4.3 |
| L6 | Rest | 232.22 | 34.9 | 318.33 | 53.0 | 150.00 | 23.0 | 105.00 | 16.5 |
| L7 | Ceremony | 0.00 | 0.0 | 0.00 | 0.0 | 180.00 | 27.5 | 180.00 | 28.3 |
|  | *Total* | 666.11 | 100.0 | 601.67 | 100.0 | 653.75 | 100.0 | 636.88 | 100.0 |

Could these be the key indicators of a social transformation, at present the practices of a small minority? Is the "rest" of a nonchurch-going working-class the beginnings of a re-apprehension of time different from the mode of apprehending time as the "rest" of atonement? And does not the dramatic increase in the duration of secular amusement among both men and women of the nonchurchgoing middle class—almost three hours for men and a doubling of the time for women, with less time spent on "rest"—give cause to Colonel Rabuka's fear that the market is a threat to a Fijian identity embodied in race and nation?

The dramatic shortening of the duration of "meals" by two-fifths among men and women of the middle class, and a decrease by half in the "sociability" of middle class men, when placed in the context of the "chief" and "land" discipline of commensality and solidarity, lends further credence to the view that market work and leisure pose political problems requiring a control of time.

But the overwhelming majority of urban Fijians continue to practice church-discipline, and in doing so to reproduce Colonel Rabuka's vision of Fijian nation-ness as the legitimizing force of the state. True, the incipient discipline of "market" is discernible, but it is a fraction of the duration of nonchurchgoers of both classes, especially for men, and below the average for all urban Fijians (Table 4). What the non-churchgoing minority has taken from "church" time to increase "rest" or "market" time, the churchgoing majority has more than compensated for by taking from those same activities to attend "church." And

**Table 4**
**Duration of Sunday Leisure of Churchgoers**
(average minutes per person and percentage of total)

|  |  | Churchgoers (N = 74) | | | | | | |
|  |  | Working Class (N = 26) | | | | Middle Class (N = 48) | | |
|  |  | Men (N = 16) | | Women (N = 10) | | Men (N = 22) | | Women (N = 26) |
|  |  | min | % | min | % | min | % | min | % |
|---|---|---|---|---|---|---|---|---|---|
| L1 | Church | 342.35 | 44.3 | 443.00 | 60.6 | 264.09 | 37.8 | 264.81 | 40.0 |
| L2 | Meals | 117.94 | 15.3 | 106.00 | 14.5 | 135.00 | 19.3 | 137.41 | 20.8 |
| L3 | Sociable | 146.76 | 19.0 | 39.00 | 5.3 | 95.45 | 13.7 | 65.19 | 9.9 |
| L4 | Amusement | 57.65 | 7.5 | 45.00 | 6.2 | 82.73 | 11.8 | 50.37 | 7.6 |
| L5 | Travel | 10.00 | 1.3 | 16.00 | 2.2 | 25.45 | 3.6 | 24.44 | 3.7 |
| L6 | Rest | 87.35 | 11.3 | 58.00 | 7.9 | 95.45 | 13.7 | 119.26 | 18.0 |
| L7 | Ceremony | 10.59 | 1.3 | 24.00 | 3.3 | 0.00 | 0.0 | 0.00 | 0.0 |
|  | *Total* | 772.65 | 100.0 | 731.00 | 100.0 | 698.16 | 100.0 | 661.48 | 100.0 |

here, too, the trend is reversed, with the duration in "church" of working-class men and women significantly higher than that of middle-class men and women (the women by nearly half again as much).

In sum, urban Fijian Sunday practices have changed relatively little despite the dominance of capitalist time-discipline and the emergence of class loyalties. In the face of hardships imposed on urban Fijians by the Sunday Observance Decree, they overwhelmingly supported it because they understood the symbolic power of time in their struggle for control of the state.

## The Struggle for Sunday: Reaction and Response

The coup is reactionary in the sense that its aim was to place the national market economy and its rhythms in the service of Fijian institutions that had failed repeatedly during the 20th century to compete in the market. Capitalism long ago had accommodated its rhythms to religion by opening a time—Sunday—for the church to practice its own discipline. But even here Fijians had given temporal ground to the market, which already had begun to absorb more time on Sunday than church-discipline would allow. The tension between market-discipline and church-discipline on Sunday can be gauged by the reaction of market institutions to the Sunday Observance Decree.

Collective reaction to the decree came from those segments of society whose Sunday practices were most disciplined by the market— sugar, tourism, and organized labor. The sugar industry has been the mainstay of the national economy for over a century.[10] Technical requirements of sugar production in a competitive international export industry force canegrowers, canecutters, lorry drivers, and mill workers to work on Sunday. Notwithstanding a "special clearance" to plant, the National Farmers Union renewed its threats to boycott the mills if the bans were not lifted. In June 1988, several weeks into the crushing season, the growers' boycott proved effective as delivery of cane to the mills was only half that expected. Within weeks, the mills were forced into costly shutdowns on Sunday.[11] Colonel Rabuka held out as long as he could, but in the face of mounting opposition, he eventually agreed to a partial lifting of the decree under the combined pressure of the Fiji Sugar Corporation, the National Farmers Union, the Sugar Growers Council, and canecutting gangs.

Tourism, both symbolically and materially, represents the most intrusive effect of the market on Sunday practices.[12] Airlines run seven-day schedules, and cruise ships are accustomed to calling at Fiji ports on Sunday. Hotel guests arrive, depart, and remain in Fiji on

Sundays. As the tourist sector grew over the past two decades to challenge sugar as an earner of foreign exchange, many concessions had to be granted the industry, including tourist access to secular amusements on Sunday.

Less organized, but no less symptomatic of the market's capacity to absorb Sunday, was the reaction of working-class and middle-class individuals to restrictions on their secular leisure. In the towns and cities, the practice of Sunday was regulated by civil ordinances that closed schools, banks, businesses, factories, and offices. Within the bounds of local law and custom, however, the 1970 Constitution guaranteed every citizen the freedom to practice Sunday as s/he wished.[13] As mentioned above, the concession of local governments to Sunday tourist business had opened many shops, restaurants, hotel bars, and theatres to the citizenry. Perhaps the most symptomatic struggle over time was the Sunday soccer league in a country that had grown very accustomed to spectator sports. Fiji had begun to develop a public and civic culture by the time of the coup.[14] Although there was only weak organized public reaction against a restriction of personal freedoms on the use of leisure time, after the decree urban spaces grew silent and empty.[15] People expressed in personal terms a demoralization and sadness that had surfaced in their lives.

The Fijian response to these and other reactions of the market might itself be viewed as an indicator of the temporary nature of the setback suffered by the market. Colonel Rabuka's response was to grant special clearance or temporary relaxation wherever it became politically necessary. But his resolve was strengthened by the response of Methodist fundamentalists within the church who supported his refusal to revoke the decree. The growing struggle went inside the Methodist Church in Fiji, where grassroots support for Fijian nationalism and a faction of the church leadership that backed Colonel Rabuka successfully routed their more moderate democratic opponents.

Their response to reactions against the decree and demands for its revocation was an organized vigilance to ensure its enforcement. In the cane districts, they organized roadblocks to prevent lorry drivers from delivering cane to the mills on Sunday. Stones were thrown at cane growers, and cane fields were burnt. When one of the organizers was arrested and jailed, Colonel Rabuka personally released him and flew the accused by helicopter back to the scene of action. In May 1988, over 3000 Fijian Methodists illegally marched through the streets of the capital accompanied by a police escort to the government buildings in order to present a petition reaffirming the church's support of the decree. The petition, called "a statement of faith," had 6000 signatories from throughout Fiji and claimed an additional 105,000 members who pledged support through their divisional organization. The petition said that the members were saddened by the government allowing economic considerations to dominate "the expressed values of the Fijian Methodist. We would like, therefore, to urge the government to consult with the Methodist Church in Fiji should there be any need in the future to introduce new measures concerning Sunday."

## Conclusion

The Sunday Observance Decree, as a political "episode" in the making of a modern Fijian nation-state, gives an ironic twist to Fabian's (1983:25) thesis that anthropological knowledge is political ideology. Fabian argues that anthropological theories deny the coevalness of other cultures with those of the West, distancing them by placing them in another time. And for what purpose? In order, Fabian argues, to validate one's own structure of knowledge in relations of power between conqueror and conquered. The politics of time, it would appear, is ubiquitous. All practice, Habermas (1979) might say, presupposes a structure of legitimation. There is an urgent (political) need, Fabian concludes, to open a dialogue by insisting on the "co-presence" of other cultures and those of the West.

But the coup and the decree are an ironic twist to this thesis. The Fijian way of life, partially an invention of the colonial era, nurtured and maintained as an emergent Fijian nation-ness in competition with Indians and Europeans (Clammer 1972; Cohn 1981; France 1969; Rutz 1987; Spate 1959), came to resist the coevalness of others. The coups and decree were a culmination of attempts by Fijians to control the political economy of temporal relations in "their own land." The coups and decree have denied coevalness to Indians as "present" in Fiji.[16] Herein lies the significance of the Sunday Observance Decree—an instrument, in the hands of Fijians, that marks the separation and temporal distancing from Fijians of Indians, in a rear-guard action against a victorious capitalist time-discipline.

## Postscript

On 25 July 1990, the Constitution of the Sovereign Democratic Republic of Fiji was decreed. Under its provisions, the President is appointed by the Great Council of Chiefs (Chapter V, Section 31:36). Parliament is composed of two houses. The House of Representatives is composed of 70 members, 37 of whom are Fijians elected by Fijians (Chapter VI, Sections 40, 41:41). The Senate is composed of 34 members appointed by the President, 24 of whom are Fijians (Chapter VI, Sections 54, 55:57). Explicit provision is made for preferential treatment of Fijians with respect to educational and business opportunities (Chapter III, Sections 1, 2:31). The letter and spirit of the new constitution guarantees civil rights to all, withholds political rights from Indians, and grants preference to the social rights of Fijians.

Under section 12 of Chapter II, *Protection of freedom of conscience,* freedom of religion is guaranteed to persons. Laws pertaining to freedom of conscience must make provision "for the purpose of protecting the rights or freedoms of other persons, including the right to observe and practice any religion without the unsolicited intervention of members of any other religion" (1990:18). The Sunday Observance Decree, however, remains in effect.

## Notes

1. Foucault (1977) develops the concept of "disciplinary power" to understand the tendency in the modern era for administrative forms of power to expand and dominate individual lives. His attention is drawn to the discipline of the body in spatial confinement (i.e., the carceral). We are concerned with a less totalizing temporal confinement and the contestation of different disciplines of a citizenry within the time horizon of the nation and state. There are two aspects of the Fiji case that facilitate our analysis. The first is the character of a political crisis. The coup was a moment of re-apprehension of the nation-state, and the decree a corresponding re-apprehension of the time-discipline of the nation. The second, related to the first, is the manner in which agents, intentions, and interests that remain concealed in ordinary times become revealed during political crisis. In this instance, a single agent in the body of Colonel Rabuka was unusually candid about his aims, interests, and objectives.

2. For a clear description of how the 1970 Constitution retained the racial politics of the colonial period and the numerical composition of Parliament, see Lal (1986:74–106). As of 31 December 1988, Fiji's population was 718,119, with 342,965 indigenous Fijians, 340,121 Indians, nearly all of whom are Fiji born, and 35,033 others, most of whom are Fiji born (see Garrett 1990:110). "Fiji" is used here to refer to a place and a sovereign state. What is usually termed "ethnic group" in the literature on cultural pluralism is referred to in Fiji as different "races" (i.e., different kinds of people). "Fijian" refers to citizens of Fiji who also are indigenous people. "Indian" refers to citizens of Fiji who are descendants of immigrants from India. English is the official language of government in Fiji. During the British colonial era from 1874–1970, white settlers, missionaries, traders, administrators, and all their descendants referred to themselves as "Europeans," and to Indians variously as "Indo-Fijians" or "Fiji Indians."

3. Fijians own 83% of the land in Fiji. Ownership is communal (i.e., vested in local lineages). A Native Lands Commission and Native Land Trust Board administer the laws governing communal ownership. There also is a Ministry of Fijian Affairs that evolved out of an earlier Fijian Affairs Board. The 1970 Constitution made provision for the perpetuity of all these forms of

institutionalized Fijian power. Constitutional change in these institutions of "land" and "chiefs" required three-quarters of the votes of both houses. No less than six of the eight nominees of the Great Council of Chiefs to the upper house must support the final vote (Lal 1986:77).

4. The metonym "church" is polysemic. We use it as a term synonymous with Christianity, more narrowly Fijian Wesley Methodism, and still more narrowly Colonel Rabuka's self-professed brand of Christian fundamentalism. The context makes clear our usage. The Fijian word *lotu* is usually translated as religion. It never has this broad a connotation in Fijian speech habits. Colonel Rabuka, for example, has referred to Hindu or Moslem Indians as "heathens."

5. The normal Fijian response to change or crisis is to "go slow." Slowing down economic development so that Fijians can "catch up" is a leitmotif of development in Fiji.

6. In an appeal to all Christian churches to evangelize Muslims and Hindus, he stated that he wanted "the Indians to be converted to Christianity" (Dean and Ritova 1988:121).

7. The most probable proximate cause of the chief's election defeat was a shift in relatively small numbers of Fijian votes in four urban constituencies of the capital. Colonel Rabuka viewed with alarm the rural exodus of Fijians to Suva and the emergence of class loyalties with their effect on racial politics.

8. For the methodology and sampling procedures used in the collection of time-budget data among urban Fijians, see Rutz (1989) and Balkan and Rutz (n.d.).

9. He perceived that the market was eroding respect for chiefs as leaders and that secular leisure had threatened sacred rest.

10. In Fiji, sugar production relies on smallholders, 80% of whom are Indian. Most tasks are performed by family labor, some of which is employed on weekdays and deployed to work in the field on Sundays. The peak demand for Sunday labor is during planting and harvesting periods. Planting schedules are staggered and timed to fit harvest schedules which, in turn, are timed to keep the machinery of crushing mills operating seven days a week.

11. The Fiji Sugar Corporation, a government-owned monopoly, estimated that it would lose $67F million if sugar growers failed to deliver the crop on Sundays. The government twice devalued its currency after the first coup. Civil servants were forced to take a 25% reduction in their wages. Foreign reserves fell to five months' worth at current levels. One year after the coup, the Fiji Monetary Authority calculated a real shrinkage in the national economy in excess of 11%. In the end, however, the sugar harvest was the largest ever and brought record earnings.

12. Tourism is labor-intensive. Fijians are the preferred labor force in hotels, but Indians dominate transportation, restaurant, and other tourist services. Indians also totally control duty-free trade that depends upon Sunday business hours. Market reaction also came from organized labor, urban transport owners, and shopkeepers. The Fiji Trade Unions Congress, whose leadership is supported by the Australian labor movement, insisted that "Nothing short of total lifting of the bans is acceptable" (*Fiji Times* 5/13/88).

13. Sunday was observed differently by different segments of society, but overall it could be said that, except for Fijians, Sunday was a day of secular leisure. Hindus, the largest religious community in Fiji, have no designated holy day in the weekly cycle. They were accustomed to using Sunday for weddings, feasts, and other collective rituals made difficult during workdays. Muslims, whose holy day is Friday, were in much the same position as Hindus with respect to Sunday. Thus, the vast majority of Indians were left to Sunday practices that fit a public and civic culture.

14. The two most popular spectator sports, rugby and soccer, are organized along racial lines. Rugby, played by Fijians, holds league play on Saturday. Soccer, played by Indians, had held its club play on Sunday.

15. The Fiji Council of Churches called for an immediate revocation of the decree, receiving the endorsement of seven Hindu organizations and the Fiji Trade Unions Congress. In its public plea, the Council stated that "In a multi-racial, multi-lingual, multi-cultural and multi-religious democratic society like ours, every individual should enjoy the freedom of worship according to his own conscience. . . . The imposition of the Sunday decree shattered all this. It has polarized the races and sounded the death knell for mutual trust that had existed between the races" (*Fiji Times* 4/7/88).

16. The Fijian community never has accepted the coevalness of Indians. During the colonial era, Fijians made periodic demands that Indians be repatriated. In the early independence period, Fijian nationalists made inflammatory speeches about pushing Indians into the sea. Even with citizenship, Indians who were able kept enough liquid assets to flee the country on short notice. Colonial Rabuka insisted that Indians were welcome in Fiji. They were needed, he said, to make money, but they shouldn't expect full political rights.

## References Cited

Anderson, Benedict
    1983   Imagined Communities. London: Verso.
Balkan, Erol M., and Henry J. Rutz
    n.d.   Development and the Commoditization of Leisure Time. Manuscript.
Clammer, John
    1972   Colonialism and the Perception of Tradition in Fiji. *In* Anthropology and the Colonial Encounter. Talal Asad, ed. Pp. 199–222. London: Ithaca Press.
Cohn, Bernard
    1981   Anthropology and History in the 1980s. Journal of Interdisciplinary History 12(2):227–252.
Constitution of the Sovereign Democratic Republic of Fiji (Promulgation) Decree 1990.
Dean, Eddie, with Stan Ritova
    1988   Rabuka: No Other Way. Suva, Fiji: Marketing Team International, Ltd.
Fabian, Johannes
    1983   Time and the Other. New York: Columbia University Press.

Fiji Times
    1987a  Chiefs to Hold Talks on Constitution Changes. May 25:3.
    1987b  Sunday Observance Decree. November 12:1.
Foucault, Michel
    1977  Discipline and Punish. Alan Sheridan, trans. New York: Pantheon Books.
France, Peter
    1969  The Charter of the Land. Melbourne: Oxford University Press.
Garrett, John
    1990  Uncertain Sequel: The Social and Religious Scene in Fiji Since the Coups. *In* As the Dust Settles: Impact and Implications of the Fiji Coups. Brij Lal, ed. The Contemporary Pacific 2(1):87–112.
Gounis, Kostas, and Henry J. Rutz
    1986  Urban Fijians and the Problem of Unemployment. *In* Fijians in Town. Chris Griffin and Michael Monsell-Davis, eds. Pp. 50–88. Suva: Institute of Pacific Studies of the University of the South Pacific.
Habermas, Jürgen
    1979  Historical Materialism and the Development of Normative Structures. *In* Communication and the Evolution of Society. Thomas McCarthy, trans. Pp. 95–129. Boston: Beacon Press.
Lal, Brij V.
    1986  Politics Since Independence. *In* Politics in Fiji. Brij V. Lal, ed. Honolulu: Institute for Polynesian Studies at Brigham Young University-Hawaii Campus.
Nai Lalakai
    1987  Vakaro me baleta na Siga Tabu. November 12:1.
Nation, John
    1978  Customs of Respect. Canberra: Australian National University.
Rutz, Henry J.
    1987  Capitalizing on Culture: Moral Ironies in Urban Fiji. Comparative Studies in Society and History 29(3):533–557.
    1989  Culture, Class, and Consumer Choice. *In* The Social Economy of Consumption. Henry J. Rutz and Benjamin Orlove, eds. Pp. 211–252. Lanham, Md.: University Press of America.
Sahlins, Marshall
    1976  Culture and Practical Reason. Chicago: University of Chicago Press.
    1985  The Stranger-King; or, Dumezil Among the Fijians. *In* Islands of History. Pp. 73–103. Chicago: University of Chicago Press.
Spate, O. H. K.
    1959  The Fijian People: Economic Problems and Prospects. London: HMSO.
Thompson, E. P.
    1965  The Making of the English Working Class. London: Victor Gollancz, Ltd.
Williams, Raymond
    1973  The Country and the City. New York: Oxford University Press.
Williams, Thomas
    [1858] 1982  Fiji and the Fijians: The Islands and Their Inhabitants. Volume 1. Suva: Fiji Museum.
Zerubavel, Eviatar
    1985  The Seven Day Circle. New York: Free Press.

# 5

# Seizing the Moment: Power, Contingency, and Temporality in Street Life

## ANNE M. LOVELL

Anthropologists have always been somewhat uncomfortable with the category of marginality, perhaps because its application depends upon the vantage point of the person using the label. Nevertheless, marginality as defined in contemporary urban anthropology in the United States usually involves such a positioning in relation to dominant groups. An older approach, based on Parks' concept but still in use (see Hannerz 1980), sees marginality simply as a positioning *between* worlds. More recently, the category of marginality encompasses worlds or subcultures themselves, whose members are excluded from actual or potential means of effecting power, either because of their absence from the mainstream labor market or their lack of access to resources or commodities. Implicit in this second definition is the effect of cultural hegemony on definitions of marginality, and the structural differentiation between dominant, or powerful, groups and marginal ones.

Time functions as a major principle of segmentation in modern societies, not only by differentiating spheres of everyday life, such as private and public, but also by separating individuals and social groups from one another (Zerubavel 1981). As such, analyzing the intersection of marginal sociotemporal orders with those of dominant groups should provide clues about relations of power—how groups are included or excluded from access to resources—in modern societies. The far-reaching effects of time as a materialization of power is perhaps nowhere better illustrated than in Goffman's analysis of total institutions; in fact, he considers time the most significant dimension of the encompassing tendencies of all institutions (Zerubavel 1981:143).

In anthropological studies of poor or marginal groups in the contemporary United States, time is usually treated as a social construction, a concept, or an image. Studies of Skid Row alcoholics emphasize their present-orientation as opposed to future-orientation (Wiseman 1970) or a sense of nonrepetitive time (Spradley 1970) as opposed to the past-present-future orientation that is hegemonous in American society. On the other hand, homeless men's image of time has been described as cyclical, in contrast to the more conventional linear one (Murray 1984). Mental patients are thought to experience undifferentiated time, without the separation of work and leisure (Estroff 1981) that characterizes industrial time (Thompson 1969). The poor are supposedly present-oriented, while the unemployed are seen as lacking *any* temporal regularity or reference points (Jahoda et al 1972). In studies of heavy drug users, time is presented as a void, oblivion, or escape from industrial schedules.[1]

One commonality can be culled from these analyses of marginal sociotemporal orders. If industrial and postindustrial societies are overscheduled, temporally highly segmented and rigidly ordered, marginal time is far more flexible. In fact, as Estroff (1981) points out, having large chunks of "free" or highly unallocated time, as opposed to dividing one's time into well-defined periods of work and leisure, characterizes those who are least integrated into modern societies.

An understanding of how time both reflects and materializes relations of power is hampered by methodological and theoretical shortcomings in these studies. First, by limiting themselves to representations of time as a social construction, without analyzing the objective *uses* of time, social scientists are left with negative concepts or residual categories: marginal temporalities as dislocations from, rejections of or reactions to standard sociotemporal orders. The positive effects (in a Foucaldien sense) of time, as a materialization of power, cannot be collectively constructed. Zerubavel (1981) intentionally concentrates on highly rationalized, rigid temporal orders, while ignoring the nonrational or nonnormative uses of time—an approach that limits us to a one-sided understanding of the effects of power through the temporal segmentation imposed by dominant practices and ideologies. It ignores individually and collectively constituted temporalities that might intersect with dominant ones, thus revealing underlying power relations.

Second, theoretical models such as Zerubavel's (1981) are too often static (Rutz 1984): once established according to convention, time cannot be altered. By contrast, it can be suggested that the "hidden rhythms" of sociotemporal orders provide a window on power relations only if the models are dialectical—if temporality is attributed some agency. Power, after all, is the possibility of altering temporal patterns within the set of cultural rules that govern them.

It is such a *practical* model of time, one that can account for the negotiation of relations of power through temporal alterations, that is presented below. It utilizes both the social construction of time by one marginal group and that group's use of time as observed by the anthropologist to produce a dynamic model of control over resources in relation to which marginality is socially defined.

## The Sociotemporal Order of Marginality: Street Time in New York City

My analysis of sociotemporal orders of marginality and power concerns a group of homeless street people in one postindustrial setting, New York City,[2] all of whom have been identified by mental health workers as being psychiatrically severely disordered. Similarly, urban dwellers and other street people they encounter label them as "crazy," "mentally ill," "space cases" and so forth (Segal et al 1977; Snow et al 1986).

The label of "street person" appeared in American policy discourse around the early 1980s[3] to differentiate those homeless who prefer makeshift arrangements over sleeping in large municipal shelters. Like others who comprise the by-now recognized very heterogeneous "population" of homeless people, they lack access to stable spatial resources. Unlike some homeless persons, however, their predilection for street life, even if interspersed with stays in shelters, expresses a desire for autonomy and for some minimal control over their day-to-day lives (Baxter and Hopper 1981; Lovell et al 1984). And unlike many street persons and most homeless, they are cognitively "different";[4] that is, at various times (or, in some cases, always) they perceive both their internal and external worlds differently than do so-called normal persons in various American subcultures.

Street people spend much of their time (see Table 1)[5] figuring out sleeping arrangements and obtaining food, as well as eating, sleeping, and occasionally scavenging; selling found objects; and hanging out in fast food places, donut shops and coffee shops. Some attend mental health program activities, and many spend a lot of time sitting and waiting, depending in part on how much they consume services from souplines, emergency rooms, clinics, and welfare offices. They may watch television, shop or look around at things they can't afford to buy, spend hours in movie houses, watch people, "hang out" on the street, take walks, ride buses and subways, drink, smoke cigarettes,

**Table 1**
**Type and Site of Daily Activities Reported by Fourteen Street People**

| SITE OF ACTIVITY | TYPE OF ACTIVITY | | | | |
|---|---|---|---|---|---|
| | Work (Paid and Unpaid) | Resource Acquisition | Resource Consumption | "Pure" Sociability | Other |
| *Outdoor Public Spaces*[a] | Canning Selling found objects on sidewalk Selling tokens ("carfare") | Scavenging for food Collecting magazines, clothes, etc. | Eating Consuming alcohol and other drugs Window-shopping Riding-bus, subway Engaging in sex | Talking, "hanging out" | Sitting and waiting Playing chess Writing poems Sleeping Daydreaming Washing up Talking to oneself Walking Watching people |
| *Indoor Public Spaces*[b] | Bartending | Buying food Buying small items- (toiletries, pen, etc.) | Eating Consuming alcohol and other drugs Doing laundry Playing pool | Talking, "hanging out" | Sitting and waiting Napping Washing up |
| *Homeless Programs and Facilities* | Volunteering (dishwashing, serving, etc.) at soup kitchen | Collecting food, clothes, "carfare", etc. | Eating Participating in structured activities (psychosocial groups, medical information groups, etc.) | Talking, "hanging out" | Sitting and waiting Napping |

*Table 1 continued on page 90*

**Table 1** (*continued from page 89*)

| | | | | | |
|---|---|---|---|---|---|
| | Volunteering (setting up cots, etc.) at private shelter<br>Volunteering (making sandwiches, etc.) at drop-in Center | Obtaining letters of introduction, other documents<br>Picking up money from public assistance | | | Sitting and waiting<br>Napping<br>Accompanying a friend (to hospital, etc.) |
| *General Health and Social Service Facilities* | | Negotiating welfare and other forms of assistance<br>Obtaining medical, dental care | Eating<br>Participating in structured activities (Alcoholics Anonymous meetings, therapy group, etc.) | | |
| *Domiciles*[c] | | | Eating<br>Consuming alcohol and other drugs<br>Engaging in sex | Talking, "hanging out"<br>Visiting | Sleeping<br>Washing, showering<br>Giving away food, other gifts<br>Storing items to sell later |

*Note:* This table is based on responses to the next-day interview

[a] Includes streets, parks, plazas, atriums, playgrounds, etc.

[b] Includes fast food joints, coffee shops, bars, stores, churches, libraries, university buildings, transportation terminals

[c] Includes abandoned buildings, welfare hotels, public and private shelters, friends' apartments

smoke dope and consume other drugs, listen to street musicians, attend other free performances, generally observe and sometimes interact with the flow of urban life in the streets. Some spend time in libraries, reading or sleeping, or sit in public places and private spaces
such as corporate plazas, university lounges, and bus terminals. Some
draw or read or daydream or talk to themselves or converse with
voices.

Most time is spent with other people like themselves and with
other marginal people, who might be welfare hotel dwellers, homeless
persons, ex-psychiatric hospital patients, or street-level drug dealers,
and their frequency of contact is great. Street people also pass long
periods of time talking to waiters, street vendors, building supers, others whose names they might not even know, and some who comprise
what network analysts call "an anonymous fringe" (Sanjek 1974).
Some, albeit considerably less, time is consumed in encounters with
service providers.

An analysis of homeless periodicities in terms of their divisions
and the sites to which the activities that comprise them are anchored
belies the typical categories produced by historical and sociological
studies of time. Notably absent in the sociotemporal order of these
street people is the clear division of everyday life into activities of production and reproduction, or the conventional dichotomy of work and
leisure.[6] On a typical day, for example, one man would obtain second-
hand clothes at a homeless drop-in center, spend several hours gathering and washing empty cans and bottles, and might happen upon a
pile of magazines, a piece of broken furniture, or other used objects
thrown out on the street. Cans and bottles were then redeemed at su-
permarkets the same day. The other items were stored in a friend's
room, in return for divvying some of them up, or they might be laid
out and sold on a heavily-trafficked sidewalk during the night hours.

While resource consumption, "pure" sociability, and other activities (see Table 1) can be thought of as leisure, such a category is mean-
ingless within a marginal sociotemporal order that is not centered on
industrial (or postindustrial) work discipline.[7] In fact, for street people
the supposed work week and weekend differ, for the most part, not
in terms of leisure versus work or even production versus consumption activities, but according to whether or not time is spent in and
around social service and health facilities. While a few persons literally
organized their day around the 9 to 5 schedule of psychosocial programs for mentally ill homeless persons, most came and went from
these facilities, depending on whether their friends happened to be
there, the coffee was brewing, or help with a public assistance application was needed. When programs were closed, soup kitchens, drop-

in centers, and other services open evenings or weekends were used
in similar ways. The schedule of productive activities followed by the
social service and health sectors may therefore limit the times when
street people undertake certain activities, without determining what
comprises them.

Much of street people's time is people-oriented. Hours are filled
with sociability. While these interactions often involve exchanges of
concrete goods or of information, many consist of sociability in a
"purer" form—talking, visiting with people, simply "hanging out."[8]
Here is an example from one activity log:

> . . . ran into Susie in the Park, talked for a while. Saw some of the dope
> dealers—hung out with them most of the afternoon. Bought a nickel bag
> . . . Rob, Lionel, Dan came by . . . we talked . . . walked over to Broad
> Street [a drop-in center for homeless mentally ill]. Said hello to Arturo
> and Julie [clients], Mrs. Quinones [secretary], Penny [a case manager].
> Someone was giving out free donuts. Took an extra one, took it to Maria
> over at the Kingston [a welfare hotel . . . ran into my sister's old boy-
> friend . . . walked over to the Avenue [an abandoned building], hung out
> with the guys . . .

When material resources do not exist, sociability—in the form of
greetings, jokes, story-telling, gossip, etc.—becomes a resource, the
exchange of which creates bonds of reciprocity.[9] Such sociability operates according to unwritten rules of positive and negative reciprocity, providing social insurance over the long run. For the street person,
such insurance might include sharing marijuana when broke, visiting
a psychiatric ward after another signed himself in, and social recognition—an appreciation of friendliness and "crazy" antics. Negative
reciprocity can also be at work, as another activity log illustrates:

> After breakfast at the shelter, I always sit by myself. [Q: Who was there
> yesterday?] Helen, Rhoda, Bonnie, Juanita . . . but I don't talk to them,
> because then they'll ask for cigarettes or change . . . [Later she continues]
> I had lunch at the coffee-shop near Broad Street. The Broad Street people
> passed by, but I didn't wave because they might think I have money to
> buy them lunch . . .

Sociability occurs between street people and nonmarginal persons, as well, providing another form of social insurance. Many New
York neighborhoods (and those in other cities as well) boast of well
known homeless personalities: Poet-O, the King of Sixth Street, and
Princess (several street persons carry this last nickname), among others. To residents and merchants of the neighborhoods whose street
corners or empty lots they inhabit, some street people express their
"craziness"—bizarre dress, rapid role-switching, colorful disjointed

dialogue—as performance, in exchange for the protection of tolerance or advocacy when, at some future point, agents of social control, such as police, threaten forcible removal from public space. One man recounted his tactics:

> I used to costume a lot, dressed as Saturn, Earth, the Blue Marble Man. And I would go *all over*. The only place I didn't go was the [mental] hospital. I did it for nine months, with almost a different costume everyday. It was like a phenomena [*sic*], a hallucination . . . I was a known street person . . . I made myself known *everywhere*. Because then if anything happened, if the cops tried to put my number in a computer, people would say, "He did *what?* Not *him*. He isn't like that."

Rather than time being set aside for sociability, as a form of leisure, then, the sociability itself opens up a temporal space. The rules of reciprocity that underlie this sociability produce a future-orientation, a time when scarce goods will be exchanged or withheld, social ties expressed or denied.

## Contingency and the Matter of Timing

The patterning of everyday street life contrasts starkly with the bureaucratic and organizational schedules that govern the city. The self-identified "known street person" cited above succinctly summed up his day in the following account:

> I would try to schedule things on a physical footwork path. I could stop in at Dunkin' Donuts, which is a real good thing because it's open twenty-four hours and you can eat and they're pretty nice. Then I could go the Y, and I know a lot of people at the social agencies . . . or I would be sleeping soundly and peacefully, and all of a sudden it was like pins being stuck in me. I would go to a phone and call the mental health hotline, and all I would get was a lot of jazz. And with the weather bad and being stuck with pins, you can ride a bus all day. . . . Then there's this bar that opens at 10:00 A.M. and I know the owner and the people who work there and the habituées, so I could sit there and have coffee or a drink. Or if I run into another person who is living out we might go find a cheap grocery and buy food. I never had any regular meals or anything. Then you're at Riverside Park, at the fountain, and you want to wash up, but this woman is standing there, and she's talking real paranoid. At night friends of mine might want to stay up and they want company. Or like say maybe they're working on this building and I'd find the back entry unlocked and all this scaffolding and building material . . . An element of it is timing. Maybe it would be some very late hour even for New Yorkers and there was no evidence of anyone so I would lie down there.

Absent from his personal use of time is any regularity in the patterning. Contingency, not the hegemonic quality of temporal regularity, characterizes the sociotemporal order of street life.

Contingency is the occurrence of the unpredictable or unexpected. In the lives of these street people, it stems from several sources: (1) the internal, cognitive experiences of the individual; (2) the immediate settings for and nature of subsistence activities; (3) the larger context and arbitrary and unpredictable nature of formal organizations and institutions. Contingency is further produced by the potential ubiquitousness of social contact, suggested in Table 1, rather than its anchoring to a few well-defined sites. Such contact is increased by the mobility, enforced or chosen, engendered by the first three sources of contingency.[10]

The interaction of internal, cognitive experiences and the unpredictable nature of resource availability produces the circulation described for another man. In part because of his persecutory fears, he maintained sleeping quarters in several places. As his caseworker put it: "He stays all over. We're talking shelters and subways. We don't even know if he stays at the Columns [a serviced welfare hotel] because they see him going in and out of there all night long."

To this man, his day-to-day life pivots on external circumstances as well:

> It's a nightly kind of thing. I haven't had a permanent residence at any men's shelter or anything. [During the day] I'll go down to Mrs. Green [a shelter caseworker] and see if I can get some carfare or clothes. Or I may go down to the Bowery and inquire if there's detail work to break the monotony for myself. Or I'll go see why my SSI or welfare was dropped. It's a one-day-at-a-time-Sweet-Jesus kind of thing.

A temporality marked by contingency is ordered not by the regular sequencing, spacing and duration of events—the hegemonous quality of bureaucratic time (Zerubavel 1981)—but rather by a matter of *timing*. The precise moment for beginning an activity must be selected on the basis of when a maximum effect can be produced. Temporal location cannot be rendered expectable in a contingent order. What recurs are the multiplicities of places where, and ways in which, even the most necessary activities are accomplished.

As street people invest much time in obtaining sleeping arrangements, these activities can further illustrate the effects of contingency on time. A young woman may abandon a rented room that took months to find because she hears voices telling her that Nazis are invading it. She may pick up a trick on the street in exchange for a shower and a floor she can spend the night on. A man may run into an old acquaintance and talk so long that he misses the bus to the men's shelter. Or he might move from the spot in the park where he has been bivouacking because a homosexual couple has invited him to join them in their sexual revelry. And so on. The permutations are endless.

While marginal time is fluid, the temporality of formal organizations is usually considered highly rational and structured (Schwartz 1975; Zerubavel 1981). In reality, however, the formal organizations street people interact with operate according to both rigid rhythms and to arbitrariness and contingency. They are governed by at least two sociotemporal patterns: the schedules of daily, weekly, or even monthly activities; and the eclipsed time of management technology, such as data banks and telephones.

Rules governing hours of operation, duration and accessibility to services such as shelters are often so strictly patterned that social workers will not refer street people whose psychiatric symptoms include a poor orientation in time. However, the services themselves also create contingency. One way is through the arbitrariness of the rules governing its activities. For example, meals at a women's shelter, delivered from another facility, were never served at the same time nor were they announced. Shelter residents in various parts of the building or even outside who did not exercise a good sense of timing risked missing dinner. Rules may also change overnight. An extremely psychotic man found himself with no place to go when a shelter whose curfews he managed to keep quite regularly ruled only elderly men eligible. Another, who alternated between sleeping at a men's shelter and "catting" (sleeping on the floor of someone else's rented room), lost what little he owned when, unbeknownst to him, the shelter eliminated a three-month time limit for storing possessions in lockers. Turnovers in social work staff at small programs have caused many homeless to start the weeks-long application process for Supplemental Security Income all over again from scratch. And one public shelter closed its doors practically overnight, scattering women who had begun to settle there.

The arbitrariness of data management systems connected to these services often contradicts the rational principles on which they are based. While homeless men have described a cyclicity created by the monthly arrival of welfare checks (Murray 1984), more characteristic of poverty in New York City is the unpredictability of these very sources of income. For example, computer breakdowns and human error stall check arrivals for months. Data banks in the public shelter system have been notoriously unreliable, and in fact lend themselves to subversion by clients, through the use of aliases and other fabricated information.

## Waiting, Scheduling, and Power Relations

The temporal patterns of street people described above intersect with the schedule of city life—its trains and subways, its eateries, libraries, social service offices, and the myriad of other places where street people spend their time. To the extent that these metropolitan institutions control desired resources, the meeting of marginal and standard sociotemporal orders articulates relationships of power. These relationships are materialized in the use of time through both exclusion (delay in accessing resources) and inclusion (regulation of the use of resources). The control generated through these structural processes is in turn reinforced by the meanings attributed to them by street people themselves.

Because no one institution responds to the multiplicity of their needs, in the way, for example, households might, street people must turn to a variety of services as well as to makeshift arrangements. As a result, they circulate between numerous situations and places, often becoming caught between the conflicting schedules of organizations, which in turn produce further circulation. As a result, street people either occupy the fringes of these organizations or they remain too briefly for the politics of regulation and discipline to take effect. Thus, theories of power and domination implicit in the analyses of the temporal effects of totalizing institutions (Foucault 1979; Goffman 1961; Zerubavel 1981) bear little relevance to the marginalization of street people.

Nevertheless, street people continue to depend on large organizations for limited goods, in particular for shelter and income maintenance. Like any social organization that distributes scarce resources, institutions used by poor people control access to goods or services through temporal exclusion, specifically through queuing systems, or the systematic organization of delay (Schwartz 1975). Waiting is the subjective experience of this delay by the disadvantaged party. And in the everyday lives of street people, waiting is rampant, counted in the weeks and months it takes to process public assistance applications, the hours of sitting in an emergency room before receiving medical assistance, and the years a name remains on waiting lists for public housing. The monopoly over services for poor people held by these public bureaucracies further increases their power to maximize client waiting, thereby cutting the costs incurred by their service staff. And in many cases, maximized delay further contains costs by deterring potential clients from claiming resources. Thus delay serves both economic and political functions.

The arbitrariness of public bureaucracies lies partly in the uncertainty that their resources will *ever* be made available to the potential client. In this context, delay takes on a somewhat different significance than it might in a more regulated order. The significance of waiting is further shaped by the particular elements of street time, for the strategy of organized delay operates by preventing alternate uses of time.

Much street time is spent sitting and waiting, an experience that reinforces feelings of powerlessness and humiliation. In the overscheduled city, with its confusing busyness, the sight of people waiting for hours connotes their marginalization from activities of production and consumption. This awareness of the dominant values of busyness can also be shared by street people themselves, as reflected in bizarre presentations of self, such as the sheaves of dirty, dog-eared documents ("my business papers") carried by the dishevelled former psychiatric hospital patient or the bureaucratese that dots his word-salad.

Without resources or the prospects of them, street people have no goals in relation to which they feel "behind time" or "out of sync." In fact, waiting itself becomes a routine. What is accentuated is not necessarily the resource one is waiting for. It is the *site* of that activity, or the place where one waits that makes the difference. Depending on the situation, particular places are particularly attractive: university lounges with comfortable seats, park benches occupied by mothers and children where some street persons can "pass," and so forth. Even the anxiety of waiting for a resource is mitigated by the poor chances of receiving it, for, as one person explained, "you can only worry if you've got something to worry about." And, within the context of scarce resources, the introduction of a new one does not change the emptiness or boredom of "sitting and waiting." "Coming here keeps me out of the cold for two or three hours," one homeless man commented about a drop-in center with free lunches that he had started frequenting. "But it hasn't made any difference in my life . . . just a difference of routine, instead of hanging out in the library or on the streets until the shelter opens."

Over the long run, waiting becomes autonomized. Here, the effects of power are no longer traceable to their source, the institutional exclusion from resources. But rather, waiting has become a way of life. Some street people experience this as a paralysis of time, the "chronic ailment" of the boxman in Kobo Abe's (1974) novel that metaphorizes homelessness in modern Japan. They are struck not so much in a repetitive cycle as in "dead time." One middle-aged man, ravaged by years on the street and incomprehensible (to him) psychotic experiences, described such a paralysis:

> I feel petrified, helpless most of the time, being as I'm stuck down in the Bowery for the last five years. I have no money so I have no social relation. I can't change no clothes everyday, that's my habit. I feel dead, cause that's what dead people do. They never change. It makes me feel like my skin is going to fall off. I don't feel like living. And that's consistent for the past five years. . . . it's all been like one god damn long humble day.

Domination through the temporary exclusion from resources has become replaced by a permanent temporal dislocation, the origins of which have long since disappeared from sight.

The ability of an organization to control the time of its potential clients through delay is also dependent on factors other than competitiveness. In particular, the desirability of its resources and the desirability of its potential clients *as* resources will shape its temporal strategies. When delay can potentially affect institutional functioning in a negative way, domination is accomplished through inclusive temporal strategies, or the regulation of the client's use of its resources. This is evidenced in the operation of mental health programs for homeless persons who are labeled "mentally ill," which provide a range of resources, some of which are less desirable than others.[11] For these programs, the politics of inclusion take the form of structuring clients' time. When this time is filled with services that street people do not desire, such as recreational therapy activities (Schiller 1984) or the dispensing of psychotropic medication, or with services they can obtain elsewhere, such as free food, strategies must be developed to keep clients. Field notes from a staff meeting observed at one such program illustrate the problematic nature of temporal regulation as one such strategy:

> Ruth asked if all clients had to attend the program all day since some could not tolerate eight hours of participation. Jon [the director] answered that a contract/schedule should be developed for each client. Each client will have scheduled times to attend the appropriate group included in his or her treatment plan . . . Harold [a case manager] said that they would lose clients who had unscheduled time, that if a client had a group in the morning and then had to leave for a few hours before the next group on his schedule, it was unlikely he would return, especially if it were cold weather and the client needed a warm place to stay.

This concern with scheduling resonates with a belief held by some of the staff that clients with unstructured time on their hands would encounter more psychiatric problems. Schwartz's social psychological analysis of waiting (1975, Chapter 8) is also applicable to the dangers of unstructured time that mental health providers often fear. Drawing on the psychoanalytic literature, Schwartz suggests that time emptied of any purposeful activity shifts the individual's psychic energy from external objects to internal ones, thus allowing, among other possibilities, the arousal of unrepressed fantasies. The effectiveness of scheduled time depends, then, on its desirability versus the extent to which fantasy, in the absence of schedules, is experienced as unpleasant. Yet to many street people, daydreaming, talking to oneself or with voices, and other forms fantasy takes (see Table 1), may or may not be unpleasant, or in psychiatric terms, ego-dystonic. Simply filling up empty time with scheduled activities, then, will vary in its attractiveness. Thus scheduled activities as such may or may not be desirable resources.

Scheduling utilizes the time of the client as a resource. And time is the only resource street people possess. For the larger public service bureaucracies, this time represents a potential burden. For many smaller mental health programs, client time is functional to the organization's operation. In the example just cited, the mental health program is reimbursed according to a minimum quota of client contact or services rendered. Scheduling through the allocation of client time to an activity slot becomes a prerequisite for organizational survival. Yet the possession of a resource, of something that can be exchanged, provides street people with a base from which to negotiate. Rather than filling activity slots by scheduling themselves, they use the program far more sporadically, as a place to hang out, run into people, and seek shelter from the elements. Thus the matter of timing so crucial to survival on the streets introduces circumstance into the highly regulated schedules of the mental health program.

## A Practical Model of Time: Negotiating Inclusion in the Postindustrial City

The social construction of a temporal order, established according to convention, is not easily altered. But just as relations of power are negotiated and renegotiated through the strategies of the powerful and the tactics of the subordinated, so can the hidden rhythms of a subculture shift. The possibility of negotiating power relations through time is implicit in De Certeau's (1984) notion of practice (tactical uses of time in subversive and clever ways) and in Bourdieu's (1977) concept of strategy (the reintroduction of "time, with its rhythm, its orientation, its irreversibility" when conventional rules are replaced). The implications of these *practical* notions of time lead to alterations in any of the elements that structure a sociotemporal order: the sequencing of events, their duration, their standard location, or their rates of occurrence. It is to this *practical* model of time that we now turn.

The salient characteristic of street people is their homelessness, a marginality defined not so much by their exclusion from the labor market as by their lack of access to space. In New York, the urban context for the sociotemporal orders analyzed here, such exclusion is a sociospatial consequence of an economic restructuring of cities induced in part by postindustrialization. As discussed elsewhere (Lovell and Makiesky Barrow 1990), the city's economy has shifted with the loss of manufacturing jobs to the production of advanced services, insurance, finance, public relations, information, and management control. Furthermore, it has become internationalized through the exportation of manufacturing, the channeling of investments, and the importation of an immigrant labor force for the secondary market. The resultant of these economic processes is a polarization of the work force, with a concentration of high-income professional and service jobs on the one hand, and low-wage work on the other. Postindustrialization also encourages the development of a secondary, informal market with low-income jobs that service the upper-income groups, while expanding the so-called underclass (Sassen-Koob 1984).

One major (although not necessarily inevitable) sociospatial consequence of this economic restructuring has been the disappearance of low-income housing. Given the need to maintain a critical mass of high-income workers, private and public resources alike are reoriented toward a goal of gentrification; that is, the conversion of residential and commercial spaces into higher income housing, services, and leisure facilities. This logic, and its inherent refusal to consider an alternative urban policy, has facilitated and reinforced disinvestment from low-income neighborhoods, if not outright abandonment.[12]

Equally important to the postindustrial shift is the necessity to render public space aesthetically pleasing, safe, and attractive to the new professional classes that are necessary to a global, service economy. In the interest of assuring the attraction of leisure and consumption for the city's new professionals, public space is more and more invested with private meaning, aided by governmental regulatory and planning mechanisms (Kasinitz 1984).

Finally, marginal space retracts as it is reconverted for high-income use. Thus the Skid Rows of an earlier era, industrial buildings, even transportation tunnels, no longer provide cheap or free urban niches.

Street people's access to space, in turn, is affected by each of these consequences. But if time can be conceptualized in spatial terms—as niches of accessibility (Zerubavel 1981)—then in a context where space is retracting, marginal persons should be able to territorialize by altering temporal patterns. This possibility, of occupying time like space, has been suggested by the historical trend toward occupying nighttime as a new frontier when land areas became settled (Melbin 1978). Where time limits the accessibility to personal or "home" territories of the propertied, trespassing in time alters these power relations of inclusion and exclusion. Three examples of the strategic temporal practices of street people illustrate these premises.

Prolonging the duration conventionally accorded to the use of public space constitutes a first strategy. Goffman (1971) defines as "stalls" those specific public amenities that can only be occupied by one person at a time, such as chairs in waiting rooms or telephone booths. Street people territorialize by stretching out the time they spend in stalls. They may sit for hours in emergency room chairs when it is cold; use telephone booths to eat in, talk to voices, engage in sex, read newspapers; occupy a toilet stall for sleeping, rearranging personal belongings, or dressing. The dominant response may be the famous "move on," symbolized by the policeman's tapping his nightstick against a wooden bench, or the more systematized sweeps of public bathrooms, subway cars, and waiting rooms. In other cases, by an unvoiced public consensus, certain public amenities are eventually left to this long-term, unintended use. This became the case for bathrooms and lower levels at major New York City transportation terminals, which commuters would wander to only out of ignorance, and only to quickly retreat.

In the second case, the daily rhythms of public and private time are inverted. Nighttime, especially for the middle class, is a private time anchored in private spaces, such as bedrooms and living rooms. Nighttime for the nonpropertied becomes frontier space for carrying out private business in public places, such as sleeping in doorways, stairwells, on the sidewalks in front of stores and corporate skyscrapers. This temporary privatization of space involves negotiating, especially at the margins of the night, such as when someone washing up at a park fountain confronts the early morning jogger or dogwalker. Appropriation of public space in daytime is best achieved by "passing," making up for the loss of a night's sleep by stretching out in the park among noontime sunbathers. Systematic responses have ranged from curfews on city parks to confrontation with police (Freitag 1989; Rimer 1989). Yet, in an ironic time-sharing arrangement with the propertied, hundreds of street people continue to bed down in band-shells, tunnels, rotundas, or the bushes of green areas (Kifner 1989).

Finally, territorialization is accomplished by appropriating the time of others. Social workers categorize street people who overuse their resources as "social service junkies." One such resource is the time of the service provider—time as sociability, not as primarily material or informational transaction. The value street people place on the time of others is reflected in a concern with busyness. "A lot of times you go to [a social service] needing help and they block you out—they're too busy" is a common complaint. The accusation of being thus occupied can extend to family members, domiciled friends . . . everyone except other street people.

One way to alter another person's use of time is simply to occupy it. Out of loneliness, street people may appropriate the time of strangers they accost on the street or of waiters in a coffee shop. Or they may sit on a social workers' desk outside the hours scheduled for clients, use the bathroom right before closing time, or talk non-stop.

One response to the appropriation of another's time is to routinize the transgression. One elderly homeless man would pace for hours in front of a social agency before it opened and then before service providers were ready to see clients. The agency eventually engaged him in their early morning grocery runs for coffee, thus routinizing the transgression. Like occupied space, time that is occupied by more than one person becomes inclusive. Although time is further segmented by scheduling the transgression, this segmentation only includes those who were previously excluded.

The successful renegotiation of temporal patterns within a contingent order depends on the tactics of circumstance. In contrast to the strategies of delay and regulation by which dominant groups alter the time of the subordinated, temporal alteration by the subordinated themselves is a matter of good timing, of finding the niche that can be occupied at the margins of sociotemporal orders or the moment in which negotiation will prove most fruitful. The dominant response is more systematized control of marginal time, new regulations that may in turn be subverted or altered, in a dialectic set in motion by the agents of marginal as well as dominant temporalities.

The denial of coevalness on the part of anthropologists who study urban marginality lies not so much in a denial of different and contradictory forms of consciousness, as Fabian (1983) would have it, but rather in the imprisonment of those temporalities within a static, subject-less concept of time. By recognizing marginal temporalities as active, we can further understand how the dialectics of inclusion and exclusion are played out at the intersection of dominant and marginal sociotemporal orders.

# Notes

*Acknowledgments:* This paper would never have been written had the author not engaged in a series of exchanges with Henry Rutz and Kostas Gounis. In addition to Henry, Sue Makiesky Barrow, Samuel Bordreuil, Byron Good, Rayna Rapp, and Peter Stastny provided much-appreciated critical readings of earlier drafts. Christine White and David Blaustein painstakingly prepared the manuscript. Some analyses in this paper were made possible by a Dissertation Grant (#1R03HS05663-01) from the National Center for Health Services Research. Some data were gathered under the auspices of a National Institute of Mental Health grant (1R18MH38924-01) to E. L. Struening and S. M. Barrow.

1. More recently, though, heroin use has been posited as creating its own sociotemporal order, constituted by busy, productive schedules organized around the goal of avoiding symptoms of withdrawal (Pearson 1987).

2. Fieldwork upon which this paper is based took place in several New York City neighborhoods during five months in 1981, and then from 1984 to 1986. Participant observation, particularly at programs for homeless persons labeled mentally ill, was supplemented by a series of structured interviews, administered at zero and six months as part of an evaluation study, reported elsewhere (Barrow et al 1989). In addition to my own field notes, I drew upon those gathered by the project interviewers.

3. Although researchers such as Segal, Baumohl, and Johnson used the term as early as 1977.

4. This difference of cognition is based on a model that Kleinman and Good discuss in relation to depression (1985) and also on studies that indicate the different perceptions of schizophrenics (Estroff 1989; see other articles in the special issue of Schizophrenia Bulletin 1989). If one prefers the symbolic interactionist perspective, such "different cognition" can also be the result of relations between the psychotic or depressed person and others. For the purposes of this paper, the particular genesis of cognition is less important than the way it affects the subject's actions in the social world. For the application of popular psychiatric labels in general, see Estroff (1981), and with reference to homeless persons, see Snow et al (1986) and Segal, Baumohl and Johnson (1977).

5. To obtain a sense of both the social construction of street people's time and their use of time as "objectively" observed, the next-day interview, or activity log, was used in combination with data drawn from a structured network interview (Lovell et al 1984), unstructured interviewing, and participant observation. Although the next-day interview is too labor-intensive to use with a large sample or for a broad timeframe, it generates valuable information about both time allocation and its social construction (Rutz 1984). The next-day interview was filled out for fourteen individuals. They were asked to describe each of their activities, from when they awoke in the morning until they went to sleep at night. The interview included probes for determining where each activity had taken place and who was present. All responses were recorded. If the previous day fell on a weekend, another activity log was filled out for the second previous day, and if this was a Saturday, the third previous

day. The categorization and sequencing of activities, rather than their precise time and duration, were sought. Results of the fourteen interviews are summarized in Table 1.

6. Only one person was engaged in wage work: bartending on weekends in the neighborhood where he formerly resided. Four others spent several hours daily or nightly in marginal production activities. Other persons volunteered at programs for the homeless, sorting out donated clothes, making sandwiches, typing, setting up cots, putting out food. Sometimes this guaranteed first choice of a new shipment of clothes, fewer hours waiting in the food line, or entry to a church shelter in cold weather before the doors officially opened. As unpaid work, it constituted hidden production within the context of the social services provided by the programs.

7. Although in postindustrial economies, the clean division between productive and unproductive time and perhaps even the pervasiveness of industrial time discipline (Thompson 1969) can be questioned, as work becomes "decentralized," no longer the major source of personal and social identity and integration (Gorz 1988).

8. The degree of sociability is apparent in a comparison of names elicited through next-day interviews to those mentioned in response to Social Support and Social Network Interviews (Lovell et al 1984). On average, eleven names came up in conjunction with daily activities but not in the network interview. These were mostly friends, acquaintances, and others who, in the course of a day, street people ran into, talked with, visited, phoned, or kept company with over lunch, in the park, at a shelter, and so on. In fact, some consistency is found between the type of social relations mentioned in the next-day interview and those reflected by exchanges in network interviews for the social relations involved in exchanges. The network interview asks about exchange relations in sixteen substantive areas, ranging from material goods to information to companionship. In both the next-day and the network interviews, most of the names mentioned are of persons who, like the respondent, could be categorized as marginal. Seventy-four persons were administered the network interview. Out of 732 names elicited from them, 30% were of persons who could be categorized as marginal. A smaller proportion of network members were health and social service providers. That they appear less frequently in accounts of daily activities can be explained by the specific resources they are tied to and the greater amounts of time street people invest in sociability as opposed to in the direct accessing of resources. This breakdown is corroborated in interview data on most of the fourteen persons who responded to the day-after interview. (The network study is reported elsewhere, in Lovell [forthcoming]).

9. The use of sociability as a resource is also suggested in Laé and Munard's (1985) ethnography of a French transitional housing project.

10. This contingency of ubiquity symbolizes a larger one, the "homelessness" of modern men and women who have yet to transform contingency itself into their personal destinies. The modern person who does not make such a choice lacks a telos, a destiny comparable to that determined by blood ties and domicile, or home, in "pre-modern" times (Heller 1989:55 ff).

11. For the contrast between the ways homeless persons prioritize their need as opposed to mental health workers' hierarchization, see Lovell (in press).

12. In Marcuse's words, gentrification works by "siphoning off people and resources, public and private, and by inflationary pressure in the remaining areas where higher prices and declining incomes in turn produce abandonment" (Marcuse 1988). For an analysis of the complex relation of gentrification and urban policy, see Bordreuil (1991).

## References Cited

Abe, Kobo
   1974   The Box Man. New York: Knopf.
Barrow, Sue M., Fred F. Hellman, Anne M. Lovell, Jane D. Plapinger, and E. L. Struening
   1989   Effectiveness of Programs for the Mentally Ill Homeless: Final Report. Epidemiology of Mental Disorders Research Department, New York State Psychiatric Institute.
Baxter, Ellen L., and Kim Hopper
   1981   Private Lives/Public Spaces. New York: Community Service Society.
Bordreuil, Jean Samuel
   1991   Soho, Lower Manhattan, et la question de la gentrification. Paris: Plan Urbain, Ministère de l'Equipement.
Bourdieu, Pierre
   1977   Outline of a Theory of Practice. Cambridge: Cambridge University Press.
De Certeau, Michel
   1984   The Practice of Everyday Life. Berkeley: University of California Press.
Estroff, Sue E.
   1981   Making It Crazy: An Ethnography of Psychiatric Clients in an American Community. Berkeley: University of California Press.
   1989   Self, Identity and Subjective Experiences of Schizophrenia: In Search of the Subject. Schizophrenia Bulletin 15:197–200.
Fabian, Johannes
   1983   Time and the Other: How Anthropology Makes Its Object. New York: Columbia University Press.
Foucault, Michel
   1979   Discipline and Punish. New York: Vintage.
Freitag, Michael
   1989   For the Homeless, Public Spaces Are Growing Smaller. New York Times, October 1, p. E-5.
Goffman, Erving
   1961   Asylums. Garden City: Anchor Books.
   1971   Relations in Public. New York: Basic Books.
Gorz, André
   1988   Metamorphoses du Travail, Quête du Sens: Critique de la Raison Economique. Paris: Galilée.
Hannerz, Ulf
   1980   Exploring the City. New York: Columbia University Press.
Heller, Agnes
   1989   The Contingent Person and the Existential Choice. Philosophical Forum 21:53–69.

Jahoda, Marie, Paul F. Lazarsfeld, and H. Zeilsel
    1972[1933]   Marienthal: The Sociography of an Unemployed Community.
        London: Tavistock.
Kasinitz, Philip
    1984   Gentrification and Homelessness: The Single Room Occupant and
        the Inner City Revival. Urban and Social Change Review 17:9–14.
Kifner, John
    1989   Worlds Collide in Tompkins Square Park. New York Times, July 31,
        pp. A-1, B-5.
Kleinman, Arthur, and Byron Good, eds.
    1985   Culture and Depression. Berkeley: University of California Press.
Laé, Jean-Francois, and Numa Murard
    1985   L'argent des pauvres. La vie quotidienne en cité de transit. Paris:
        Seuil.
Lovell, Anne M.
    Forthcoming   Marginal Arrangements: Homelessness, Mental Illness, and
        Social Relations. Ph.D. Dissertation. Columbia University.
    In Press   Classification and Its Risks: An Analysis of Psychiatric Categori-
        zation in Homelessness Research. In Homelessness. A Critique of Amer-
        ican Health and Welfare Policy, Volume III. Aaron Rosenblatt, ed. Al-
        bany: Nelson A. Rockefeller Institute of Government.
Lovell, Anne M. and Barrow, Susan Makiesky
    1990   Portable Images: Post-industrial Constructions of Home and Home-
        lessness. Paper delivered to the Section of Anthropology, New York
        Academy of Sciences, New York.
Lovell, Anne M., Sue Barrow, and Muriel Hammer
    1984   Social Support and Social Network Interview. New York: New York
        Psychiatric Institute. Epidemiology of Mental Disorders Research De-
        partment.
Marcuse, Peter
    1988   Abandonment, Gentrification and Displacement: The Linkages in
        New York City. In Gentrification of the City. Neil Smith and Peter Wil-
        liams, eds. Pp. 153–177. Boston: Allen and Unwin.
Melbin, Murray
    1978   Night as Frontier. American Sociological Review 43:1, 3–22.
Murray, Harry
    1984   Time in the Streets. Human Organization 43(2):154–161.
Pearson, Geoffrey
    1987   Social Deprivation, Unemployment and Patterns of Heroin Use. In A
        Land Fit for Heroin? Drug Policies, Prevention, and Practice. Nicholas
        Dorn and Nigel South, eds. Pp. 62–94. London: Macmillan Education.
Rimer, Sara
    1989   Pressed on the Homeless, Subways Impose Rules. New York Times,
        October 25, pp. B-1, B-5.
Rutz, Henry J.
    1984   Units of Time Budget Analysis: The Social Construction of Time and
        Its Allocation by Fijian Households. Paper delivered at the 83rd Annual
        Meeting of the American Anthropological Association, Denver, Colo-
        rado.
Sanjek, Roger
    1974   What is Network Analysis and What Is It Good For? Reviews in An-
        thropology 1:588–597.

Sassen-Koob, Saskia
    1984    The New Labor Demand in Global Cities. *In* Cities in Transformation: Class, Capital, and the State. Michael Peter Smith, ed. Urban Affairs Annual Reviews 26. Beverly Hills: Sage Publications.
Schiller, Nina Glick
    1984    Invisibility and Compliance: Strategies of Survival in a Program for the Homeless. Paper delivered at the 83rd Annual Meeting of the American Anthropological Association, Denver, Colorado.
Schwartz, Barry
    1975    Queuing and Waiting: Studies in the Social Organization of Access and Delay.
Segal, Steven P., Jim Baumohl, and Elsie Johnson
    1977    Falling through the Cracks: Mental Disorder and Social Margin in a Young Vagrant Population. Social Problems 24(3):387–400.
Snow, David A., S. G. Baker, L. Anderson, and M. Martin
    1986    The Myth of Pervasive Mental Illness among the Homeless. Social Problems 33:301–317.
Spradley, James
    1970    You Owe Yourself a Drunk: An Ethnography of Urban Nomads. Boston: Little, Brown.
Thompson, E. P.
    1969    Time, Work-discipline and Industrial Capitalism. Past and Present 38:56–97.
Wiseman, Jacqueline P.
    1970    Stations of the Lost: The Treatment of Skid-Row Alcoholics. Chicago: University of Chicago Press.
Zerubavel, Eviatar
    1981    Hidden Rhythms: Schedules and Calendars in Social Life. Berkeley: University of California Press.

# 6

# Time, Talk, and Class:
# New York Puerto Ricans as Temporal and Linguistic Others

BONNIE URCIUOLI
*Linguistics Program*
*Hamilton College*

## How is Time Like Language?

In American public life, time and language are powerful signs of social value. To begin with, both are (culturally speaking) "natural" objects in the "real" world. Correct uses of time and language are measured against a standard of linear order and rational organization: one should use time punctually and efficiently; one should speak clearly and logically. Magazines, best-sellers and self-help entrepreneurs offer programs whereby a person can take control of time or language to rid oneself of obstacles and impurities (distractions leading to procrastination or wastes of time; accents, bad grammar and slang leading to misunderstanding). In this chapter, I show how New York Puerto Ricans are put at risk by these quintessentially American ideologies of time and language. Anglo supervisors, teachers, social workers and others in authority pass judgments about time and language in a strikingly parallel manner. Such judgments are especially problematic in that rational uses of time and language are supposed to be neutral and objective, equally accessible to anyone with the requisite energy, drive and work ethic.

This ideology of temporal and linguistic rationality links ethnicity and class in a manner that Puerto Ricans (like African Americans) have always been particularly vulnerable to. The American social science literature is replete with examples, the most vivid (and influential) being *La Vida*, Oscar Lewis' study of a Puerto Rican culture of poverty.

The misuse of time turns up squarely in the middle of Lewis's culture of poverty criteria:

> a high incidence of maternal deprivation, orality, weak ego structure, confusion of sexual identification, a lack of impulse control, *a strong present-time orientation with little ability to defer gratification and to plan for the future,* a sense of resignation and fatalism, a wide-spread belief in male superiority, and a high tolerance for psychological pathology of all sorts. [1965:xlvii; italics mine]

Lewis nicely illustrates Fabian's (1983) argument that anthropology has made time a sign of the incommensurable. In fact, Fabian explicitly equates time with language as signs that place the ethnographic object in an "Other" frame of reference:

> Time, much like language or money, is a carrier of significance, a form through which we define the content of relations between the Self and the Other. . . . Time may give form to relations of power and inequality under the conditions of capitalist industrial production. [p. ix][1]

Both time and language have come to be typified by Euro-Americans as linear, a rigid sequence of segments following segments. Zerubavel (1981:46ff) shows how time came to be objectified as a schedule of minutes, hours, days, and weeks. Friedrich (1986:135ff) shows how language came to be idealized as a sequential structure of phonemes, morphemes, and words. Time can also be exchanged for money, and its value varies with the user's status (Schwartz 1975). Similarly, linguistic signs—words, sounds, phrases—are objects of social and political value. Irvine (1989) argues that in language, both semantic and social functions are built into the power structure of human relations, so that signs themselves can become objects of exchange.[2] Finally, time can be "spatialized" (Fabian 1983:16) so as to put, in Fabian's terms, the Other in a timeframe beyond and incommensurate with the analyst's. By the same token, labels like "bilingual" or "Spanish-speaking" move Puerto Ricans to places on the social map incommensurate with, and certainly less valued than, the Anglo power center (Urciuoli 1991). In the public imagination, the ideal language of America (and of the Anglo power center) is what Silverstein (1987) calls Standard Monoglot English, a naturally logical and pure English that carries no contaminating accents, slang or illogical bad grammar, and that everyone should be able to learn if they work hard enough. The ideology of this monoglot is so overwhelming in the public imagination that any other form of language is a mistake. Pulling a page from Fabian and a page from Silverstein, I would argue that the American public imagination holds to a parallel hegemony of time, which might be called a Standard American Monochron, a naturally organized, logical time that everyone should be able to achieve if they discipline themselves.

## Local Voices

Puerto Rican and Anglo relations are tightly structured by class. Indeed, class has been an issue between the United States and Puerto Rico since the latter became a U.S. colony in 1898 as a result of the Spanish-American war. From the 1920s to the 1970s, American investors regarded Puerto Rico as an unskilled labor pool, and it was as unskilled labor that the Puerto Rican labor migration to the continental United States was encouraged after World War II (Carr 1984:201–214). As a result of several decades of such policies, many Puerto Ricans find themselves in economically constrained situations, the worst of which are found in large cities like New York, where Puerto Ricans and African Americans are increasingly segregated. Even poor housing is expensive and hard to find. Wages for unskilled day labor and low-level clerical jobs are low and benefits limited. People's lives become increasingly subject to regulation because of the administrative requirements of welfare, Medicaid, and public housing, and subsidized job training programs. It is usually women who deal with public agencies, especially welfare, since it is meant to subsidize mothers living alone with dependent children.

Puerto Rican relations with "whites" or "Americans" (as they usually typify Anglos) can take a variety of forms. Younger men and women (especially unmarried or childless) are likely to have Anglo bosses or coworkers; whether these become friendships is less easy to tell. Women with children are most likely to encounter what they see as the archetypal white: the middle-class agency representative, probably college-educated, male or female though more likely female. Actually, the agency representative is as likely to be Latino or black as white. But the position is structurally white so to speak, in that it represents the hegemonic concerns of U.S. society. If the woman is on welfare, she has to present her situation in a way that middle-class Americans typically regard as dysfunctional: no husband, no job, unskilled, etc. (In fact, many women on welfare do work and/or have common-law working spouses whose existence must be hidden.)

The agency representative sets the terms of the petition process and the petitioner must constantly present her or his reality so as to fit those terms. However much the agency representatives might sympathize with their clients' plight, and they very often do, they must operate within clearly defined parameters. The American concepts of time and language from which they work are the bases for bureaucratic policies, which institutionalize the homogenous coordination of personal and collective schedules and rhythms (Zerubavel 1981:64). In other words, they must work within an institutionalized Monochron, allowing no other time rhythms, as they must use the agency's version of a Monoglot English that disallows departures from a "just right" denotational English Standard (Silverstein 1987:10).

The interviews cited below represent two sets of voices. The Puerto Rican voices belong to families from the central-south Bronx and the Lower East Side of Manhattan. Dolores Fonseca, her husband, and young daughter live in Manhattan; he works "off the books" (no benefits or Social Security) in renovation jobs. Frank and Migdalia Cortez, their two young children and Migdalia's mother Selenia Colón live in the Bronx (they used to live in Manhattan); he has a clerical job with an import-export firm. Both families have received support from AFDC (Aid to Families with Dependent Children). Peggy Adams is a Puerto Rican woman whose husband was black. She lives with her grown daughters in the Bronx and works in a neighborhood agency. Mercedes DeLeón lives in the Bronx with her husband and three young children. She works in Manhattan as a legal secretary and he works as a grocer. Their joint income and housing are more comfortable than those of the other families. All are fairly young: Mr. and Ms. Cortez are 28 and 27; Ms. Colón is 45; Ms. Fonseca is 23; Ms. Adams is 38; Ms. DeLeón is 30. I have known them all for over twelve years. I worked with them on the Lower East Side in 1978–79 and in the Bronx in 1988 in studies of language and discrimination.

Most of the voices represented here are women's, in part because I had greater access to women's networks than to men's, in part because mothers are the primary players when the local Puerto Rican world touches the bureaucratic Anglo world. Local men are not altogether visible outside the neighborhood. The 1980 Census for the 15–35 age bracket shows the proportion of women to men on the Lower East Side about 5% greater among Latinos than among the general population. Some men die young; some are in jail; many are simply never listed on the census.

The Anglo voices belong to Mr. Smith, Director of Continuing Education in a local business college where Selenia Colón attends evening classes for a high school equivalency and business skills; Ms. Jones, who supervises a high school equivalency and neighborhood job training program which Dolores Fonseca attends; and Ms. White, who administers a public outreach program to establish neighborhood gardens.

## What Do People Do with Their Time?

Public education and outreach programs are built on the notion of linear individual progress. Agency representatives see Puerto Rican "culture" or "tradition" or the fact that they are not "European" as interference with that natural progress. They are likely to see their clients' time as unstructured and controlled by others. Mr. Smith comments:

> I don't want to stereotype but I think that a lot of the Hispanic females in the Bronx have particular concerns, I don't want to say problems, but concerns that I think only now they're realizing because of culture. . . . One thing I think I should mention is that the female population in the evening, since most of them are working, they come to us not straight out of a high school. They've been working and then something happened and they wanted to finish their education so they haven't been used to a structured schedule of classes, work, family.

Ms. Jones observes that many of her students are unable to continue in the program because "things come up at home":

> A lot of times the family's sending really mixed messages to the person in the program. I've had some women who were in the program who were married, one . . . whose husband was really not supportive of her at all for being in the program because she was doing very well, and she was trying to get a white collar job and she was very bright and she was succeeding. . . . They had a child and it was very threatening to him. They worked it out. She finished the program and got a job and got a promotion and everything and they ended up working it out . . . it's not always like a husband. It may be the mother who isn't supportive of the person being in the program. I've had examples of students—their mother is relied on to do a lot of work around the house in terms of taking care of younger siblings, and helping out with errands and housework. And so in a sense they want the person to go out and get a job but in another sense they don't because the person is so valuable in the home place also and takes over a lot of the mother's responsibility.

Mr. Smith and Ms. Jones are concerned with progress, and with the degree to which students are surrounded by people who interfere with their progress. Gender is a particular problem. Ms. Jones:

> . . . a third area that I've seen a lot is with very traditional Puerto Rican families in which they do not like their daughters coming to the program, in many instances just because they want to keep their eye on them wherever they are. So they can never go out at night or anything, so even coming to school, coming into this program and coming all day is threatening, because they don't know where their daughter is.

Mr. Smith makes an almost identical assessment, which resonates with Lewis's "wide-spread belief in male superiority":

> We have many male Hispanics who do not go to the school, calling, is she there, does she attend? Fathers, brothers, husbands, because it's a cultural thing that the women—

Ms. White sees gender and race as obstacles to social progress:

> It's not like the Europeans coming over and saying "I got this far and now you have to move the ball forward." Even thinking about moving the ball forward is sometimes a threat to the mother and the father. Especially to the father.

How does women's time come to be seen in such terms? Two separate but related factors affect women's use of time.

First, the greater one's status the less time one has to wait, the less one has to actively pursue, the more one can control the sequencing of one's own time (Schwartz 1975:13ff).[3] Public agencies instituted for the disadvantaged, like welfare, public housing, Medicaid, clinics, GED programs and youth employment programs structure the terms of meeting, set appointments, make clients wait. One of the principal differences between being poor and being middle-class in the modern United States is that middle-class people deal with housing, food shopping, and employment with relatively little institutional interference, whereas poor people have no such option (Susser 1982). All the families I worked with were used to institutional dealings, some having had them for years. Since women are the contact people, women do the waiting.

Second, women's time is governed by their networks, in which resources, obligations and emotions are strongly invested among kin, especially between generations. For example, Ms. Cortez divides her time and resources among her mother, husband, sisters and nephews. Women are responsible for organizing and scheduling activities. I have often seen Ms. Cortez, Ms. Fonseca and Ms. DeLeón sandwich large numbers of errands into small amounts of time, getting everyone up, dressed, fed and ready to go where they are going when they are supposed to be there, in time for another family member to do what he or she has to do. This is especially difficult for Ms. Cortez and Ms. Fonseca, who have no cars. Outings are layered and intercalated: stops at relatives' houses, rides for people without cars and so forth. Just getting ready to go out for the day can be a nightmare of coordination. Ms. DeLeón, before going to work, picks up the sitter for her youngest child (except when the sitter cannot come, in which case she drives the child to her mother's), takes the older children to school, and drives from the central Bronx into Manhattan to be at work by 8:00 A.M. Her husband (who has his own car) walks to work. After work, she picks up her middle child from school (the oldest takes the bus) and drives the sitter home.

Women do this organizing because women are responsible for all relationships that grow out of the household (including feeding and lodging husband's kin or even friends, or friends of one's children, who might be staying in the household). Men may help if asked and many offer, but men do not have primary responsibility for organizing the household. Women are also responsible for negotiating with the landlord about repairs, a considerable investment of time and effort. Ms. Cortez's landlord had ten housing violations against him. She was on rent strike for months, finally succeeding in taking him to small claims court and forcing him to paint and put in new cabinets: a lot of time and a small return. Similarly, Ms. Fonseca spent several weeks on rent strike to get her landlord to paint; shortly after that, new building violations began to accumulate, particularly broken hall lights, so she helped organize another rent strike.

The same principle covers the dispersal of time and money: the simultaneous claim of relationships for which women are primarily responsible. (Both women and men bring money into the system, but women are the chief dispatchers; see Sharff 1986.)[4] These claims cannot be sequentially ordered: the mark of value is to be there when needs arise, and one never knows when that will be. Women are frequently asked to take in relatives' children, often without compensation. Ms. DeLeón took in her sister's daughter for several weeks during a family emergency, expending a great deal of time and effort to find her a job and car. Ms. Adams was asked to take in her brother's two children at a time when she just could not afford to do so, which worried her enormously. For years Ms. Cortez has been trying to save for a house, and for years, as soon as her savings become appreciable, emergencies and sudden needs arise to siphon off a considerable part. The pattern seems to be, roughly, that as soon as enough money builds up it is dispersed simultaneously along several points, to Ms. Cortez' husband, to her sisters, in addition to the constant exchange between her and her mother. Large sums do not accumulate.

Personal recreation (not involving family) takes a back seat to other claims. Ms. Cortez and I spent nearly a month planning a day trip to Chinatown. This depended on when her mother could watch her daughter. She postponed twice when other family claims on her mother's time arose, and almost postponed a third time because she had to buy school clothes for both children and birthday clothes for her son. At the last minute, she combined these errands with the day trip so that we could have four hours to take the train into Manhattan, walk around, have lunch and be back before her son came out of school. Scheduling two or three day trips that included her husband and children was much easier because she did not have to budget her time around them.

While most of the women I worked with were wizards at organizing time, little of it was scheduled in a linear sense. Linear scheduling is antithetical to this ideology of relations and responsibilities: if one is going to be a good mother or daughter or aunt or sister, one's time cannot be linear. No friend or relation could impose a schedule. Schedules can only be imposed by welfare, housing authorities, clinics and other public agencies. While clients cannot afford to miss appointments (or bring the wrong documentation), agencies need not be on time. Institutional schedules are for benefit of the institution, not the client (see next section). As for the clients, as Schwartz (1975:174) points out, waiting of this sort is degrading because "it reawakens the social context in which these permissions and constraints are originally felt."

When women seek time that no one can touch, a *"niche of inaccessibility,"* (Zerubavel 1981:142) they usually seek respite not from family but from socially hierarchic obligations outside the family. Guarding time from welfare is nearly impossible, but time can sometimes be guarded from, say, one's employer. Ms. White relates an incident that took place at her office:

> I worked with a gal from Ecuador and she took off quite a bit of time from work and her boss one day called her home to find out if she was really at home and she wasn't, and this woman got really upset and she got everyone in the office, black and Hispanic, banded together to give the boss a really hard time.

The intrusion is from public office to private home; the privacy boundary is across, not within, class/race/authority lines.

Antithetical as the American Monochron is to the structure of local lives, many women see its prestige value. Ms. DeLeón comments that families whose time (and money) is habitually disorganized reinforces "lowlife" stereotypes of Latinos, and when she complains about people being disorganized and late, her husband tells her she's "thinking white." Ms. Adams disapproves of relatives who intrude on her time, or treat her time as if it were unimportant by being late or not appearing at all. She is proud of the fact that she is always prompt, and proud that her daughters (both working their way through college) use time well. She too is sensitive to the "lowlife" image of unstructured time:

Around here there's a few people that hang out in front of our building, and sometimes some of them don't even live around here, just hang out in front of that building. They just sit there, they don't do anything, and somebody that passes by that building would say, "oh, they have the worst people living there." And they're putting me in there, and I don't hang out in the street and they're putting my daughters in there, they don't hang out in the street. And there are plenty of people in this building that go to work every day.

## Parallels and Interplays of Time and Language: Turning People into Nonpeople

The ideal Anglo trajectory for non-Anglo success is triply linear: learn proper English, organize time, get a good job. Time and language become parallel, and their value leads to money. The more one departs from this ideal, the more one risks becoming a total Other, so completely defined by "what is done wrong" that one becomes a nonperson. Mr. Smith examines the uses to which his evening division students put time and language:

> Since we're dealing predominantly with two groups I don't have that wide a range to compare, basically just Hispanic and black. Yet I don't want to stereotype but I think that a lot of the Hispanic females in the Bronx have particular concerns, I don't want to say problems, but concerns that I think only now they're realizing because of culture. Because of culture. Again, not to put anyone in a group. . . . One thing I think I should mention is that the female population in the evening, since most of them are working, they come to us not straight out of a high school. They've been working and then something happened and they wanted to finish their education so they haven't been used to a structured schedule of classes, work, family. And it's very difficult for them. As you said before, very few have support systems behind them. So you run into a problem not only of child care but once you tackle that, of just structuring their time to do all the things they now have to do . . . Our students tend to have a lot of I guess what you'd call inner city problems? And when they leave here the problems are always there and just crash in on them. It's not the academics so much as the personal problems . . . "I can't get the babysitter in today so I can't get to class"; "Cat ate the homework." Conflicts among themselves within the class. I don't know if you'd want to say lack of maturity, I wouldn't want to say that—

Mr. Smith is trying very hard to find fair and neutral terms in which to talk about his students, finding "culture" and "inner-city" less "stereotypic" than "Hispanic or black." "Inner city problems," a phrase often heard from teachers and social workers, conveys a sense that the "culture of poverty" model, of which the phrase is reminiscent, seems relatively neutral to Mr. Smith.

Women's lives are most typically nonlinear: they have children (often several children, often starting in their mid-teens), leave school, and so are unaccustomed to a "structured schedule." The principal problem lies not in conflicting duties, nor in circumstances that bring about conflicting duties, but in students' inabilities to learn to structure time. Thus, "you run into a problem of not only child care. . . ." Child care is objectified as a glitch in a schedule, a time problem that can, or should be, encapsulated and solved. Yet child care is not seen to be as basic a problem as being culturally nonlinear: "but once you tackle that of just structuring their time." Lack of linearity becomes evident in the equation of "no babysitter" to "cat eating homework" as equally schedule problems. The students are, as Fabian would argue, placed in an Other time, a sort of going-around-in-circles time. Insofar as this "should" be controllable, it is not coeval with the sequential scheduling of the Monochron "because of culture." Not finding a sitter should seem familiar to middle-class Americans, but its familiarity is distanced by equating it to cats eating homeworks, personal conflicts in class and, above all, being immature (i.e., in the wrong phase of life for one's age.)[5]

Mr. Smith is a sympathetic person who acknowledges that these are real problems. But his own monochronic perspective is inseparable from the fact that he must administer a program serving diverse needs on a minimal budget. From his structural vantage point it is absolutely imperative to observe a schedule. Thus, any reason for a disorganized schedule is equivalent to any other reason. This basis for action is not readily compatible with that of the women students, who are responsible for everyone and everything in their households, all of which they experience as simultaneous claims, all of which have to be dealt with in an intercalated fashion.

Ms. Colón now presents her perspective. At this time, she was taking a sociology requirement. The sequence of requirements which the school had assigned was (1) a basic English requirement, which she had taken the previous semester; (2) a basic social science requirement (the sociology course she was now taking); (3) a writing requirement; and (4) Technical Writing, which she was scheduled to take the following semester. She had wanted to take Technical Writing before Sociology because Sociology required a great deal of writing and she had no confidence in her writing skills. She could not persuade her advisor to let her take the courses out of sequence, although when I talked this over with Mr. Smith, he said that had he realized how insecure she felt about her English, he would have allowed her to do so. Normally, he said, the school did not like to make exceptions because they feared students sought reasons to put off Sociology which they

regarded as difficult and vague. A further problem had arisen when
Ms. Colón wanted to enroll on a part-time basis, but was only eligible
for AFDC subsidy as a full-time student:

> Last night I went to bed at four o'clock in the morning. Sometimes I go
> to bed at six o'clock in the morning. Studying, studying because I know
> it's difficult for me if I don't study, because if the teacher says something
> and I don't understand it I have to sit down and I have to study and to
> see, to look the ways what is this? . . . And I am, I am killing *myself*. Bon-
> nie, I don't hardly eat. I don't hardly do nothing. I don't hardly clean my
> house. . . . My house is a big mess. I don't have time for myself, I don't
> have time for nothing. They don't see that. The welfare is *pushing* me,
> like stop motherfucker, you have to be here. You have to be cleaning
> here, have to be washing toilets.

Mr. Smith sees each student as ultimately responsible for control over
her or his own time, just as in the next portion of his interview (below)
he sees each student as responsible for his or her own language. Any
individual can succeed so long as he or she overcomes the constraints
of culture. By contrast, Ms. Colón sees several conflicting claims on
her time. She lives in a small apartment with two of her grandsons
near her daughter's place. During the day she shops, cooks, takes care
of her grandsons, and baby-sits her granddaughter while her daughter (Ms. Cortez) shops and runs errands. She cannot work during the
day due to constant interruptions, and if she leaves books or papers
out they might disappear. So she works at night, after her grandsons
are asleep. Since AFDC requires full-time status for her subsidy, she
has more work than she can handle. AFDC controls the amount of
time she must commit, just as the school's area requirements control
the distribution of her time. Time for herself means time that need not
be accounted to an outside authority (AFDC), like the woman in Ms.
White's anecdote. There is a schedule fetishism at work here, based
on a utilitarian logic (Zerubavel 1981:54ff) that gives the institution a
naturalized right to control, and to discount her rationale.

Mr. Smith constructs language, like time, as a linear and utilitarian object that can be controlled:

> I look over their transcripts and I perhaps see College English One, B;
> College English Two, B+ . . . they have to go into a course that involves
> technical work, they'll come to us and say "my English is not that good,
> I have a concern with this and that," and I'll look at their transcript and
> say "but how, you did well" . . . I think again it goes back to how they
> perceive themselves and some of them, I can't stereotype but I think
> some people, Hispanics, think of the accent, "I have an accent, I'm very
> conscious of it and I don't want to let that accent out, I don't want to *axe*
> you something because everyone will laugh at me" . . . If the student
> fails English, we call them in and find out right away what the prob-

lem . . . there are workshops, the teacher refers them to us and we would catch it. So I think it's a problem that's unique to the student. They always have this feeling that they're down here and the American born, if there's such a person because there is no accent, is better.

Language is linear in that the student can pass tests showing that she or he knows the correct pieces and puts them into correct sequences. As with time, an individual can overcome "culture" to learn to put pieces of language in the right order. This is a utilitarian rationale in that each piece has its use. Proper use can be tested, and corrected in workshops. Since accents do not detract from use, students should not be concerned with their accents. Such problems are "unique to the student," which is to say, a nonrational cultural ("Hispanic") concern. Both time and language present a linear object that can be used in a rational manner once the student breaks free of "culture."

Ms. Colón sees language, as she sees time, in terms of multiple and conflicting functions:

> I went in and I asked them if they have bilingual classes. . . . They accept me, but I told them, my English is not that good . . . then the man told me, "are you understanding what I am asking you?" I say "yes, I understand you. But you know, my vocabulary is not, it's not that big. I need English." And he said, "oh, you're gonna do it. I'm sure you're gonna do it, because you understand everything. You'll do it, you'll do it, Mrs. Colón." And I haven't seen nobody asking me, "are you getting better in English, Mrs. Colón?" . . . Nobody comes to me. I have to go to them.

Ms. Colón is alarmed precisely because the school only perceives the linear structure and an adequate linear structure at that, not adequate for texts or exams or term papers:

> Like when you said "Selenia, you speak good English, I don't know what is your problem" . . . that was like elementary English. It was something that I knew it from when I was little. . . . But I need more English, I need more explanations, I need more examples. . . . Like when you are building a house, you need a lot of things. You need the land. You need wood, or cement. You need nails, you need people who help you, because by yourself you won't be able to do it. You have to have the structure, or how you are going to build the house.

The crowning insult is that they rob her of time. She spends her time going to "them" and even then:

> I ask for help. But in school they won't help me. They said we have tutoring on Saturdays. I went over there on Saturdays, who was helping me? Nobody. Nobody was there.

Ms. Colón introduces a theme that does not arise in Mr. Smith's construction: the interplay of language and time. She must invest time into study in inverse proportion to her linguistic skills. The school is in a position to certify her language as acceptable and so owe her no further time. The school has "help" officially scheduled and that ends their responsibility; it is up to her to make it accessible. The "disorganized" time it costs her to make them give her language is her (cultural) problem. The school need do nothing about it because they have already certified her language as acceptable:

> They don't give a fuck, they just want to grab the money from the government. That's it.

The money motive she introduces is the key to the interplay of time and language. The school can sell her bogus English in exchange for the AFDC subsidy because they can set up a double standard for English.

I have said the Monochron parallels Silverstein's Monoglot, both natural, rational, linear and ideally free of "cultural" interference. As the reader may have noticed, the parallel is askew in that a strictly Monoglot English would not have a "foreign accent" and here Mr. Smith certifies an accent as acceptable. But the point is that the school *can* so certify language. Schools that serve the disenfranchised do not have resources to maintain both organized time and "good" English so they make a tradeoff. They maintain the Monochron by fetishizing schedules, and select (through tests) the bits of student English closest to the Monoglot for certification. Accent is certified to not interfere with rational comprehension. To draw an analogy from another fetish-making industry, fashion, students are sold a knock-off discount Monoglot; at those prices, they should not mind that they get "factory seconds" made of cheap polyester instead of silk. Ms. Colón, that unsatisfied customer, knows quite well that while what she is getting is cost effective, it will not pass for "good English" because it lacks complex structure ("I need more examples, more explanations) and is limited in function ("like elementary English"). "Good English" requires the vendor to invest time ("by yourself you won't be able to do it").[6]

While students are made incommensurate in time through being nonlinear, they are made incommensurate in language both by speaking a different English and by having to accept a discount standard. In both cases, the agencies certify what is real, what matters. The students' worries and anxieties cannot matter because the institution cannot afford to have them matter, so they become problems "unique to the individual." The fetishism of time and language as commodities turns on the value of capital after all (see Note 2).

The discount standard is unlikely to be bought by bilinguals sensitive to the fact that any sign of being Latino puts them at a distance. Mr. Cortez's Anglo coworkers criticize him for speaking Spanish with the cleaning women at work:

> . . . Right away they say, "uh-oh, English, English. We're in America." And I say, "that's right, we are in America and you are allowed to speak whatever language you want to speak." They say, "Oh, you should speak English. It's not polite to speak next to someone who doesn't understand." I say, "put yourself in my shoes. If I don't speak English do you think you guys will care two cents about me not knowing what you say about me?"

Mr. Cortez has to make the effort to be commensurate with his coworkers (through language), just as Ms. Colón and other students have to make the effort to be commensurate with the school's time standards. The same logic applies to accents. Ms. DeLeón:

> When people tell you you have an accent, they're judging you. If you have an accent you belong to a stereotype, you're scum. People do this to you no matter what, just because you're Hispanic. They especially resent it if you're Hispanic and doing well. They feel like you shouldn't be equal to them, they look for extra ways of putting you down, like making a big deal out of how you sound.

The particular source of resentment lies in the fact that many Americans prefer to see Puerto Ricans as utterly incommensurate. If they "do well"—become commensurate through capital—an accent becomes an even more important sign of Otherness.

Incommensurability at its most extreme and least negotiable turns one into a nonperson. Mr. Smith does not quite do that to Ms. Colón: she can talk to him, he does explain policy, and if she is very persistent, she may get language help. She remains in the interaction, if at a distance. When one becomes a nonperson, one is regarded as not worth bothering with or simply not there. One becomes a nonplayer in the interaction. Thus, Ms. Fonseca describes her landlord as someone she cannot answer back:

> Like the way the landlord comes and tries to put me down in words and even if I don't know the words I can tell from his voice and if I respond to him the only words I know are bad words, I can't talk to him in big words like on his level so he might be thinking I'm a lowlife, "she's a lowlife girl."

One can be construed a "lowlife" through "bad words" as readily as through "wasted time" (cf. Ms. Adams and Ms. DeLeón, above). Once in that category, one becomes an object, a nothing. Ms. Fonseca neatly parallels becoming a nothing through language ("I can't say anything") and time ("they think you're not working"):

> I can't say anything back to [the landlord] anyway because he could throw me out of the apartment because of welfare. . . . If you're in the welfare they have all this opportunity to take advantage of you. Or like with housing, they think you're not working, we're supporting you, we can't give you a good apartment.

Ms. White gives a vivid example of a white agency representative using temporal dislocation to turn clients into nonpersons:

> It really bothered me to see Ms. X turn off those Puerto Rican women in the street. I'll never forget the way they said "thank you very much for giving me some of your time." Ms. X was condescending to those women in front of us . . . all the [residents] wanted was 30 seconds about the water in the garden [and she said] "I can't talk to you now, you have to make an appointment." And it would have taken a minute, not even a minute. How can you turn people off like that?

Any index (socially/culturally interpreted signal) of being "Spanish" can create distance. These indexes can be creative in Silverstein's (1976) sense, bringing into being new social lines. They can be perniciously creative in situations where a "Spanish accent" or "bad words" make one a nonperson. If indexes acquire a politicized value in the process of social exchange, as Irvine (1989) argues, then these indexes have a negative value that entirely outweighs the value of any potentially positive indexes. One's persona is so completely represented by such indexes that no other index can count: totally incommensurate, totally Other.[7]

The advantage that public institutions have is that they can and do certify indexes, linguistic and temporal. Clients and students may perceive a different reality, as Ms. Fonseca does here, but the problem is to convince someone of that reality:

> DF: Another thing about that program is that they talk bullshit at you. They talk so much bullshit in the program, in the classes about good communication and good this and good that, and they don't even do it. Like for the working world? They don't do it. Why do they teach us something that they don't even do? Especially in the same program. I'm gonna tell [Ms. Jones] about that.
>
> BU: Do you think she's aware of it?
>
> DF: She should be, as long as she been working there. She been working there I think it's gonna be almost two years. She should be aware of it. So I feel that they're telling us like a lie?
>
> BU: Or trying to pretend it's something that it's not?
>
> DF: Right. I'm gonna tell her. "Why do you teach us a lot of communication skills and that we have to be organized in our work? And this

program, the whole staff, they're not even organized, they see people like if they wasn't even there.

While Ms. Jones does not regard Ms. Fonseca as a nonperson (since they can talk), this does not always apply to the rest of the staff. The program's criteria for "organization" and "communicative skills" seem more format than substance, matching the clients against a template that is itself invisible. The staff's actions do not match it. Communication and organization should make connections, lead somewhere. The staff ignores, misunderstands, or otherwise fails to make connections with its clients ("like if they wasn't there"). More to the point, they have trouble making connections outside the program, placing people in jobs. The program implies that its clients' treatment of time and language is unproductive; Ms. Fonseca argues that the staff's is no different. But the staff have jobs that many clients never get, so something else must be responsible for jobs. To paraphrase Schwartz (1975:169), Ms. Fonseca and the other clients need something to *do* (like a job) but what they are given is *something* to do (like magazines in a waiting room). The irony is that while the staff tells the clients that they live in an incommensurate place, a "going around in circles" time, this is exactly the position into which the program puts the clients.

Like the discount standard that Ms. Colón's school sells, the program's organization and communication "skills" are an institutionally certified reality that need not match the actions of the people who represent the program. The program sells it because it is what the program can afford to sell. Ms. Fonseca can see this, as clearly as Ms. Colón could see what she was being sold. But their programs at least have the resources to create public and official constructs. They do not.

## Conclusion

Utilitarian ideologies of time parallel utilitarian ideologies of language, drawing from the same sources in Euro-American cultural history. Deviations from the Monoglot and the Monochron are taken as illogical (and ethnic and low-class) unless the deviator operates from a position of safety, as when upper-class British can say "he don't" or "he ain't" and Very Important People can be busy enough to be excused from being on time.

Both men and women are at risk, women in particular because so much of the burden of dealing with institutions falls on them. They are seen by agencies only as clients and they have to appear "deviant": mothers with no (legal) husbands. Nearly everything about them is seen and framed in those terms. It is not simply that their time is "disorganized" or that their English is "nonstandard." It is that these things become aligned with the very reasons why they must deal with agencies to begin with.

Time and language become indexes of tremendous risk. Women must show maximum control over those indexes. At the same time, women have the most to lose if they do it wrong: they must sit and wait and be wiped off the roster and start again if they mis-speak or mis-time. Men's time is less at the beck and call of public agencies than is that of women, but if they are not (officially) working, their time has no reality to the middle-class world, and they risk the appearance of "hanging around doing nothing."

While Gramsci's idea of cultural hegemony has some ambiguous recensions, its central concept is useful here: the powerless may be co-opted as well as coerced; class domination may be achieved through both labor and cultural practices, cultural practices which are reproduced by institutions of information, education, law, and so on as well as by relations of material production (Anderson 1977). Ways of knowing are grounded in the routines and relational structures of ordinary production insofar as such routines and relations materially affect the degree to which a person is trapped in institutional and class-based definitions of who one is, what one's options are, and what recourse one has. They are not Others because their time and language are different. They are Others because they lack the wherewithal to stand within the charmed circle of interactive social definition, the dialog constantly carried out among the privileged. Through the institutionalization of poverty, their time is cut up and controlled and their language boxed in (particularly through poor public schooling). Since they have no recourse, anything that does not appear to fit the middle-class template of natural and rational becomes grounds for Otherness. Ethnicity, like jewelry, is allowed as an accessorizing touch here and there—a splash of an accent; a dash of fashionable lateness—only so long as it does not disturb the overall American structure.

## Notes

*Acknowledgments.* The 1988 research on which this essay is based was made possible by the Spencer Foundation Small Grants Program. My thanks to Henry Rutz and Wendy Weiss for reading and commenting.

1. So (as Fabian also argues) is the inability to handle money: "they're all on welfare"; "they don't know how to save, they spend it all on color TVs and fast food." Sex is also a criterion: "they breed like rabbits." Sometimes sex and

money are combined criteria: "they have babies as soon as they're old enough so they can spend the rest of their lives on welfare."

2. Saussure and Benveniste between them describe the value of the linguistic sign in terms highly comparable to those which Marx applies to the value of commodities. Saussure (1966[1915]) argues that sign relations are arbitrary and that the value of the linguistic sign lies in its capacity for exchange; Benveniste (1971[1939]) argues that for the speaker, the sign must be the reality and that while value is relative and derives entirely from form, it must seem necessary to the user. Cf. Marx: "Could commodities themselves speak, they would say, 'our use-value may be a thing that interests men. It is no part of us as objects. What however does belong to us as objects is our value. Our natural intercourse as commodities proves it. In the eyes of each other we are nothing but exchange value' " (1906:95).

3. The status attached to controlling one's own time led Mr. Cortez to observe that the very fact that I was interviewing him and his wife illustrated one of the chief advantages that whites had. Mr. Cortez knew no Puerto Rican with the time, money or education to do a study like this.

4. An interesting angle on the dispatch of resources was given to me by a legal affairs supervisor for the public transport system who told me that plaintiffs in lawsuits against the transit authority were more likely to be poor and nonwhite, reflecting (1) transit user demographics; (2) the fact that middle-class people generally settle out of court as they cannot afford time for protracted lawsuits. Some plaintiffs are frauds but most are poor people with a legitimate case. These generally lose a large proportion of their settlement to lawyers and go through the remainder within six months to a year, "as soon as all the needy relatives show up." Note the central elements: poor people have more time to litigate than middle-class people, and poor people cannot hold on to their money.

5. Ms. White makes a comparable comment about a comparable clientele: "their attention span is not very long."

6. I became acquainted with Ms. Colón when Ms. Cortez asked me to help her with her sociology paper. I strongly suspect that my relations with Ms. Cortez and Ms. Colón developed in this time-exchange: while they had been mildly interested in my project before I started tutoring Ms. Colón, they took a far more active role after.

7. Thus, by certifying accented English as good enough for the students, the school is really selling them a bill of goods!

## References Cited

Anderson, Perry
    1977   The Antinomies of Antonio Gramsci. New Left Review 100:5–78.
Benveniste, Emile
    1971[1939]   The Nature of the Linguistic Sign. *In* Problems in General Linguistics. Pp. 43–48. Coral Gables: University of Miami Press.
Carr, Raymond
    1984   Puerto Rico: A Colonial Experiment. New York: Vintage.

Fabian, Johannes
   1983   Time and the Other: How Anthropology Makes its Object. New
      York: Columbia University Press.
Friedrich, Paul
   1986   The Language Parallax. Austin: University of Texas Press.
Irvine, Judith
   1989   When Talk Isn't Cheap: Language and Political Economy. American
      Ethnologist 16:248–267.
Lewis, Oscar
   1966   La Vida. New York: Random House.
Marx, Karl
   1906   Capital: A Critique of Political Economy. New York: Modern Library.
Schwartz, Barry
   1975   Queueing and Waiting: Studies in the Social Organization of Access
      and Delay. Chicago: University of Chicago Press.
Sharff, Jagna
   1986   Free Enterprise and the Ghetto Family. In Annual Editions in An-
      thropology, 1986–1987. E. Angeloni, ed. Pp. 139–143. Guildford, CN:
      Dushkin Publishing Group.
Silverstein, Michael
   1976   Shifters, Linguistic Categories and Cultural Description. In Meaning
      in Anthropology. Keith Basso and Henry Selby, eds. Pp. 11–55. Albu-
      querque: University of New Mexico.
   1987   Monoglot "Standard" in America. Working Papers and Proceedings
      #13. Center for Psychosocial Studies. Chicago.
Susser, Ida
   1982   Norman Street. New York: Oxford University Press.
United States Department of Commerce Bureau of the Census
   1983   1980 Census of Population and Housing: Census Tracts New York,
      N.Y.–N.J. Washington, D.C.: U.S. Government Printing Office.
Urciuoli, Bonnie
   1991   The Political Topography of Spanish and English. American Ethnol-
      ogist 18:295–310.
Zerubavel, Eviatar
   1981   Hidden Rhythms: Schedules and Calendars in Social Life. Chicago:
      University of Chicago Press.

# 7

# Temporality and the Domestication of Homelessness

## KOSTAS GOUNIS

I will begin with a song that I heard outside a public shelter for homeless men in the South Bronx. The song, by "El Gran Combo," a popular Puerto Rican band, is entitled "Y No Hago Mas Na"—"And I Don't Do Anything Else." The lyrics describe the ideal-typical life of a man whom some urban sociologists would call one of the "dependent poor" and Ronald Reagan would have used as an illustration of the corrupting effects of welfare. The song can be read as a time budget detailing the good life: our man wakes up late to a good breakfast; goes out with his guitar to look at the girls; comes back at noon for lunch followed by a siesta until 3:00 P.M.; smokes a cigar; hangs out with friends until 6:00 P.M.; has a dinner of steak, fries, and salad; and then enjoys himself sitting on the porch with his woman. The chorus declares that it is indeed great to live this kind of life "without having to work," and explains that he can afford all this through food stamps and disability benefits that he collects by pretending to be crazy. This essay explores the temporal themes of the song, that is, the temporal construction and experience of social dependency, in the concrete setting where the men who were listening to it actually lived—i.e., the shelter.

Since the rise of homelessness during the 1980s, shelters have become a common feature of the urban landscape of the United States. Many of the "dependent poor" found themselves with no other option than the streets or one of these facilities. Homelessness, here understood as spatio-temporal dislocation, in addition to socioeconomic marginalization, and shelters, here identified as the *institutionalization* of homelessness, make a temporal perspective a particularly relevant framework of analysis. On the one hand, following Goffman (1961), there is the question of how shelters, as institutions, order and appropriate time. On the other, since shelters and the condition of homelessness denote an experience of social dislocation, we have to address the extent to which the temporal orientations of those subjected to this experience conform to, diverge from, or oppose dominant temporal orders and the normative systems in which these are embedded. The latter question will be addressed utilizing the framework provided by Thompson's (1967) influential study of time and work-discipline.

According to Thompson, a utilitarian approach to time and the simultaneous elaboration of a moral order mediated the growth of industrial capitalism against the background of *pre*industrial, medieval resistances to, and disregard for, the new work ethos. For our purposes, however, the epoch has changed—we are now dealing with the *post*industrial world. Whereas Thompson inquired into the ways that emerging industrial capitalism sought to recruit a generally reluctant population into new habits of working and living (or producing and consuming), the present study, much more limited in scope, deals with a population that has been made redundant by the very same economic system, at a much later and "advanced" stage.

In 1967, Thompson himself, inspired by "recurrent forms of revolt within Western industrial capitalism, whether bohemian or beatnik" (relatively harmless forms of revolt, if I may add), wondered whether the "Puritan valuation of time will begin to decompose as the pressures of poverty relax." Is our opening song a guide to understanding the valuation of time by today's urban poor—especially of the marginalized populations that inhabit the devastated neighborhoods of the inner city in the current, postindustrial phase of Western capitalism? To rephrase the same question in Thompson's terms: is the song a reflection of the decomposition of the work-ethic that, unlike the traditions of resistance to the imposed rationality of time-thrift, amounts instead to a glorification of dependency?

Thompson's question remains valid only if an important term in his equation is radically reversed: namely, the fact that the pressures of poverty have increased rather than relaxed. It is precisely the increase in poverty that contributes to more serious "revolts" in the heart of what were previously the centers of industrial capitalism. "Social pathologies" such as crime, the drug epidemic, and the persistence of homelessness are definite indications that the material basis of legitimacy of bourgeois institutions and of the dominant ideology, including its valuation of time, is rapidly eroding.

The focus on temporal dimensions of shelter life that pertain to these issues will be informed, first, by the empirical validation of Goffman's view that places the appropriation of time as primary among the "encompassing tendencies" of "total institutions" (Goffman 1961:4;

Zerubavel 1981:143); and second, by a modified appreciation of Thompson's perspective on time in the modern capitalist world.

In the discussion that follows, after a brief outline of the background of homelessness, a description of the shelter system for men in New York City will be presented, focusing on the formal and informal characteristics that justify the depiction of this system as a kind of "total institution." Evolving patterns of use of the system in general and the social ecology of a particular shelter site will be described in order to clarify the nature and extent of displacement from normative patterns of living and working experienced by the men who use New York City shelters.

After a *spatial* ethnography of the shelter is presented, a *temporal* approach will be adopted. In this context, I will examine the temporal dimensions in the formal and informal organization of shelter life and the ways in which the temporal orientations of residents are shaped, altered, or accommodated by the shelter. The extent to which shelter life informs attitudes and behaviors toward work will be addressed along these lines. By focusing on the temporal order of shelter life we can begin to elucidate the interplay of social forces that contribute to the reproduction of social marginality as a permanent state of captivity.

## The Institutionalization of Homelessness

The social rhythms that have defined the contemporary landscape of urban poverty and the rise of an "underclass," of widespread social dislocation, and of homelessness are the structural embodiment of the urban capitalist process (Harvey 1973), intensified by current political and economic policies (Hopper and Hamburg 1986; Wilson 1987). Deindustrialization and unemployment, exacerbated by the dismantling of the welfare programs that were intended to protect the poor (Piven and Cloward 1982), are the background against which "cycles of deprivation" have culminated in the emergence of social problems of catastrophic proportions since the mid-1970s (Wilson 1987). As Wilson has convincingly argued, the "truly disadvantaged" have remained so, in increasingly deteriorating conditions, despite civil rights victories and the creation of the "Great Society." The vision of the good life, the "universals" that have been celebrated as the main ingredients of the American dream and have been offered as principles of self-definition (Ewen 1976), are definitely beyond reach—through legitimate means at least—for the populations that comprise the "new poor" of contemporary America and who are increasingly

reduced to the category of the "underclass." The poor, primarily minority, populations of the inner city remain entrapped in the impoverished space of the ghetto, while employment opportunities and the
middle class have fled to the suburbs (Harvey 1973; 1989). Drugs,
crime, and the AIDS epidemic further devastate the material and
moral economies of these already depleted communities.

Undoubtedly, the most visible portion of today's poor are the
homeless. No longer confined to the traditional Skid Rows, during the
1980s homelessness emerged as a widespread social problem and as a
new niche in the postindustrial, poverty-stricken landscape of American cities. Homelessness and the "survival economics" of the urban
poor have introduced new patterns of appropriation and use of urban
resources (Morrissey and Gounis 1988). In New York City, where the
scale and the visibility of the problem have been most pronounced,
public spaces such as sidewalks, parks, subway cars and stations,
other transportation terminals, bank lobbies housing cash-dispensing
machines, and a host of other sites have become contested territories
between their "normal" users (e.g., commuters) and "the homeless."
The latter not only live "private lives in public spaces" (Baxter and
Hopper 1981), but also engage in survival strategies and behave in
ways that are experienced by the public as disruptions at best, and as
dangers—real or imagined—at worst.

## New York City Shelters

Beginning in 1981, after advocates for the homeless took their case
to the courts and forced New York City authorities to make shelter
space available on demand (Hopper and Cox 1982), the largest municipal shelter system in the United States was established in New York.
Initially, the focal point of this system was the Shelter Care Center for
Men (SCCM) on East 3rd Street in the Bowery, which had been operating since the late 1940s. For decades, East 3rd Street was the desti-
nation of marginalized men who had made the Bowery synonymous
with Skid Row (Bahr 1970). Since the 1970s, however, the reshaping
of the urban ecology of New York City introduced new clients and
new functions into the public system of institutional relief that the
SCCM exemplified (Morrissey and Gounis 1988). During the past decade, shelters of a variety of types and sizes developed into an elaborate
institutional apparatus.[1]

By the mid-1980s, the shelter system radiated out into armories,
old schools, abandoned hospital wards and other facilities throughout
the city. Most shelters were located in neighborhoods in advanced
stages of urban decay where community opposition to the presence of

these facilities was minimal or ineffective. The nightly distribution of shelter applicants to the different sites became the primary function of the East 3rd Street Center. By the late 1980s, the municipal shelter system for single men—the ethnographic context for this analysis—included more than fifteen individual sites and on an average night accommodated over 8,000 men. Shelters evolved into an emergent form of "public housing" and the traditional denizens of New York City's Skid Row—primarily older, white, and alcoholic—became a minority in the New York City shelter system. The data provided by the Survey of New York City Municipal Shelters (Struening 1986) show that by 1985 most of the users of the men's shelter system (74%) were under 40 years old. Seventy one percent were "black" and 19% were "hispanic."[2]

By 1987, East 3rd Street no longer represented the main point of entry, as new arrivals were not required to go through this facility in order to be admitted into the system. A computerized system linked all the shelters, making obsolete many functions of the East 3rd Street facility. Whereas East 3rd Street continued to be the center of the system until 1990, it functioned primarily as a point of entry for specific subgroups rather than for all new or returning clients. For instance, it was used heavily by men entrapped in long-term dependency on the shelter system who continued to be denizens of the Bowery. Also, East 3rd Street served as the point of reassignment for men who were barred admission to a certain shelter, usually as a punishment for violating shelter rules.[3]

Individual shelters share a number of generic features. Primarily they function as custodial institutions where the provision of bed, food, and an appearance of order and security are the operators' main concerns. Staffing patterns, accountability procedures, and formal rules and regulations are uniform across the system.

In each shelter, custodial staff—Institutional Aides and security guards from a private security agency under contract with the Human Resources Administration, the New York City agency that runs the shelter system—far outnumber the social service staff. Institutional Aides mop floors, clean the bathrooms, serve meals, distribute clothing, and do some clerical work. Security guards are stationed in various posts throughout each facility and their main function is to provide a visible surveillance force that is considered necessary for maintaining control over the resident population. Social service workers process the paperwork required for clients to receive shelter services: issuing and renewing the shelter identification cards known as "meal tickets," authorizing the distribution of clothing or of carfare, and the

like. Moreover, social service workers provide referrals to outside services and entitlement programs.

In practice, the social distance between shelter dwellers and staff
implied by these formal roles is often suspended. Chronic deficiencies
in resources create vacuums that staff have to fill on an *ad hoc* basis.
Staff depend on clients to perform tasks such as cleaning tables after
meals, locating other clients and "going to the store" for them. Residents volunteer their help to the Institutional Aides and do various
errands for staff in exchange for favors and privileges such as not
standing in line for services, having access to additional portions of
food, or securing favored sleeping arrangements.

Often, both residents and staff participate in a number of activities
that constitute a thriving informal economy inside and around the
shelter. Field observations suggest that in the shelter's underground
economy, which is largely based on drugs, the roles of provider and
client—in this case, of seller and buyer, respectively—are sometimes
reversed, and some staff members become regular "clients" of shelter
residents. In a few cases, staff involvement in the underground economy may go further, as suggested by the arrest in one shelter of a staff
member who was accused of running a male prostitution business in
the shelter. In another instance, shelter residents spoke of a staff member who was renting out a nearby room to men who used it as a
"shooting gallery" (i.e., a place to inject drugs).

The *marginal affinity* between shelter staff and residents is in fact
a distinguishing characteristic of the shelter as an institution. Besides
the interdependence and the exchanges that are centered inside the
shelter, front-line staff, especially the security guards, often share
common backgrounds and interests with residents. The marginal nature of the shelter limits accountability and standardization, granting
considerable flexibility in defining roles. Thus, an understanding of
the informal organization becomes relatively more important than the
formal structure in the description of shelter staff and of their roles.

Within this permutable system of relationships, seemingly arbitrary shifts of behavior by shelter staff toward the men are common.
Staff maintain several divergent and even contradictory roles. As
"custodians" their role is to control a rather difficult population. But
they also relate to the residents as friends, depend on them for help,
and may collaborate in the underground shelter economy of drugs,
thefts, Medicaid fraud, and extortions. In addition, there is great var-
iance in the way different shelter staff in similar positions treat the residents. The changeable and unpredictable nature of the ways in which
staff relate to residents tends to confuse and demoralize the latter, especially those men who are mentally disabled or otherwise vulnerable.

In the next section I will present a brief description of one New York City shelter for men, where extensive fieldwork was undertaken. These highlights are intended to help contextualize the preceding observations and to provide a concrete anchoring for the subsequent discussion of temporality.

## A Shelter for Men in the South Bronx

The physical site of the Franklin Avenue Shelter is one of the New York State armories that were converted into municipal shelters for homeless persons during the 1980s. The armory is located amidst the burned-out abandoned buildings and vacant lots of the South Bronx, one of the poorest congressional districts in the United States. Whatever remained of the armory's old grandeur provided a striking backdrop to its contemporary makeshift appearance and current uses. The shelter's capacity was about 600 men. Approximately 300 of these men slept in closely spaced cots on the drill floor, an area of almost two acres, that also served as the dining room, the recreation area (there was a pool table, a ping-pong table and two television sets), and the "hanging out" area. At one end of the drill floor and the sea of cots that filled it was the local Social Services Unit, housed in a prefabricated structure of its own—literally, a building within a building. Daily, scores of men lined up outside this structure to meet with shelter caseworkers for various services.

The rest of the beds were in relatively smaller dorms in the upper three floors of the armory building. During the time of field research (1986–87), the dormitories on the upper floors of the armory, isolated as they were from the rest of the shelter, had evolved into almost autonomous territories of distinct subgroups: residents who were employed and those who participated in the shelter work program occupied one of these floors; yet another floor was the domain of drug addicts and young male prostitutes. Even on the seemingly undifferentiated space of the drill floor, territorial divisions were formally and informally established and enforced. For instance, shelter administrators had designated two clusters of cots near the Social Services Unit for two particularly needy groups of residents—the physically disabled, usually older men, and those with mental disabilities—who needed increased supervision and protection. The rest of the cots on the drill floor were also divided into three additional areas and each was referred to by a color code. Different groups, mainly divided along ethnic lines (i.e., black or hispanic), occupied different color-coded areas. A hierarchical organization of space was also evident: undesirable areas, such as those near entrances, bathrooms, and other parts where traffic was greater, were given to residents with limited negotiating power (e.g., newcomers and loners).

Ethnicity played a critical role in the informal organization of the shelter. The overwhelming majority of shelter staff was black, and more than half the residents were black as well. (An additional 40% of the residents were hispanic, and the rest were white.)[4] There was very limited interaction between ethnic groups, and relationships of inter-dependence were found predominantly between black staff and black residents. Hispanics often expressed discontent for being discrimi-nated against and resentment at being excluded from this system of exchanges and privileges. For example, on one occasion in early 1987, HRA staff perceived the hispanic men in the shelter to be on the verge of "rioting" over alleged harassment perpetrated by a black HRA staff member against some hispanic residents.

The short history of the Franklin Avenue Shelter encompasses distinct stages in the rapid evolution of the shelter system. Through-out 1986, various sections of the upper floors were under construction to open new bed space in the shelter. Overall, during 1986–87, the Franklin shelter underwent extensive renovations and the makeshift appearance of its early days gave way to a more efficient and perma-nent institutional look. After decentralized admission into the shelter system became an accepted practice, men from the South Bronx be-came the majority at the Franklin shelter. Men displaced from housing in the deteriorating environment of the South Bronx could simply walk over to the shelter. Many maintained an ongoing involvement in the surrounding community, with social networks and social supports there. Thus the shelter evolved into an extension of community beds that men could utilize as a place of last resort, or as a place to return to sporadically, when precarious arrangements in the community col-lapsed.

At the same time, the activities inside the shelter became an ex-tension, albeit in an intensified form, of the phenomena intrinsic to the survival economy of the South Bronx's "underclass." Men moved be-tween the shelter and the surrounding community in their efforts to secure resources such as a place to stay, food, and medical or social services. They also did so in the pursuit of illegal activities—such as buying and selling drugs, stealing, and prostitution—that defined a large part of their economy.

Although connected to the community, the shelter also main-tained a partially autonomous internal economy. The drug economy—dealing, using, and whatever activities are engaged in procuring ille-gal drugs—constituted a major sphere of the shelter's economy. Other aspects of this economy included the barter between residents of such goods as food, transportation tokens, clothing items, and of course cigarettes—the staple of institutional currencies. Small-scale entrepreneurial activities ranged from selling loose cigarettes—a dime a piece or three for a quarter—to a makeshift barbershop run by a resident who even "employed" an assistant/apprentice and specialized in styles currently popular with the younger black men.

The Franklin Men's Shelter encapsulates in an extreme form the lived reality of many young men of the South Bronx and of other similarly marginalized populations of New York City. Shelters have become an extension of the community, and the problems, experiences, and orientations that shelter users bring with them can be construed as a sample of the collective misfortunes of these marginalized communities.

The pathologies that are observed inside the shelter—crime, drug and alcohol abuse, untreated mental disabilities, AIDS—are simply an extension and an intensified form of the collective misfortunes of the marginalized populations that comprise the so-called "underclass." The functions of shelters are determined by the "survival economics" of households in communities subjected to the combined assault of the economic forces of the market and the social neglect of the state.

For the most part, shelters serve as collective "community bedrooms" by partially removing the burden of caring for individuals whose presence—either because they can no longer contribute to the income of the household, or because of their behavior and special needs—presents an extraordinary strain on the viability of these embattled households. In this environment, chronically unemployed males, drug addicts, or persons with mental disabilities are among the most likely shelter candidates.

At a certain level, the creation, expansion, and elaboration of the shelter system represents the most comprehensive of the various administrative measures aimed at limiting the disruptions caused by the appropriation of the city's public spaces by "the homeless." Also, it could be argued that, to some extent, this system, in its present size and scope, is the "unintended consequence" of the activities of advocates who forced the city to make shelter space available on demand. Without doubt, questions of intentionality become relevant to the understanding of the development of this expansive institutional apparatus. An initial approach to such questions may be suggested by distinguishing between the manifest functions of shelters (i.e., the provision of beds, some food, and a few other basic services), and the latent ones. These latter functions, I will argue, include the constitution and elaboration of an emergent order aimed at the *domestication of urban marginality* and, in the face of the dismantling of the "safety nets," a refiguring of the "moral economy" that regulates the conditions of social existence of today's urban poor. By the late 1980s, the shelter system had evolved into a hybrid between a degraded type of "public housing" and a new form of "institutionalization."

## Rhythms of Shelter Life

A variety of sociotemporal perspectives inform the institutional life of a shelter. First, I will address changes of space over time and seasonal variations in the outlook of these institutions as instances of such perspectives.

Initially, shelters were a poorly planned emergency response and were presented as a "temporary" measure. But contrary to alleged original intentions, they emerged as an increasingly rationalized institutional arrangement that continued to grow, despite repeated denunciations of the role shelters play in entrapping residents into a life of dependency. In the context of this evolution, shelters have changed in response to a number of pressures: changing constituencies of clients; legal challenges concerning the "quality of life" and the rights of residents; and above all, the persistence and exacerbation of homelessness and its attendant pathologies (mental disabilities, drug and alcohol abuse, AIDS, etc.). Any description of the shelter milieu must then be understood against a background of change of the system as a whole, and relative differentiation of the roles of individual shelters.

At another level, the encounters, confrontations, and exchanges between persons with different roles and objectives within the formal shelter structure constitute shelter life as an informal and highly fluid social organization that varies from site to site. Shelters that are located in isolated, nonresidential parts of the city tend to "specialize" in populations with limited ties to the outside. These shelters become inwardly focused and closely resemble "total institutions" such as mental hospitals or prisons. On the other hand, as noted earlier, shelters in poor, minority neighborhoods, such as the Franklin Avenue shelter in the South Bronx, tend to become something of an extension of the community: they accommodate men drawn from the surrounding area who can move between the shelter and their social networks on the outside and utilize the shelter only as a place to sleep.

Furthermore, the demand for shelter beds is partly subject to seasonal variations. Thus, the shelter system must be flexible enough to accommodate such fluctuations. The profile of a shelter at any one time varies according to weather conditions that affect the demand for shelter beds. Shelters can be entirely different places on a cold winter night from what they are on a spring or summer night when rooftops, abandoned buildings, park benches, and all kinds of open spaces can serve as alternative sleeping places.

## Temporal Inversions of Experience and Meaning

Beyond changes in their spatial configuration over time, shelters provide a distinctive sociotemporal framework for experience and meaning. Indeed, it is this framework that is the embodiment of the unique institutional logic of the shelter system.

Most of the conventional temporal designations—the weekly cycle, the month, holidays, etc.—have some meaning in the shelter. These meanings, however, rarely coincide with conventional ones. The weekend and holidays in a shelter are more likely to be experienced as a vacuum—access to resources is limited, and staff with whom one has established an ongoing relationship tend to be absent. In other words, in the shelter there is an inversion of the "normal" weekend. For people with homes, the weekend is "full" because they can make themselves inaccessible to the demands of the market and escape the realities of the workweek. The "Thank God It's Friday" (TGIF) syndrome reflects the fact that, in Zerubavel's terms, the weekend normally constitutes a "temporally defined niche of inaccessibility" (1981:142). For shelter residents, however, Fridays offer little to be thankful about. This is aptly illustrated by the experience of the clients of a shelter-based mental health program for whom Fridays were particularly difficult days. Most of these men agonized over the imminent separation from workers on whose continuous support they had become dependent. One particular week in the life of one of these clients serves as a dramatic example of the significance of the weekly cycle. He began the week with what his caseworker called "Monday-ism": he was distressed on Monday because the staff was away during the weekend. Although he began to relax as the week progressed, by Friday he was a wreck again, besieging his caseworker with "gifts" and calls for attention, anxious over the coming "long weekend" (the following Monday was a holiday). On Sunday he attempted suicide.

Shelter dependency, a condition that has been described as "shelterization" (Gounis and Susser 1990), engenders an inversion of the value of time insofar as it is divided between workweek and weekend. Unlike those with homes (and regular jobs, steady incomes, stable households, etc.) for whom the norm is to look forward to the weekend for pleasure and escape, the shelterized men's experience of the weekend is one of deprivation. The fact that the last thing many of these men want is an "escape" from the institutional routines of the shelter is an inevitable and ironic consequence of their dependency. In the shelter, as in all "total institutions," temporal access to basic resources is not controlled by the individual. Therefore, discontinuities in the routine of shelter life have a profound effect on the residents' ability to satisfy essential needs that are constant and surface without conformity to staff schedules.

The first of the month is another temporal location invested with a particular meaning in the shelter. Shortly after I had started fieldwork in the New York City shelter system, the director and various residents at one site encouraged me to return the following evening, a first-of-the-month, so that I could get an idea of how rough things can get. They explained to me that a number of shelter residents would be receiving their monthly disability check on that day and would return to the shelter either drunk, high on drugs, robbed, or as candidates for robbing and other more subtle ways of expropriation. Indeed, on the following evening, and on similar evenings over the following years, the shelter lived up to their description. In general, "pay-days," whether a first-of-the-month or other regular times, tend to raise tensions. On these occasions, almost all residents who have come to possess some money engage in "consumption binges," usually of a variety of foods, alcohol, or drugs. Drugs and alcohol usually cause a lot of trouble, either among residents or between residents and staff. However, as prevalent as it may be among these men, it is not "addiction" alone that accounts for this telescoping of consumption. Money in the shelter does not last long—it is either consumed fast, or else it marks its possessor as a target. The pressure for immediate consumption is understandable, even rational, under these circumstances. For the most part, money and other goods are consumed either in a group with friends, or in buying protection and privileges from other residents or from staff members. The circulation and consumption of goods constitute a way of buying a form of social insurance in an environment where one needs all the help one can get in avoiding danger and deprivation.

## Temporal Domination and Control

Field research in New York City shelters substantiates Zerubavel's observation (which follows Goffman's) that time is "probably the most significant dimension of the 'total' aspect of 'total institutions' in general" (Zerubavel 1981:143). The shelter does function according to the principles that characterize a "total institution"—even if these operate somewhat more loosely. (Unlike typical "total institutions," such as prisons or mental hospitals, entry is theoretically voluntary, and the shelter does not formally bar social intercourse with the outside world.)[5] The large scale of the shelter—in some cases, up to 1000 men—and its primary function as a custodial institution make the regulatory use of time an indispensable organizational principle. Curfews set boundaries of exclusion and inclusion, as do formal temporal constraints such as the obligation to show up at specific times in order to sign up for a bed, eat meals, or receive clothing, carfare, and other services. All these tasks normally involve long waits in line, since anywhere from 200 to 1000 other men are also engaged in the same activity at the same time. Shelter staff supervise clients as they follow the daily shelter routine, moving from one line to another: for food, to signup for a bed, or to be searched by security guards as they enter. Renewing one's shelter identification card, which is known as a "mealticket" and is valid for a specific time period, is a monthly ritual that reinforces the regulatory function of time. Discipline and punishment for violations of shelter rules often take the form of being refused access to the shelter for varying periods of time.

But a shelter is a type of "total institution" out of "Alice in Wonderland." The permutable, unpredictable, and arbitrarily shifting institutional rigor of the shelter is reflected in the ways in which it accommodates very different patterns of use and allows individual residents considerable flexibility in defining their short- and long-term temporal orientation. The following examples should offer some insight into this dimension of shelter life.

Until a few years ago, city officials insisted that the shelter system was a "temporary" arrangement and they wanted to discourage men from "settling in" and becoming "comfortable" in any one shelter. This approach, a form of temporal alchemy attempting to evade the true dimensions of homelessness, was at odds with the interests of local shelter directors. For the latter, a relatively stable population offered better possibilities of control and internal stability and was preferred over the unpredictability of an ever-changing population. Thus when an administrator from "downtown" was expected at the shelter, the local staff would instruct residents to remove pictures from the walls above their cots and temporarily hide all evidence that would suggest long-term occupancy. (Some men had to hide such items as hot-plates, ironing-boards, arm-chairs brought in from the streets, and other bulky "household" items.) What is interesting about this unenforceable and subsequently abandoned policy is that a kind of moral intelligence was operating, which informed the imposition of these temporal restrictions: it is as if city officials were trying to prevent shelterization by keeping shelter clients on the move. A similar effort, on a smaller scale, was the policy of "fresh-air time": shelter residents were forced to go outside for a certain period of time during the day. I suppose the same perspective inspired an assistant director at a certain shelter who would not allow men to lie on the floor during the day. Everybody had to be above floor-level, although they were allowed to sleep on top of the pool table, the ping-pong tables, and every other available surface, as long as it was above floor-level.

Length of stay at a particular shelter inevitably translated into relative advantages, as indicated by the contrast between "permanent" and "transient" residents. Even in the early 1980s, when official city policy discouraged lengthy stays at any one shelter, field research revealed that in most shelters there were already many "permament" residents who formed the core of the shelter population. Not surprisingly, these residents were the ones who were able to translate their regular presence into relative benefits such as access to favored sleeping areas, familiarity and friendship with staff and other regular clients, and turf control in the underground economies of the shelter (drugs, thefts, extortions, and the like). In other words, time became the means for making territorial claims. Transient users were at a disadvantage. Their irregular or sporadic presence at a given shelter prevented them from entering into interdependent relationships with other residents or shelter staff. Both regular residents and staff could, therefore, easily prey on these men.

Shelter life encompasses a whole range of activities that are temporally structured. This structure dominates the lives of shelter residents. Daily, large numbers of men are processed through the shelter routine and, at each phase, violence and disorder is a real and ever-present possibility. Scale and considerations of control imply a formally established temporal order to which residents must submit.

*The Daily Shelter Routine*

On a day-to-day basis, residents become immersed in the organizational routine of the shelter, which is characterized by extensive temporal segmentation and requires a considerable investment of time in order to secure timely access to scarce shelter resources. The intensely competitive, predatory, and impoverished shelter milieu makes daily subsistence a full-time occupation. The apparent paradox of this condition is that activities which for those with homes are normally classified as "leisure" or "home production" become the "work" of homeless people. At another level, very much like in the ideal-typical "total institution," for many residents prolonged stays in the shelter result in an almost complete temporal dislocation and a mere mechanical compliance with the institutional routines of shelter life. This complete immersion in the role of a shelter resident is the manifest dimension of shelterization.

The daily routine begins with an early wake-up call—the scratchy sound of badly functioning loudspeakers provokes all kinds of curses by residents, jolted into the awareness of their surroundings. After the mobbing of the bathroom facilities, an experience that certainly deters many from showering and keeping clean, breakfast is served, and that entails waiting in long lines for those who want to eat. All this usually happens before 8:00 A.M. when the day shift of shelter staff arrives. Then, residents who need to see a caseworker wait around until the workers make themselves available. Access to workers and to the resources they command requires knowledge on the part of the residents of these workers' schedules. A most common sight around the social services unit is that of men being told that the worker they are looking for will not be in until the evening shift arrives at 4:00 P.M.; or that the particular resource they are applying for will not be dispensed until a later time (or day, or week).

During weekdays, the period between 8:00 in the morning and 4:00 in the afternoon, the day shift, encompasses activities and services that link the shelter to the outside world. Interagency affairs such as applications for welfare benefits, linkages to medical, psychiatric, or detoxification professional services, and job or housing referrals are examples of activities that must be accommodated during the day. This necessity stems from the established temporal rhythms of the outside agencies with which the shelter's activities must be coordinated.

Because many services, such as mental health programs and medical clinics, are commanded by "professional" staff, as opposed to staff whose responsibilities are of a more "custodial" nature, the day shift becomes a more likely temporal location for these services for the simple reason that these "professionals" tend to prefer "normal" schedules of work. The institutionalization of this preference is illustrated by the example of an on-site mental health program at the Franklin Men's Shelter that was directed by the regulations of a City agency to discontinue the practice of keeping the program open until 10:00 in the evening because liability insurance for the program ended at 5:00 P.M. every day.

The departure of the day shift signals a radical change in the atmosphere of the shelter. With the arrival of the evening shift, the shelter begins to prepare for the night: cots are assigned once again; men who were out for the day return to catch dinner; and new arrivals appear and try to orient themselves. The population increases, and the air thickens with smoke and the characteristic institutional smell produced by the mixture of unwashed bodies and clothes and the ammonia-based disinfectants used to wash floors, toilets, and other surfaces. The social density of the shelter milieu reaches its highest point as the evening progresses; more men return and the crowding and the incredible proximity—cots are only inches apart, bathrooms are communal—fuel an explosive atmosphere where shouting, arguments, and fights erupt all over the place.

The evening shift is the time when the shelter reveals itself as an institution with a precarious stability. Indeed, this stability is regularly shattered and the arrival of ambulances or police cars signifies the need for extra-shelter mechanisms of control to be deployed in order to reestablish the institutional order.

The day comes to an official end at curfew-time, usually at 10:00, and the subsequent turning off of lights. By the time the night shift begins, at midnight, the shelter is relatively calm and most of the residents have retired to their cots for a night of uneasy sleep, always aware of the danger of theft and of the violence that surrounds them.

The sequential ordering of shelter life and the extensive periods of "waiting" are therefore key aspects of the daily shelter routine. It should be noted that for shelter residents, the duration of "waiting" is invariably disproportionate to the duration of the activity for which one has waited. Although many people are willing to stand in line for long periods of time in order to gain access to some scarce resource, as for instance those who favor trendy restaurants or exclusive night-clubs in New York City, "waiting" for most of those with a "home" is an unwelcome disruption of a usually busy schedule. For shelter residents, on the other hand, "waiting" becomes the dominant temporal moment, and with it comes a negative or resigned experience of the passage of time. After breakfast is served, shelter residents who cannot find an activity to occupy themselves just "hang out," asking now and then if lunch time has come yet. They line up then, eat up their lunch in a few minutes and go back to "hanging out" until it is time to line up again in order to sign up for a cot for the night, or to have dinner. Besides "hanging out," the periods between these standard temporal locations can easily be filled with "waiting" for things such as an appointment with a caseworker, getting fresh clothing, using the showers, getting soap or clean linen, etc. In the shelter, "waiting," a distinctly temporal form of power and control, becomes, quite literally, "the order of the day."

At the same time, there is an abundance of needs that the shelter cannot meet (for instance, cash for personal expenses, medical and psychiatric care, detoxification services, etc.). Catering to these needs takes time—time that needs to be wrested from the competing demands of the shelter. This surplus time is often bought or negotiated through a number of different exchanges. For instance, a resident helps a staff member with his assigned duties in exchange for not standing in lines, or not having to be present at the appointed hour in order to sign up for his bed. Skipping curfew is another temporal restriction that is often negotiated in these exchanges.

Whether busily negotiating the temporal boundaries of the shelter or resigned to the timeless ennui of shelter life, the men who use a public shelter become subject to the centripetal forces of shelterization. The successful negotiation of, and resistance to, these forces depends on the presence of alternative sociotemporal perspectives that can serve as an anchoring of these men's lived experience.

### Forms of Resistance to Shelterization

For a variety of reasons, many shelter users do not spend their day in the shelter. Some of them do so in an effort to escape the atmosphere of the shelter; for obvious reasons even a temporary respite from this atmosphere becomes a strong need.

In the first place, the shelter completely reverses the temporal definition of public and private. Private time—what Zerubavel calls the "temporally defined niche of inaccessibility" is normally the container of certain activities that are considered personal or private: sleep, sex, showering, or going to the bathroom. In the shelter, it is precisely these activities that are generally denied a private domain. The invasion of "the boundary that the individual places between his being and the environment" and the "exposure [that] follows from collective sleeping arrangements and doorless toilets" (Goffman 1961:23–24), are conditions of shelter life not easily reconciled with.

On the whole, new arrivals to the shelter system keep going away during the day, lest they become, in their words, "like the rest of the guys in here," meaning those who languish inside the shelter. These initiands resist shelterization, and they are quite vocal about it. But sooner or later the imaginary prospects of "making it back to society"—self-deluding myths of the sort: "I'll be out of here as soon as I take care of some things"—do not materialize. Their clothes become worn out, they become demoralized, and the short-term, and perhaps more tangible, goals of improving their position inside the shelter take priority over the long-term goals of getting jobs, finding apartments, reuniting with families, or kicking drug or alcohol habits.

Others go out because they are employed in legitimate or illegitimate work. "Hustling cans" (i.e., collecting returnable bottles and cans), wiping windshields, dealing drugs, defrauding Medicaid, prostitution, temporary jobs in construction or unloading trucks, or working as security guards are examples of these men's work. Others visit with family or friends, often trying to patch things up and be allowed back into the household. Many attend programs: school, job training, mental health, detoxification—in fact, there is a whole array of services in an ever expanding industry that endlessly prepares them for reentry into an imaginary community.

The perception of the temporal boundaries of one's experience of homelessness and of one's "moral career" as a homeless person are dialectically related to patterns of shelter use. The experience of shelterization varies, depending upon when someone begins using the shelter in the context of his life-cycle. For instance, the younger black men—blacks are the majority of shelter clients—tend to look constantly busy, "hustling" in and around the shelter, moving between the shelter and the community. It is largely men from this subgroup that are involved in the underground economies of drugs, thefts, or extortions. Therefore, they are the ones who effectively control the shelter-based extensions of these economies. Also, the high prevalence of crack addiction in this subgroup entails a heightened level of activity (Hamid 1990).

Men in their thirties, on the other hand, tend to be more concerned with "reentering" society. They are looking for work and are willing to travel three hours each way to a job that pays minimum wage. They also express interest in dealing with drug or alcohol addictions. These men have aged-out of street life or have lost the precarious hold on jobs that they may have had at some previous time.

*The Uses and Meanings of Work*

The case of those men who are employed "on the outside" illustrates the point made earlier regarding the shelter's flexibility. These residents are exempt from many temporal restrictions of the shelter. If necessary, curfew regulations are relaxed for them and special arrangements are made on their behalf when it comes to bed sign-up, getting food, having access to shelter case-workers, etc. They are also allowed relative privacy at night by being assigned to special sections, when the physical shelter layout permits such arrangements. In recognition of the fact that they work, these men enjoy certain privileges, primarily in the form of the removal of temporal restrictions.

Another category of men who share similar benefits includes those who work in the shelter work program, which is pointedly called the Work Experience Program. This program paid the "trainees" who participated $12.50 a week for 20 hours of work. WEP, as the program is commonly referred to—an unfortunate abbreviation that conceals the suggestive power of its full title—is a controversial proposition among the men. Because of the benefits it accrues—a little cash, privileges similar to the ones granted to those who are employed, access to goods that can be appropriated and then exchanged—many residents view participation as an improved status. Yet for many others it is an insult—a form of "slave-labor" that devalues their time and only serves the interests of the city.

On certain occasions, WEP participation has been viewed as a first step toward securing regular employment inside the shelter—a kind of upward mobility. Shelter administrators have often encouraged men to think along these lines and indeed, a number of residents "made staff," that is, they were hired by the city as shelter workers. Such a change of fortunes inspires other men to invest time in pursuit of the same goal and to perceive their prospects for employment along this shelter-based continuum. Of course, this orientation is rather convenient for shelter operators who can rely on the cooperation and eagerness of these men to work, whether as paid WEP trainees or as "trustees" who volunteer their time hoping to move up the ladder.

Work is definitely a major theme in the experience of shelter life—work that one actually has, whether legitimate or illegitimate; work that one is looking for; work that one cannot find; and, to a large extent, the surrogate forms of work, or the prospects for it, inside the shelter. As such, work indeed provides an alternative sociotemporal horizon for a shelter user's experience, despite the fact that the economic and social realities shaping the lives of these men make employment—steady, reliable employment that can provide a base for a "normal" life—a rather intangible prospect. As one shelter resident once told me (and all the men around us agreed): "Maybe there is work. But there ain't no jobs out there." Nevertheless, the shelter, through the fragments of a work ethic that it manages to accommodate, perpetuates the myth of jobs as a ticket out of the condition that its very presence fosters in the first place.

Somehow many residents manage to adhere to this myth for surprisingly long periods of time. Some construe their survival economics in terms that render these activities as legitimate economic categories. For instance, collecting cans may be referred to as "running a recycling business." An interesting example of the connection between work, dominant consumption ideologies, and the valuation of time can be

found in the experience of one shelter resident who ran such a "recycling business." At an earlier time, this man would have invested the
twenty-or-so dollars he had earned after a day of very hard work on
crack. At that time, he would say that he was "hustling cans." Then
he decided to get off crack, save money, and find an apartment or
room. He intensified his work—only this time he was "running a recycling business." When he became discouraged about finding an af-
fordable place, he resigned himself to life in the shelter but did not
stop working. He began applying his proceeds toward buying a bottle
of French champagne. Could it be the case that the consumption of a
high status, luxury good—his kind of conspicuous consumption—
made the 10 to 12 hours of collecting cans more "meaningful?"

## Conclusion

In this essay, the examination of the sociotemporal construction
of shelter life for homeless men was intended to demonstrate that the
shelter is a unique arrangement that manages to incorporate seemingly incompatible perspectives: as a place of last resort for people
who find themselves socially excluded and economically redundant—
first their jobs went, then social transfer payments were curtailed,
then they were asked, or themselves decided to leave precarious
households where they "had become a burden"—the shelter *prima fa-
cie* represents a serious challenge to the legitimacy of the dominant
ideology regarding the valuation of time and its uses. Still, the shelter
is a place where dominant ideas about time and work, self and society,
and the conditions for social integration (re)assert themselves with a
surprising resilience: residents are forever "preparing" themselves for
a "normal" life on the outside. Furthermore, the shelter is an institution where the potential for "revolts" is effectively neutralized
through the institutional appropriation of the inmates' time and of its
representations.

The institutional appropriation of time is perhaps the most important dimension of shelter dependency, or shelterization. The temporal structure of shelter organization dominates the inmates' daily
life. The custodial functions of shelters make time a fundamental technology of power and control and an indispensable regulatory and organizational principle. Curfews, standardized schedules for performing one's basic functions, and waiting in lines define the daily shelter
routine. Keeping up with this routine requires considerable investment of time and effort. Activities such as eating, sleeping, or taking
a shower, which are normally classified as "leisure" for those with

homes, become the "work" of homeless individuals. By transforming the most basic activities of personal sustenance and reproduction into an all-consuming activity, the temporal organization of shelter life functions as the centripetal force that produces and perpetuates shelter dependency.

The men who reside in New York City shelters experience time and negotiate their lived reality from a number of different sociotemporal perspectives. (As Graham Greene says in *The Tenth Man*, "there were as many times as there were prisoners.")[6] These perspectives are present simultaneously, although they are embedded in radically different normative systems that are incompatible with one another. However, for the majority of these men, the end result is a surrender into the temporal order of shelter life brought about by the institutional appropriation of their time and the redefinition of their temporal perspectives. Ultimately, they are all "prisoners" of the shelter order.

## Notes

*Acknowledgments.* I wish to thank Ricardo Rodriguez, a social worker at the Franklin Avenue shelter for homeless men, for pointing out the song to me; L. Synn Stern and Eliecer Valencia, mental health workers at the same site during the period of field research, for valuable information and insights into the lives of the men whom they tried to help escape the demoralization of shelter life; Ezra Susser and Ernest Drucker, my earlier collaboration with whom is reflected in various parts of this paper; Susan Barrow and Ansley Hamid who commented on an earlier draft; Anne Lovell, with whom I began to discuss many of the ideas developed here; and Sarah Hamaty for her support and valuable editorial comments. Henry Rutz provided the inspiration to pursue the topic and continuous intellectual guidance throughout the development of this article, and for a long time before that.

1. There are municipal shelters for men, for women, and for families. In addition, a policy of "segmentation" has been enforced since the late 1980s whereby individual shelters are designated as "specializing" for a particular type of clients—e.g., mentally disabled, elderly, drug abusers, "employables," etc. Alongside the municipal system, a network of "private" shelters, usually small in size, has been operated by a variety of nonprofit, mostly religious, organizations. A 1989 survey by the New York Planning Department counted a total of 326 shelters with a capacity of almost 30,000 (Dunlap 1990).

2. The inverted commas on these ethnic categories are meant to indicate that they are socially constructed under particular hegemonic conditions and that they can become contested, as illustrated by current efforts to replace "black" with "African-American." The dialectics of racism require that those in subordinate positions constantly rename themselves in their struggle for empowerment and destigmatization.

3. In 1990, New York City transferred the use of the building that housed the Shelter Care Center for Men on East 3rd Street to a nonprofit service

agency that operates an alcohol detoxification and rehabilitation program. New York City authorities have attempted to decentralize the functions of assessing and assigning new clients that East 3rd Street used to perform. However, the future development of the city-operated shelter system is subject to changes that are impossible to predict, given the enormous budgetary problems that the city is currently (1991) facing. One likely scenario is the consolidation of smaller facilities into huge shelters with capacities exceeding 1000 beds. Another scheme points to the opposite direction: small-scale shelters of no more than 200–300 beds.

4. The ethnic composition of the Franklin Avenue Shelter reflects that of the surrounding community. The transformation of shelters into "local" or "community" shelters accounts for the higher proportion of hispanic men among the residents of this shelter, compared with the shelter system as a whole.

5. "Voluntary" should be qualified: For instance, when the temperature falls below a certain mark, the police have the power to remove homeless people from the streets and force them into a shelter—or a psychiatric hospital, if they refuse the shelter—allegedly "to protect them from themselves." Also, there is always pressure from public authorities (e.g., transportation) and by interested private parties (e.g., merchants or homeowners) to clear terminals, subways, or the streets in front of shops and houses from the disruptive and disturbing presence of homeless persons.

6. Quoted by R. Whipp (1987). Whipp draws attention to the fact that a number of literary writers "seem to have long appreciated the social basis of time and its implied order."

## References Cited

Bahr, Howard
   1970   Disaffiliated Man: Essays and Bibliography on Skid Row, Vagrancy, and Outsiders. Toronto: University of Toronto Press.
Baxter, Ellen, and Kim Hopper
   1981   Private Lives/Public Spaces: Homeless Adults on the Streets of New York City. New York: Community Service Society.
Dunlap, David
   1990   Listing Shows Homeless Sites to Aid Census. New York Times, January 22, p. B1.
Ewen, Stuart
   1976   Captains of Consciousness: Advertising and the Social Roots of the Consumer Culture. New York: McGraw-Hill.
Goffman, Erving
   1961   Asylums: Essays on the Social Situation of Mental Patients and Other Inmates. Garden City, N.Y.: Anchor Books.
Gounis, Kostas, and Ezra Susser
   1990   Shelterization and Its Implications for Mental Health Services. *In* Psychiatry Takes to the Streets. N. Cohen, ed. Pp. 231–255. New York: Guilford.
Hamid, Ansley
   1990   The Political Economy of Crack-Related Violence. Contemporary Drug Problems, Spring 1990.

Harvey, David
   1973   Social Justice and the City. Baltimore: Johns Hopkins University Press.
   1989   The Urban Experience. Baltimore: Johns Hopkins University Press.
Hopper, Kim, and L. Cox
   1982   Litigation in Advocacy for the Homeless: The Case of New York City. Development: Seeds of Change 2:57–62.
Hopper, Kim, and Jill Hamburg
   1986   The Making of America's Homeless: From Skid Row to New Poor, 1945–1984. *In* Critical Perspectives on Housing. R. Bratt, C. Hartman, and A. Muerson, eds. Pp. 12–40. Philadelphia: Temple University Press.
Morrissey, Joseph, and Kostas Gounis
   1988   Homelessness and Mental Illness in America: Emerging Issues in the Construction of a Social Problem. *In* Location and Stigma: Contemporary Perspectives on Mental Health and Mental Health Care. C. J. Smith and J. A. Giggs, eds. Pp. 285–303. Boston: Unwin Hyman.
Piven, Francis, and Richard Cloward
   1982   The New Class War: Reagan's Attack on the Welfare State and Its Consequences. New York: Pantheon.
Struening, Elmer L.
   1986   A Study of Residents of the New York City Shelter System. Report to the New York City Department Of Mental Health, Mental Retardation, and Alcoholism Services. New York: New York State Psychiatric Institute, Epidemiology of Mental Disorders Research Department.
Thompson, Eward P.
   1967   Time, Work-discipline, and Industrial Capitalism. Past and Present 38:56–97.
Whipp, Richard
   1987   "A Time to Every Purpose": An Essay on Time and Work. *In* The Historical Meaning of Work. P. Joyce, ed. Pp. 210–236. New York: Cambridge University Press.
Wilson, William J.
   1987   The Truly Disadvantaged: The Inner City, the Underclass, and Public Policy. Chicago: University of Chicago Press.
Zerubavel, Eviatar
   1981   Hidden Rhythms: Schedules and Calendars in Social Life. Berkeley: University of California Press.

# 8

# Jewish Ontologies of Time and Political Legitimation in Israel

## ROBERT PAINE

This essay is about people who experience different temporalities within the same country, Israel. These separate groups of persons each strive to define the state of Israel, so I am also writing about linkages between languages of time—all but one of which are eschatological—and political legitimation.

The groups are Jewish. The ultra-Orthodox are in no doubt about the time in which they live, but it puts them out-of-place in present-day Israel. The Orthodox, too, are certain of the time in which they live, but it is a different time from that of the ultra-Orthodox, and they are self-consciously in-place. Yet there is a serious difference, among the Orthodox themselves, over whether one is living in the age of the coming of the Messiah. Then there are Jews for whom Israel is their only home, cognitively and emotively, but they are uncertain or indifferent about its temporality—just as they may be about their Judaism.

## The Pendulum of Exile and Return

Now, the soundest starting point for an understanding of the eschatological renderings of time is through the paired concepts of the Law and the Land. The *Land* was covenanted by God to the descendents of Abraham: to the Chosen People, the Chosen Land. However, this holy space can be defiled, even by the Chosen, and the penalty is their exile (Leviticus 18; Numbers 33). Thus while their possession of the Land is inviolable, its occupancy is contingent upon a strict and encompassing code of religious and moral behaviour.[1] This code is articulated in the *Law*.[2] Thus "on the observance of the Law . . . depended the well-being of The Land" (Davies 1982:64). In this way "Israel and the Land . . . belong to one another; when united, both flourish and are blessed. The converse is true . . . when [L]and and the people are separated, then misfortune takes hold of both" (Elizur 1978:97).[3] The time-honored conclusion has been: "Israel is not a nation but through its Law" (Elam 1976:30).

Of course, the Chosen, for most of their history, have been either en route to the Land or in exile from it, so that much of Jewish consciousness has revolved, self-absorbedly, around the pendular process of *exile and return*. This historical pattern has been overlain with eschatological meaning such that the pendulum swings between "sacred centricity" in time and space, its loss, and (completing the cycle) the redemptive return to the center. As the centricity symbolizes conjunction between the cosmic and the human, so exile denotes their disjunction (Handelman and Shagmar-Handelman 1986:3–5).

**Figure 1**
**Pendulum of Exile and Return in Israel Today**

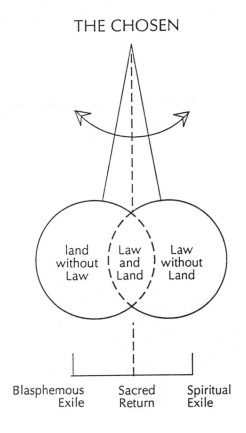

THE CHOSEN

land without Law / Law and Land \ Law without Land

Blasphemous Exile        Sacred Return        Spiritual Exile

There is what the Handelmans call a "signal irony" about such an ideational system. It is that the "privilege" of Chosen-ness carries the burden of failure "to live up to the requirements," so "centricity led inevitably to the exilic condition" (p. 6). Hence "the recurring double vision of failure and perfection, curse and blessings" (Eisen 1987:222); and what are most remembered are "the breaches of convenant that Israel has been guilty of" (Roskies 1987:581). This pendular movement, then, tells the story of both the messianic energy and, as well, the messianic predicament of the Jewish faith. Return is predicated on Exile; Return seeks an eschatological dissolution of exile—that is, of the pendulum itself.

In Jewish discourse in Israel today, the spectre of exile *(galut)* has an additional dimension. Besides exile *outside* the Land, such as the Handelmans describe, there is exile *within* the Land: living there *without* the Law, thereby desecrating the Land.[4]

Among the secular Jewish majority in Israel, however, the Law is not revered;[5] and the land, for them, is not to be explained eschatologically but historically—thus not warranting the capital *L*. Even so, it is revered by many.[6] Likewise with the motif of exile and return: eschatologically a dead letter, the historical weight of the pendular process is experientially present; emphatically, it is not dismissed from the collective consciousness as "detritus of time past" (Handelman and Shagmar-Handelman 1986:2).

In what follows, I look at each of the three Law/Land combinations of Figure 1, the association of a particular Jewish Israeli group with each, the distinctive time-space ideologies that adhere to each, and the implications each carries for the legitimation of the state.

## The Law Without the Land

"Naught has been left us, save only this, our Torah"
                                        —a penitential hymn, 1000 CE.

For the moment, our concern is with the roots through time of what is today ultra-Orthodox eschatology and its relation to the creation of the State of Israel.[7] but most of all, with its structure of temporality: this leads us from the narrow circles of ultra-Orthodoxy in Israel to the broader ranks of Orthodoxy.[8]

The secular Zionist state, for the ultra-Orthodox, is a profanation and a hindrance to the messianic redemption of the Jewish people. The Return will only happen when all Jews live wholly and solely by the Torah. Though *they* live devotional lives and do so *in* Israel, they are, nevertheless, still in spiritual exile; as for the Jewish population of Israel as a whole, theirs is a blasphemous exile.[9]

Other Orthodox than the ultra-Orthodox are devotional in their study and observance of the Torah, and some share their eschatology, but it is especially the ultra-Orthodox whose lives are dedicated to a tradition especially prominent among Jewry of pre-Holocaust East Europe and dating all the way back to the enforced diaspora following the destruction of Jerusalem by the Romans in the first century (Raphael 1983). Exiled from the Land they have been and are, but never from the Torah; and it is through the Torah that the way out of exile passes.[10] Even the biblical Exile in the "wilderness" is part of this tradition— "a *time* is remembered which, as Deuteronomy 8:7 ff. makes clear, prepared Israel for life in The Land (Davies 1982:58–59; emphasis in original).

"Preparation" in this eschatologic sense is an important part of the talmudic study circles[11] of the Orthodox as well as the ultra-Orthodox.[12] The preparation is predicated on a seamless view of time whereby "the world as experienced and the one which the Talmud describes become fused" (Heilman 1983:65). The fusion happens through processes of "traditioning" and "contemporization" (Figure 2). Memory, it seems, is transformed into experience. And by that I

**Figure 2**
**Time as Experience of Memory**

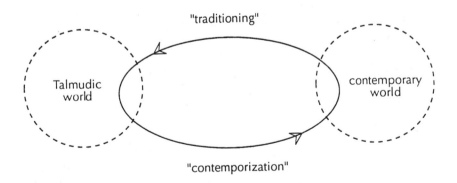

"traditioning"

Talmudic world

contemporary world

"contemporization"

Legend

*traditioning:* "there is no experience or idea in the Talmud so archaic or remote that it cannot be imagined or understood by the contemporary Jew . . ." (Heilman 1983: p. 62).

*contemporization:* "the past becomes embedded in, completed or corrected by the present, just as in traditioning the opposite is the case" (Heilman p. 63).

mean something more than Judaic edicts about religious memory as an obligation and the importance of prefigurement in Jewish experience. Heilman tells us how, in the talmudic study circles, they "replay the text"—not to learn, not for the sake of new information, for they study what they already "know."[13] Rather, in the replaying they "*hear themselves* exemplifying talmudic logic and thinking" (1983:66, 71; my emphasis). "Then was now, and now then" says Heilman (1984:64).

So the present is prefigured by the past, nothing new can be learned except how to experience that past in the present.[14] Rabbis "play with Time as though with an accordian, expanding and collapsing it at will" (Yerushalmi 1982:17). It is Time detached from the space in which they live. It produces a messianism of waiting, from which the eventual transforming release will be apocalyptic.[15]

But time is not still; even as it "waits," it moves cyclically through the Jewish calendric year. It is a calendar with eschatologically related phenomena at the heart of the Jewish experience (Passover, Yom Kippur) and it is closely tied to the Law, which—be it noted—"minutely regulates" the life of the Orthodox Jew (Dinur 1969:20; cf. note 2).[16]

## Land without Law

> ". . . the land and only the land will be holy of holies for the Hebrew soul."[17]

The secularism—even "paganism" in the eyes of some (Don-Yehiya and Liebman 1981:123; cf. Rubinstein 1984:43)—of much of the early Zionist labor movement raised the question: are they going to be "Hebrews" or "Jews"? If the former, they were, as one distinguished political commentator puts it, "entitled to break the chains and shackles of an outdated Judaism" (Rubinstein 1984:43). Ben Gurion—through his long years in power[18]—grappled—and varyingly embraced—both sides of the question.[19] He spoke of the "new Jew": a Zionist who had, indeed, broken those chains and shackles of Judaism in the Diaspora—or in Ben Gurion's own words, "these sterile and bloodless longings"—and who now worked for the "reconstruction" of his people "on the soil of the homeland . . . [as] a self-sufficient people, master of its own fate" (cited in Avinieri 1981:200). In respect to this "revolutionary" side of Zionism, Ben Gurion, too, refers to the new Jew as a "Hebrew." However, the new Jew "returns" to the Homeland with a "Messianic vision" out of which flows the "redemption" of a "unique" people.[20] These are Jewish code words. But whereas through the millennia of exilic Jewry they had, in effect, *locked* doors, now these same code words became keys with which to *open* doors. This "messianism" (no longer eschatological, yet more than a metaphor) is seen by some—e.g., Rubinstein (1984)—as "prefigured" by the mode of Jewish thought through the millennia; one spoke not of a Messiah but of "messianic action."

Let me now put the foregoing in more direct terms of temporality: (1) Labour Zionism propagates a civil religion (Bellah 1967) whose objective is the "sacred legitimation of the social order" and at whose core "stands a corporate entity rather than a transcendent power" (Liebman & Don-Yehiya 1983:4–5). (2) A consequence is a Homeland without the Law, and the subordination of time to space in the making of place. However, (3) along with the rebuttal of the eschatologic time of Orthodox (and ultra-) Judaism, there is a fervent embracement of biblical *times* in this old-new place, the State of Israel. In short, Ben Gurion scissored-and-scotch-taped time, still calling it messianic.[21]

For a while what was attained by the ambitious socioeconomic program provided "messianic" momentum; perhaps it was this which drew a distinguished scholar to write, in the middle '50s, of this Zionism as "the first redemption movement [*sic*] able to remain within the historical dimension and not compelled by initial historical failure, to translate itself to a purely spiritual plane" (Werblovsky 1956:108). Yet the void that had always been there, between the biblical "then" and this Zionist "now," began to overtake the enterprise. It was a *Jewish* void: "the secular day no longer mirrored the sacred history of the past; it was simply the secular day . . ." (Halkin 1977:170).[22]

While this Zionism sought its legitimation in history, the use to which it put this "history" was to ignite putative "memory." In this it seems like the Judaic tradition itself, but—and this is what matters—unlike it in not successfully fusing memory and experience.[23] For one thing, there was in this Zionism a strong strain of a politics of *forgetting*. Forgetting not just a "history" (of the Diaspora) but the lives of one's immediate forebears. This set in motion a process of "counter-memory" (Davis & Starn 1989)—of "interrogation" of (in this case) the long tradition of rabbinical Judaism that should end in its "dissociation from memory" (Nora 1989:10). At the same time, the erased Diaspora was to be replaced by ("memories" of the "history" of) the biblical nation; and paradoxically—as Nora found elsewhere—this was to happen in "a society deeply absorbed in its own transformation and renewal, one that inherently values the new over the ancient, the young over the old, the future over the past" (Nora 1989:12).

I borrow again Nora's insight: this experientially unsettling period of Zionism is one that "calls out for memory because it has abandoned it" (Nora 1989:12).[24]

## The Law and The Land

> "The purpose of this process is not the normalization of the people of Israel—to be a nation like all other nations—but to be a holy people, a people of the living God."
>
> —Rabbi Yehuda Amital (Rubinstein 1984:105)

Three decades after Werblovsky's pronouncement that Zionism is remarkable among political redemptive movements in not being overtaken by the "purely spiritual," there is growing compelling evidence of "the appropriation of Zionism by religion" with an eschatologic timetable (Aran 1985:4). The focal point of this development have been the *Gush Emunim:* a group of Orthodox Zionists, later joined by secular figures with whom they share the political program of a Greater Israel.[25]

I keep the Gush Emunim under review, through this section, as a foil, doctrinally and politically, to the ultra-Orthodox, the secular Zionist tradition of Ben Gurion, as well as another expression of Zionism within the Orthodox camp—*Oz VeShalom* (Strength and Peace). Rabbi Amital (above) was a prominent Gush Emunim ideologue;[26] in his disavowal of the goal of "normalization of the people of Israel," he is at one with the ultra-Orthodox—but they are non-Zionists;[27] at the same time, the disavowal puts him at odds with the majority of the Jewish population in Israel; and it is what the moral conduct, in national affairs, of "a holy people" should be that places fellow Orthodox Zionists in sharp, agonized disagreement with him. In short, mapping the Gush Emunim position in relation to others throws into relief a range of inflections—with hyphenated "how-where-when" questions—about the fulfilment of Zionism and the "redemption" of its people. Perceptions of place—reached through associations of time and space (Innis 1964; 1972)—are at the core of these issues.

The backdrop for the public emergence of the Gush Emunim and the media attention they were afforded were two wars and the ideological emptiness into which—it seemed to many—Zionism had fallen. The Six-Day War of 1967 brought the "miraculous return" of Judea and Samaria and the Old City of Jerusalem; then in the Yom Kippur War of 1973—a victory snatched from a prospect of defeat—all could have been lost. As 1967 added to what 1948–49 had won[28] and 1973 issued its warning, the Gush Emunim announced—with Joshuan trumpet blasts—that Israel had entered a time of messianic immanence, that the Homeland of Labour Zionism and the Land of Destiny (Schweid 1985) which the ultra-Orthodox seek in their *waiting* will be brought together and reach to the full extent of the post-1967 boundaries.

The Gush Emunim, then, appeared on the scene as an exultant, giddying or—depending on ideology—alarming, menacing antidote to the Jewish void that was befalling Zionism. Neither doctrinally nor experientially, however, did it arrive *de novo*. Doctrinally, it emerged through the teaching of Rabbi Abraham Isaac Kook (d. 1935), especially as expounded in the *yeshiva* (seminary), headed by his son, to which the early core of the Gush Emunim belonged. The essential points (for our purposes) of Kookian "realized eschatology" (Hertzberg) are:

1. "the certainty that the present generation is the one foretold in prophecy as the age of the coming of the Messiah" (Hertzberg 1986:417);

2. "Jewish original creativity whether in the realm of ideas or in the arena of daily life and action, is impossible except in Eretz Israel" (cited in Avinieri 1981:190);

3. "the spirit of Israel is so closely linked to the spirit of God that a Jewish nationalist, no matter how secularist his intention may be, is, despite himself, imbued with the divine spirit even against his own will (cited in Avinieri p. 193);[29]

4. thus, he sought "to transmute the profane, allowing the sacred to permeate and remold it in its own image" (Lewis 1979:43).

Ironically—except that Rabbi Kook foresaw this particular conjunction—the Gush Emunim drew experiential inspiration (as well as a measure of public justification for their actions) from the "pioneering" of the land by earlier generations of secular Zionists (*halutzim);* like those pioneers, they worked to imprint their presence on the land. Beyond that, though, philosophical and metaphysical differences separate the two movements. The imprint of the pioneers could as well have been "Hebrew" as "Jewish"; they also sought the impact of the land on themselves: it was a *natural* homeland they wanted. The Gush Emunim, by contrast, work to imprint a Jewish presence, and to transform the land into the Land, a *metaphysical* reality (cf. Benvenisti 1986 and Tal 1983; 1986).

Emerging from their seminaries to found settlements in Judea, Samaria, and Gaza, the Gush Emunim *politicized* a fusion of memory and experience.[30] The other fusion desired by Rabbi Kook between the secular and religious populations, was not fulfilled although the country as a whole was alerted to this renewal of Zionist vision. For some, a *return* to the temporality of prefiguration of prophecy—and its intrusion into the political debate—is, I assume, a comfort, an offering of psychic security, to their own sense of Jewishness. Others, though, are left to ponder the moral and political contradictions in Gush Emunimism as a Zionist message and as a Jewish one. Where some identify with its "redemptive Zionism," its transcendentalism, and its sacralization of space—others recognize irredentism, fanaticism, and idolatry.

However, the consternation that the Gush Emunim arouse in others differs markedly, in its nature, from group to group.

The ultra-Orthodox (who are themselves widely considered to be "fanatical") are especially disturbed by the messianic presumption: "To those religious Zionists [the Gush Emunim] we say, 'you presume to know what the Messiah wants, his timetable, you presume even to prompt the Messiah.' These are dreadful sacrileges!" (personal communication). Whereas the ultra-Orthodox follow a quietist ideology, the Gush Emunim follow one of action (both are eschatologically motivated). From this follows the Gush Emunim idolatry over *space*, in the eyes of the ultra-Orthodox. All will come with time (His Time), they say, but "we cannot conquer time through space"—which is what the Gush Emunim are attempting. "We can only master time in time."[31] For the ultra-Orthodox, space beyond the synagogue and the home is spurned; their recurring focal point in time is the Sabbath, which "acknowledges God as lord of time" (Houston 1978:232).[32]

Of course the Sabbath is important to the Gush Emunim, too. All branches of orthodoxy in Israel—whether they be Gush Emunim or Oz VeShalom or haredim (ultra-Orthodox)—live by the same Jewish calendar, even as they are otherwise divided. The point I wish to underscore here, however, is that the Gush Emunim, as "political" agents of an immanent messianic occasion, live with a "vision of eternity" (Heschel; see note 32) beyond—but still including—the Sabbath experience. As one would expect, there are secular times on the calendar of the State of Israel from which the ultra-Orthodox, but not the Gush Emunim, exclude themselves (e.g., Independence Day). In addition, the Greater Israel Movement in which the Gush Emunim play a leading role have their own calendric celebrations.

In sum: the ultra-Orthodox celebrate the timeless texts of Judaism without yet being able to celebrate place; the Gush Emunim proclaim place through possession of space—the justification for which, they say, can be found in those same texts.

Groups of fellow Orthodox, also Zionists, such as Oz VeShalom and also *Netivot Shalom* (Pathfinders of Peace), are no less critical of Gush Emunim's politics of space, but for somewhat different reasons to the one just reviewed. Gush Emunim practice is, first idolatrous, and second, offensive to Torah morality. Idolatrous because space is *sanctified*:

> Space . . . assumes the form of and encompasses sanctified localities and neighbourhoods and venerated sites. [Tal 1986:321]

But for Judaism "it is the other way round":

> This country is not holy because it has holy places. This country is not holy because it is associated with holy events. It has holy events and holy places because it is a holy country. [Werblovsky 1970:201]

The essential offence to Torah morality of Gush Emunim practice is that it involves Jews in ethical transgressions against the present-day Arab occupiers of the Land (Aviad 1983:26); "the pursuit of peace and justice"—Torah values—"cannot be reconciled with remaining faithful to the totality of the Land" (Simon 1983:6).

The alternative that keeps faith with the Torah recognizes territorial boundaries "as historical phenomena, as results of political and strategic as well as moral considerations, and hence, if necessary, subject to change" (Tal 1986:323), even while the Land remains divinely covenanted to the Chosen. In short, possession, within the terms of Judaism, is not dependent upon—or to be conflated with—occupancy. What is interesting is that this view introduces—in the cause of moral Judaism—a historical rather than metahistorical reading within what still is, in the final analysis, an eschatological interpretation of time and space.

Only by this route (claimed as that of the Law[33]) is there a prospect of peace—which is itself a theological imperative, say the Orthodox opponents of Gush Emunim. The politics of space of the latter—these opponents argue—are such that "the sanctification of place becomes a practical, political, not simply a theological, necessity" (Tal 1986:321).

By contrast, Gush Emunim ideologues draw war itself—with references to Gog and Magog and the Arab enemies of Israel mixed in together—into a messianic context, so that it has "only one significance: the purification, refining, and cleansing of the congregation of Israel" (Tal 1986:321, citing a sermon of Rabbi Amital).

Secular intellectuals of Labour Zionism are likely, on occasion, to denounce Gush Emunim theo-politics as an "open defiance of Herzlian[34] Zionism—and of everything the Labor movement stood for" (Rubinstein 1984:105). For example: the attempt to make the redemption of the land (now the Land) a matter "standing above reality and beyond the needs of the people" (Rubinstein, p. 112). On other occasions, though, they may blame themselves for having set a kind of precedent with "symbolic acts of possession" in their "pioneering" culture (Benvenisti 1986:17f.)—albeit a precedent that is now grossly distorted by the Gush Emunim. Considered the most dangerous of all, however, is Gush Emunim rejection and inversion of the twin values of "normalization" and "universalism": returning from Exile the Chosen choose to live in righteous exclusion.[35]

## Conclusions

"Time (not history) is the great integrator . . . it is what Jews have in common, above all else" (Handelman, personal communication 1987). What, then, of my insistence throughout this essay that Jews in Israel are experiencing *different* temporalities? Handelman continued: "space fragments." This has never been truer, or more serious, than today. Probably an unavoidable consequence of Zionism, it is one of its principal costs and the disruptive intrusion of space, in the effort to claim a place, is a large part of the explanation of the different temporalities.

When around one hundred years ago the Jews in Europe were faced with radical alternatives to their historical situation—the Zionist option was that of a small minority (Avinieri 1981; Vital 1975)—strong currents of difference were released, including versions of Judaism outside the circle of traditional values. Something of this is reflected in the presence of the *two* code words for Zionist Israel: The Land of Destiny and The Homeland (Schweid 1985). The Chosen people, embracing the Law, are pulled by destiny: their Israel is an eschatological value. But for a harried, homeless people, many of whom have forsaken the Law, Israel is simply a home—albeit one of considerable historical evocation but without eschatologic value.

On Figure 1, then, The Land of Destiny is the righthand swing of the pendulum and Homeland the lefthand swing. *Land of Destiny* expresses a temporal bias over the spatial (so evident in diasporic Jewry) but *Homeland* reverses this. Israel as Homeland (without the Law) is a secular fulfilment of Zionism; for the Orthodox Jew, however, Zionism will not be fulfilled until the Land of Destiny is conjoined with Homeland *through practice of the Law and occupancy of the Holy Land*.

Of course, it is exactly behind these conditions that there lie questions of profound significance for all (Jew and Arab) who live in Israel and along its borders. In this essay, I have looked for the religious components behind the political, and restricted myself to Jewish discourse at that. Most strikingly, we have seen eschatologic time with concomitant messianic belief, albeit with differences, as the principal of competing visions of theocratic legitimacy. Secular Zionism, too, has its visions of state legitimacy, but without a notion of eschatologic time their adherents either find themselves in a progressively weaker position or, as is the case with the Greater Israel exponents (now perhaps a majority in the Knesset), they enhance their public credibility through not challenging the messianic premise. (Ben Gurion was assuredly aware of the "messianic desire" [Biale] even in the early "secular" times of the Zionist state, and, as we saw, he evoked "messianism" metaphorically, not eschatologically, as a "basic truth" among the Jewish people.)

It is appropriate, therefore, to close with a brief recapitulation of the two principal messianic "programs" and their fundamental differences. The messianism of the ultra-Orthodox compels "a life lived in deferment" (Scholem 1971:35), but that of the Gush Emunim moves time into an active mode—one of immanence and "presentness" in action. Truly, the Gush Emunim evoke (in another Scholem image) a "blazing landscape of redemption" (p. 35). Ultra-orthodoxy, an active belief that is messianically quiescent, is "uncomplicated by the need for transfiguration into modern nationalism" (Katz 1982:20). Not so with the Gush Emunim. They use *space* to express messianic time. For them, messianic immanence is demonstrated by the recapture of Judea and Samaria and the Old City of Jerusalem (hence the aggravation, for them, of a mosque standing on the Temple Mount at the site of the First and Second Temples). And we noticed the dismay of groups of fellow-Orthodox who are also Zionists, as well as the ultra-

### Figure 3
### Presentness in Action (Gush Emunim)

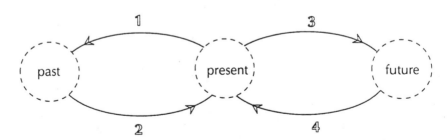

Legend

*1* traditioning—see Figure 2
*2* contemporization—see Figure 2
*3* prefigured action on basis of *2*
*4* fulfilment, with explanation in *1,* and renewal of cycle
*Note:* the fulfilment in 4 is theo-political; there is also fulfilment in terms of proper/pious personal and familial conduct at 2.

Orthodox who are not, over the determination of the Gush Emunim to "conquer time through space."[36]

Now it may seem that if this is not halted, *space*, eschatologically empowered and with the ideology of territorialism that follows politically, will eclipse time as "the integrator" of the Jews in Israel. But the imperative of space—with time, whether metahistorical or historical, brought in *ex post facto*—had "fathered" the birth of the (Herzlian) Zionist idea. This reversal of Handelman's dictum (above) is, however, as "Jewish" as the dictum itself. When in Exile or when in "the wilderness," which has been the Jewish fate over millennia, time *is* the great integrator (Davies 1982; Kaufman 1987; Sarna 1970, 1986; Yerushalmi 1982); and when returning from Exile (and the present Return is not of course the first in the history of the Jews) space may well be that.

However, inasmuch as this is an either/or thesis (either time or space), it is still inadequate. What we have seen among the ultra-Orthodox as well as the Gush Emunim is the enmeshment of space and time with each other as the mandatory course of action for the people of the Covenant. Space, as an expression of time, is part of the eschatological scheme. We must not let our attention be diverted from this by the fact that, at another level, we find the respective outcomes quite dissimilar. The ultra-Orthodox make few moves to return to that special space that is the Land because of their reading of the messianic timetable, and it is also a reading of that timetable that presents the Gush Emunim with their opposite imperative.

## Notes

*Acknowledgments.* My thanks to Jonathan Boyarin and Shlomo Deshen for their helpful readings of an earlier draft, and especially to Henry Rutz.

1. "The Torah makes clear that the religious right can by no means be identified with actual ownership. Just as the promise precedes possession so it does not cease with exile" (Simon 1983:24).

2. *Halakhah*, or Jewish Law, encompasses "the legal, that is specified and detailed rules of behavior, and the relational, that is, the yearning to give expression to the intimate covenantal relationship between God and Israel . . . [as well as relations] between the individual and the community" (Hartman 1987:310, 312).

3. A not uncommon verdict, supported by Talmudic sources, is that when the Land is in non-Jewish hands it is "deemed to be in a state of desolation" (Neriah 1978:83).

4. In ultra-Orthodox circles, the accusation runs that "Zionism has taken Jews and made gentiles out of them" (Schnall 1979:30); among religious mes-

sianic nationalists the accusation is about "Jews" who have become "Israelis," forsaking their Jewishness (Oz 1983:115).

5. Which is not to say that they wholly escape it: there is a secular judiciary, but such issues of "personal status" as marriage and divorce are under rabbinical jurisdiction.

6. And the land of Israel is referred (by religious and secular speakers alike) in Hebrew as *eretz* with explicit ideological connotation; no other country or land is so designated.

7. Centered upon Me'ah She'arim, a neighbourhood of Jerusalem, and Bnei Brak, a suburb of Tel-Aviv, are some 50,000 or more ultra-Orthodox—the *haredim* or pious ones. Their symbolic and eschatologic significance in post-Holocaust Israel outreaches their weight in numbers. Their presence is living evidence of Israel as a home for all Jews. At the same time, though, it is a reminder of both the Holocaust (in which pious Jewry were victims in disproportionate numbers) *and* of diasporic Jewish culture from which secular Zionism dissociates. Many Israelis, then, suffer ambivalence over this presence in their midst. On the one hand, the ultra-Orthodox are a legitimating force for a state which they themselves refuse to legitimate (though there is increasing inconsistency about this); on the other, they are a symbol of Jewry which most Israelis feel uncomfortable with.

8. For empathetic treatment of ultra-Orthodoxy, see Domb (1958) and Marmorstein (1952), and for sociological analysis see Friedman (1975; 1986). For the adaptation of Orthodoxy to the Zionist state see Katz (1969; 1985); also Deshen (1982).

9. Necessarily, I overlook here differences within the ultra-Orthodox world between its various sects and "houses," some of which have drawn closer to the state.

10. The Torah: narrowly defined as the Pentateuch but commonly understood to include the corpus of Jewish religious law and lore, and interpretations (cf. Talmud—note 11, below).

11. The Talmud (part of the inclusive Torah—note 10, above): "not simply another book but rather a human translation of God's Oral Law. . . . the source of real wisdom . . . [it has] preserved and protected the Jewish people since the destruction of the Holy Temple. . . . [it is] a monument of religion and culture, a symbolic of historical identity" (Heilman 1984:25, 29).

12. Torah study is also a blueprint for living here and now—a model simultaneously ethical and aesthetic (Boyarin 1989).

13. If Heilman's interpretation is too idealistic, Yerushalmi provides a corrective. Although he does speak of this Jewish memory as "reactualization," he also notes that only certain memories live on, "the rest are winnowed out, repressed, or simply discarded" (1982:43, 94).

14. If we may speak of "Jewish temporality," this, surely, is its quintessential element. For Ricoeur "the Jewish conception of time [is an] experience of nowness or presentness" (cited in Mendes-Flohr 1987:376). Soloveitchik (1983:120) speaks of "this wondrous chain [whereby] past and future become . . . ever-present realities," and the Handelmans (1986:27) of "an an-

cient present and a living past." Ravitzky (1978:98) observes how "The 'soul of Moses' exists *a priori*, as the point of departure, and the struggle is always for the realization of the vision as a return to the original source . . . future salvation is basically a return back," and Yerushlami (1982:96) notices how what is sought is "not the historicity of the past, but its eternal contemporaneity."

The difficulty the idea of an existentially present past runs into outside Jewish scholarship is itself instructive. For R. G. Collingwood a past that continued to exist (as opposed to being "residually preserved") would be a "limbo where events which have finished happening still go on;" and putting metaphor to what he regards as a derisive proposition, Collingwood sees it as "a world where Galileo's weight is still falling, where the smoke of Nero's Rome still fills the intelligible air" (cited in Lowenthal 1985:187). But Galileo's weight, if it comes to that, *is* still falling; that is to say, in the Talmudic circles studied by Heilman "they tell the story of the past that transcends time, they inhabit the ruins with meaning and motive, with living yet dead people" (1983:72). And not only that: "interpretation of the Talmud and its commentators are precisely what makes the *future* foreseeable" (p. 106; emphasis added).

For an application to contemporary political discourse in Israel, see Paine (1983).

15. On several occasions through the millennia, the waiting broke the patience of Jews and false Messiahs appeared; the Hasidic movement—closely associated with ultra-Orthodoxy today—emerged as palliative. On apocalyptic messianism and hasidism, see Scholem (1971) and Biale on Scholem (Biale 1982); see also Katz's (1961) history.

16. Even so, there is, necessarily, still "clock time" outside the Jewish calendar and Jewish Law. It is the left clock in Heilman's description of his yeshiva in Jerusalem, for instance: "On the wall across from me were two clocks. . . . The left clock was . . . to tell men when they had to get to work or had to leave home, the other told them when they could linger in the pages of a prayer book or the folios of the Talmud . . . one remained aware of the time on the left clock, but one lived in the time of the other" (Heilman 1984:43–44). Noteworthy is how the two clocks juxtapose the notions of *meanwhileness* (left clock) and *simultaneity*—suggested paradigms of modernity and premodern, respectively (Anderson 1983:29f.; cf. Paine 1990).

17. From the ideology of the early Labour Zionist settlers, cited in Don-Yehiya & Liebman (1981:123).

18. Three useful overviews (among many) of this important period in the making of the state—each different in approach—are Elon (1981); Eisenstadt (1967); and Liebman & Don-Yehiya (1983).

19. It surfaces again today—though now it is not a question of being a "Hebrew" rather than a "Jew" but an "Israeli"—see note 4, above.

20. "Anyone who does not realize that the Messianic vision of redemption is central to the uniqueness of our people, does not realize the basic truth of Jewish history and the cornerstone of the Jewish faith" (Ben Gurion 1959:113). In moving Jewish messianic fulfilment from the next world to this one, Ben Gurion was in a tradition of Jewish socialist national thought from the previous century—e.g., Moses Hess (Avinieri 1981:36–46; Buber 1985:111–122).

21. He declares that there has been a leap back in time "which makes us feel closer to David, Uzziah and Joshua bin Nun than to the shtetl in Cracow or the 19th-century ideologists of Warsaw" (cited in Weiner 1970:241).

22. Liebman & Don-Yehiya (1983:13) suggest "Jewishness contains religious overtones for the vast majority of Israeli Jews, and they seek a reflection of this content in the conduct of the state." Approaching the same point, Schweid (1973:46) believes that probably most secular Israelis "seek tradition, but not precisely [the Orthodox] tradition." More challengingly, he suggests that secular Zionists are likely to veer back and forth between attraction and repulsion for Judaism (pp. 46, 111).

23. In searching for reasons for this difference, I look especially to Pierre Nora's "Between Memory and History" (Nora 1989), which is a theoretical introduction to his monumental collaborative history of French collective memory (*Les Lieux de memoire*; 1984–xx).

24. And perhaps another formulation of Nora's captures the essence of this move away from rabbinical Judaism to secular Zionism. He speaks of a change in kinds of memory—"from a history sought in the continuity of memory to a memory cast in the discontinuity of history" (p. 17).

25. For political significance of the Gush Emunim, see the collected essays and the bibliographies in Newman (1985); for sociology of religion approach see Deshen (1982); Aran (1985, 1986); Tal (1977, 1983, 1986).

26. His position has since changed, switching to Oz VeShalom (Deshen, personal communication 1990).

27. In the modern (Herzlian) sense—discussed in Paine (1989).

28. Israel proclaimed its independence on May 14, 1948, war with its Arab neighbours followed; the borders of the new State became those reached in armistice agreements, signed between February and July 1949, and later ratified by the United Nations.

29. The Temple in biblical Israel, the rabbi used to tell his disciples, was built by ordinary workmen, its sanctity took effect only when construction was completed, and so it must be with the building of the Zionist state (Shashar 1980:61). He drew upon traditional Jewish sources to show that the pervading secularism, and apparent heresy, are themselves prophetic of messianic intervention (Don-Yehiya 1984:22).

30. Producing a condition near to Robert Alter's *poetic imagination:* ". . . the world can be seen in the glaring light of ultimacy, its shadows blacker, its bright surfaces blinding, everything tremulous with a terrible intensity that is only intimated in the realm of ordinary experience . . . representing the immediate historical moment in terms of some deeply felt, imaginatively imperative past" (Alter 1973:23).

31. These are the words of Abraham Heschel (Heschel 1951:6) whose writings celebrate the experience of exilic rabbinical Judaism.

32. Heschel (1951:8) calls the Sabbaths "our great cathedrals . . . that neither the Romans nor the Germans were able to burn." He asks (p. 16): "What would be a world without Sabbath?" "It would be a world . . . without the vision of a window in eternity that opens into time. . . . The Sabbath is not for

the sake of the weekdays; the weekdays are for the sake of the Sabbath. It is not an interlude but the climax of living (pp. 14, 16).

33. For the Law *(Halakhah)* is "an arch of holiness between the sacred and profane. [It] binds Israel's everyday, historical reality with its metahistorical vocation to be God's 'holy people' " (Mendes-Flohr 1987:379).

34. Theodor Herzl (1860–1904), recognized as the "founder" of political Zionism at the end of the last century, leading, half a century later, to the establishment of the State of Israel.

35. Rubinstein (1984:109) sees the Gush Emunim "return[ing] to Jewish singularity, shining in its loneliness against the dark backdrop of an alleged universal rejection." Aronoff (1985:64) reports how the biblical curse, "Lo, it is a people that shall dwell alone . . ." (Numbers 23:9), has been elevated by the Gush Emunim to a blessing. Such theo-politics separates the movement from its theological progenitor, Rabbi Kook.

36. The Gush Emunim of course use Judaic texts as the legitimating source for their actions (in this case, as they would say, of bringing the Law and the Land together). Something of the alarm and anguish this raises in other religious Zionist circles is indicated in the response that "we must come to grips with the quotation and not just with the quoter" (Ravitzky 1985:57). That is to say, the Judaic sources themselves must be scrutinized for legitimacy and appropriateness. Beyond the Gush Emunim (and disreputed by them) was Rabbi Meir Kahane, of whose speeches it is said "even the language of the street [gutter] is legitimated by references to holy writ" (Cromer 1988:13). And predating the founding of the state, the revered Rabbi Abraham Isaac Kook (see above) spoke of the need "to overcome many difficult statements that are scattered like giant obstacles in individual sayings [in the Jewish sources] as well as [to overcome] the superficial reading of certain laws" (Ravitzky, p. 59).

The importance of the above is in how it shows that "talking about" as opposed to "talking within" an ideology (Bloch 1977) is, in the case of religious Zionism, being urged by religious Zionists themselves—if only by a small minority at the present time.

# References Cited

Alter, Robert
  1973   The Masada Complex. Commentary 56:19–24.
Anderson, Benedict
  1983   Imagined Communities: Reflections on the Origin and Spread of Nationalism. Thetford: Verso.
Aran, Gideon
  1985   Redemption as a Catastrophy: The Gospel of Paradox. Paper presented at a colloquium on Religious Radicalism and Politics in the Middle East. Jerusalem: The Hebrew University.
  1986   From Religious Zionism to Zionist Religion: The Roots of The Gush Emunim. *In* Studies in Contemporary Jerusalem, Volume 2. Peter Y. Medding, ed. Pp. 116–143. Bloomington: Indiana University Press.

Aronoff, Myron J.
　1985　Gush Emunim: The Institutionalization and Co-optation of a Charismatic, Messianic, Religious-Political Revitalization Movement in Israel. *In* The Impact of Gush Emunim: Politics and Settlement in the West Bank. David Newman, ed. Pp. 46–69. London: Croom Helm.
Aviad (O'Dea), Janet
　1983　Religious Zionism Today. *In* Religious Zionism: Challenges and Choices. Y. Landau, ed. Pp. 25–31. Jerusalem: Oz VeShalom Publications.
Avinieri, Shlomo
　1981　The Making of Modern Zionism: The Intellectual Origins of the Jewish State. New York: Basic Books.
Bellah, Robert N.
　1967　Civil Religion in America. Daedalus 96:1–21.
Ben Gurion, David
　1959　Vision and Redemption. Forum IV:108–124.
Benvenisti, Meron
　1986　Conflicts and Contradictions. New York: Villard Books.
Biale, David
　1982　Gershom Scholem: Kabbalah and Counter-History. Cambridge: Harvard University Press.
Bloch, Maurice
　1977　The Past and the Present in the Present. Man (NS) 12:278–292.
Boyarin, Jonathan
　1989　Voices around the Text: The Ethnography of Reading at Mesivta Tifereth Jerusalem. Cultural Anthropology 4(4):399–421.
Buber, Martin
　1985[1952]　On Zion: The History of an Idea. Edinburgh: T & T Clark Ltd.
Cromer, Gerald
　1988　The Debate about Kahanism in Israeli Society, 1984–1988. Occasional Papers of the Harry Frank Guggenheim Foundation, Number 3.
Davies, W. D.
　1982　The Territorial Dimension of Judaism. Berkeley: University of California Press.
Davis, Natalie Z., and Randolph Starn
　1989　Introduction. Representations (Special Issue: Memory and Counter-Memory) 26:1–6.
Deshen, Shlomo
　1982　Israel: Searching for Identity. *In* Religions and Societies: Asia and the Middle East. C. Caldarola, ed. Pp. 85–118. The Hague: Mouton.
Dinur, Ben-Zion
　1969　Jewish History—Its Uniqueness and Continuity. *In* Jewish Society Through the Ages. H. H. Ben-Sasson & S. Ettinger, eds. Pp. 15–29. London: Valentine, Mitchell.
Domb, I.
　1958　The Transformation. London: Hamadfis.
Don-Yehiya, Eliezer
　1984　Jewish Orthodoxy, Zionism, and the State of Israel. Jerusalem Quarterly 31:10–30.
Don-Yehiya, Eliezar, and Charles Liebman
　1981　The Symbol System of Zionist-Socialism: An Aspect of Israeli Civil Religion. Modern Judaism 1:121–148.

Eisen, Arnold
    1987   Exile. *In* Contemporary Jewish Religious Thought. Arthur A. Cohen
    & Paul Mendes-Flohr, eds. Pp. 219–225. New York: Charles Scribner's
    Sons.
Eisenstadt, S. N.
    1967   Israeli Society. London: Weidenfeld & Nicolson.
Elam, Yigal
    1976   Gush Emunim: A False Messianism. Jerusalem Quarterly 1:60–69.
Elizur, Yehudah
    1978   The Borders of Eretz Israel in Jewish Tradition. *In* Contemporary
    Thinking in Israel. Avner Tomaschoff, ed. Pp. 42–53. Jerusalem: World
    Zionist Organization.
Elon, Amos
    1981   The Israelis: Founders and Sons. Jerusalem: Adam Publishers.
Friedman, Menachem
    1975   Religious Zealotry in Israeli Society. *In* Ethnic and Religious Diversity
    in Israel. S. Poll & E. Krausz, eds. Pp. 91–112. Ramat-Gan: Bar-Ilan Uni-
    versity.
    1986   Haredim Confront the Modern City. *In* Studies in Contemporary Je-
    wry, Volume 2. Peter Y. Medding, ed. Pp. 74–96. Bloomington: Indiana
    University Press.
Halkin, Hillel
    1977   Letters to an American Jewish Friend: A Zionist's Polemic. Philadel-
    phia: Jewish Publication Society of America.
Handelman, Don, & L. Shagmar-Handelman
    1986   Shapes of Time: The Choice of a National Symbol. (Wenner-Gren
    Symposium No. 100: Symbolism Through Time) New York: Wenner-
    Gren Foundation for Anthropological Research.
Hartman, David B.
    1987   Halakhah. *In* Contemporary Jewish Religious Thought. Arthur A.
    Cohen & Paul Mendes-Flohr, eds. Pp. 309–316. New York: Charles Scrib-
    ner's Sons.
Heilman, Samuel
    1983   The People of the Book: Drama, Fellowship and Religion. Chicago:
    University of Chicago Press.
    1984   The Gate Behind the Wall: A Pilgrimage to Jerusalem. New York:
    Summit Books.
Hertzberg, Arthur
    1986[1959]   The Zionist Idea. New York: Temple.
Heschel, Abraham J.
    1951   The Sabbath. New York: Farrar, Straus & Giroux.
Houston, James M.
    1978   The Concepts of "place" and "land" in the Judaeo-Christian Tradi-
    tion. *In* Humanistic Geography: Prospects and Problems. David Ley & M.
    S. Samuels, eds. Pp. 224–237. Chicago: Maaroufa Press.
Innis, Harold A.
    1964[1951]   The Bias of Communication. Toronto: University of Toronto
    Press.
    1972[1952]   Empire and Communications. Toronto: University of Toronto
    Press.

Katz, Jacob
    1961   Tradition and Crisis. New York: Free Press.
    1969   The Jewish National Movement. *In* Jewish Society Through The Ages. H. H. Ben-Sasson & S. Ettinger, eds. Pp. 267–283. London: Valentine, Mitchell.
    1982   Situating Zionism in Contemporary Jewish History. Forum 44:9–23.
    1985   Orthodox Jews—From Passivity to Activism. Commentary 79(6):334–339.
Kaufman, William E.
    1987   Time. *In* Contemporary Jewish Thought. Arthur A. Cohen & Paul Mendes-Flohr, eds. Pp. 281–285. New York: Charles Scribner's Sons.
Lewis, Justin H.
    1979   Vision of Redemption. New Haven: Four Quarters Publishing.
Liebman, Charles S., & Eliezer Don-Yehiya
    1983   Civil Religion in Israel. Berkeley: University of California Press.
Lowenthal, David
    1985   The Past Is a Foreign Country. Cambridge: Cambridge University Press.
Marmorstein, Emile
    1952   Religious Opposition to Nationalism in the Middle East. International Affairs 28(3):344–379.
Mendes-Flohr, Paul
    1987   History. *In* Contemporary Jewish Religious Thought. Arthur A. Cohen & Paul Mendes-Flohr, eds. Pp. 371–387. New York: Charles Scribner's Sons.
Neriah, Moshe Zvi
    1978   Jewish Sovereignty and the Halakhah. *In* Contemporary Thinking in Israel. Avner Tomaschoff, ed. Pp. 78–84. Jerusalem: World Zionist Organization.
Newman, David, ed.
    1985   The Impact of Gush Emunim: Politics and Settlement in the West Bank. London: Croom Helm.
Nora, Pierre
    1989   Between Memory and History: *Les Lieux de Memoire.* Representations 26:7–25.
Oz, Amos
    1983   In The Land of Israel. London: Fontana.
Paine, Robert
    1983   Israel and Totemic Time? Royal Anthropological Institute Newsletter 59:19–22.
    1989   Israel: Jewish Identity and Competition Over "Tradition." *In* History and Ethnicity. Elizabeth Tonkin, Maryon McDonald & Malcolm Chapman, eds. Pp. 121–136. Association of Social Anthropologists, Monograph 27. London: Routledge.
    1990   Time-Space Scenarios and the Innisian Theory. A View from Anthropology. Time and Society 1(1):51–63.
Raphael, Chaim
    1983   The Springs of Jewish Life. London: Chatto & Windus.
Ravitzky, Aviezer
    1978   The Prophet Vis-à-Vis His Society. Forum 30:89–103.

1985    The Phenomenon of Kahanism. Jerusalem: Institute of Contemporary Jewry.
Roskies, David G.
    1987    Memory. *In* Contemporary Jewish Religious Thought. Arthur A. Cohen & Paul Mendes-Flohr, eds. Pp. 581–586. New York: Charles Scribner's Sons.
Rubinstein, Amnon
    1984    The Zionist Dream Revisited. New York: Schocken.
Sarna, Nahum M.
    1970    Understanding Genesis. New York: Schocken.
    1986    Exploring Exodus. New York: Schocken.
Schnall, David J.
    1979    Religion, Ideology and Dissent in Contemporary Israeli Politics. Tradition 18:13–33.
Scholem, Gershom
    1971    The Messianic Idea in Judaism. New York: Schocken.
Schweid, Eliezer
    1973    Israel At the Crossroads. Philadelphia: Jewish Publication Society of America.
    1985    The Land of Israel: National Home or Land of Destiny. London: Herzl Press.
Shashar, Michael
    1980    The State of Israel and The Land of Israel. Jerusalem Quarterly 17:56–65.
Simon, Uriel
    1983    Religion, Morality and Politics. *In* Religious Zionism: Challenges and Choices. Y. Landau, ed. Pp. 16–24. Jerusalem: Oz VeShalom Publications.
Soloveitchik, Joseph B.
    1983    Halakhic Man. Philadelphia: Jewish Publication Society of America.
Tal, Uriel
    1977    The Land and The State of Israel in Israeli Religious Life. Proceedings of the Rabbinical Assembly (76th Annual Convention) 38:1–40.
    1983    Historical and Metahistorical Self-Views in Religious Zionism. *In* Religious Zionism: Challenges and Choices. Y. Landau, ed. Pp. 5–15. Jerusalem: Oz VeShalom Publications.
    1986    Contemporary Hermeneutics and Self-Views on the Relationship between State and Land. *In* The Land of Israel: Jewish Perspectives. Lawrence A. Hoffman, ed. Pp. 316–338. Notre Dame: University of Notre Dame Press.
Vital, David
    1975    The Origins of Zionism. Oxford: Oxford University Press.
Weiner, Herbert
    1970    The Wild Goats of Ein Gedi. A Journal of Religious Encounters in the Holy Land. New York: Temple;.
Werblovsky, Zwi
    1956    Crises in Messianism. Forum II:99–110.
    1970    Discussion. *In* The Jerusalem Colloquium on Religion, Peoplehood, Nation, and Land. Marc H. Tanenbaum & R. J. Zwi Werblovsky, eds. Pp. 201–202. Jerusalem: Truman Research Institute.
Yerushalmi, Yosef H.
    1982    "Zakhor," Jewish History and Jewish Memory. Seattle: University of Washington Press.

# 9

# Centralizing Agricultural Time: A Case from South Sulawesi

JOHN R. BOWEN

*(Washington University, St. Louis)*

This paper concerns the changing control of agricultural timing in a Bugis-speaking community in South Sulawesi, Indonesia, during the period 1975–85. Since the mid-1970s, the Indonesian government has sought to broaden and deepen its control over agricultural production. These efforts to increase state power at the farm level have come as part of the promotion of high-yielding varieties of rice (the "Green Revolution"). In South Sulawesi, district governments have responded to crises of pest control and water supply by assuming a greater role in the management of agricultural time: in setting irrigation schedules, rotating seed varieties, and coordinating planting and harvesting.

Prior to this extension of government control, local agricultural practice in much of the province had depended on maximizing the use of highly variable water sources through a decentralized system for timing. Village calendrical experts adapted the knowledge contained in written almanacs to local microecological variation. These experts managed the tension between the need for local variation and flexibility in the timing of planting (primarily to respond to variations in available water) and the need for regional coordination of harvests (primarily to reduce past damage).

State efforts to enforce a centralized schedule for rice planting have emphasized the imperative of regional coordination at the expense of the imperative of local variation. In an effort to enlist popular support for its program the government of Sidrap district has invoked an "ancient tradition" of farmers' meetings. Local calendrical experts are called to districtwide agricultural assemblies at which they approve uniform planting schedules. This policy has politicized agriculture in two respects. First, what had been local variations and changes

in schedule now are construed as civil disobedience. Secondly, by en-
listing the authority of the calendrical experts, the district government
has rendered itself vulnerable to their criticisms. The older calendrical
system linked success in a wide array of social activities to the state of
the cosmos and to the proper conduct of the rulers. The state now can
be held responsible for poor harvests. State appropriation of the preexisting temporal system thus is double-edged: it provides ideological
cover for the extension of state control but also widens the sphere of
events for which the state may be held responsible.

I argue here that the timing of agricultural production can be a
critical area for the expansion of political-economic control and for the
cultural mediation of that process of expansion. Yet the cultural organization of time in Indonesia has tended to be regarded as if it itself
were static.[1] Debates over the broader implications of Indonesian
time-reckoning systems have centered on Bali, and the calendars and
temple rituals linked to the provisioning of water for rice irrigation systems. It may be that the nature of the agriculture at hand has shaped
the debate over the cultural organization of time. In such finely tuned,
well-watered irrigation systems as those studied in Bali, the provisioning and timing of water flow can be guaranteed to farmers. Anthropological debates about Bali time reckoning have turned on the significance of such certainty and control: whether the progression of temple festivals and their supporting calendrical systems serve to organize
the practical activities of wet-rice farming (Geertz 1973; Lansing 1987),
or, on the contrary, to disguise the real cause of farming failures behind a mask of celestial control (Bloch 1977; Hobart 1978).

The politics of time have been quite different for those farmers—
perhaps the majority of Indonesia's farmers—who depend on rainfall
or on undependable irrigation systems.[2] Water supply is not assumed,
it is problematic, and the science of prediction is a major component
of agricultural knowledge. Those who interpret the cosmos for the
farmer do not share in its inevitable dispensations; they risk misread-
ing its enigmatic signs and misleading their clientele. In assuming control of agricultural timing the state thus inherits a highly erratic set of
variables and the responsibility for failed predictions.

The Sulawesi case broadens the scope of inquiry into agricultural
time in two ways. It features a system whose inherent uncertainties
highlight the vagaries of prediction rather than the powers of allocation. Furthermore, it focuses on the role of temporal culture in political-economic change rather than its function in a presumably static local setting.

## Timing in a Rainfall-Dependent Economy

The province of South Sulawesi is one of the major rice-producing areas of Indonesia. As of the mid-1980s it was one of only two provinces that consistently produced a rice surplus (Whitten et al. 1987:585). Yet about one-half of the rice-growing area in the province depends on rainfall for its water supply (ibid). I examine here the changing relation of rice cultivation and politics in the 1980s for the subdistrict of Panca Rijang, and in particular for the village of Rijang Panua.[3] Panca Rijang is located in the northern part of Sidrap district, on the edge of the highly productive Sulawesi "rice bowl." Most farmers in Panca Rijang, however, rely on rainfall or highly rainfall-dependent village irrigation systems for their rice crops.

Before Indonesian independence in 1945 the area now called Panca Rijang was the domain of the lord *(arung)* of Rappang. Rappang rule was relatively decentralized. Whereas rulers in the kingdoms to the south and east appointed their successors, a group of four local chiefs selected the lord of Rappang from among candidates of high rank. Moreover, whereas rulers in the more centralized kingdom held the residual rights to all lands in their districts (and claimed tribute on the basis of those rights), the corresponding rights in Rappang were held by village governments. The war for independence, attempts at restoration of earlier rulers, and a militia-led rebellion against Jakarta's rule kept the area in turmoil in the 1940s and 1950s. The military has played a large role in local government since the installation of Suharto's New Order regime in 1965.

Although residents of the district engage in a wide variety of occupations, rice continues to be the major source of wealth, either directly or indirectly through the proliferation of rice mills, transport, traders, and storage facilities. In the village of Rijang Panua, about 70% of the 711 household heads grew rice as their major source of income in 1981 and in 1985.[4] Riceland is not in absolutely short supply in Rijang Panua village (an average of one and one-half hectares is available for each farming household), but less than one-third of that land received irrigation water, and only 12% of village households had access to irrigated land.[5] Prior to the mid-1970s, farmers in Panca Rijang planted one crop of rice, usually in March or April, to benefit from the spring rains. Only in the mid-1970s, after the introduction of quickly maturing rice varieties and improvement of irrigation facilities, did some Panca Rijang farmers begin to plant rice in the dry fall season.

Decisions about when to plant were and are governed by two major imperatives: plant when the rains are about to fall, and harvest together to minimize past damage. In Rijang Panua, even the 12% of farmers who received some irrigation could not depend on obtaining sufficient water as reservoirs were not replenished by a good downpour. Rice plants require a steady water flow to supply nutrients for most of their growing season. But too much water during the harvest can produce rot in the standing crop. Thus planting should occur before or during the rains, but harvest should occur during a relatively dry spell.

Rainfall in this part of Indonesia is, unfortunately, both highly variable by region and erratic over time. The timing and amount of rainfall shift particularly sharply in South Sulawesi as one moves across the thin arm of the province (Whitten et al. 1987:23). Farmers thus must possess highly localized knowledge of the seasonal likelihood of rain, wind, and pests. Rainfall also is quite variable from year to year relative to other rice-growing areas in Indonesia (Whitten et al. 1987:21–28; see also Lineton 1975:152–153). Table 1 shows rainfall amounts for three successive years in Panca Rijang. The table shows that in successive Februaries, when most farmers prepare the fields and sow the rice seeds, rainfall was 180, 100, and 50 mm. In the planting month, March, rainfall was 140, 300, and 200 mm. Dry season variation was even greater: in October, the dry season sowing month, rainfall was 90, 170, and 3 mm over the three years. Even short dry spells at critical moments in the rice cultivation cycle may wreak considerable damage on the plants despite an overall good rainfall during any particular month. Such a series of dry spells destroyed many crops in 1982. Conversely, heavy rains at harvest time led to high amounts of rot damage in 1981.

Because of the uncertainties surrounding rainfall, even after consulting calendrical experts farmers often wait for the first rains of the season before planting. But a delay by some farmers threatens the second major imperative: harvest simultaneously across as large an area as possible. Simultaneous harvests spread out pest damage over a

### Table 1
### Rainfall Variation in Panca Rijang, 1980–83

|      | Jan | Feb | Mar | Apr | May | June | July | Aug | Sept | Oct | Nov | Dec |
|------|-----|-----|-----|-----|-----|------|------|-----|------|-----|-----|-----|
| 1980 | 176 | 184 | 136 | 273 | 248 | 253  | 16   | 61  | 32   | 92  | 115 | 194 |
| 1981 | 33  | 101 | 308 | 190 | 415 | 93   | 462  | 25  | 146  | 173 | 106 | 162 |
| 1982 | 131 | 52  | 201 | 173 | 150 | 72   | 0    | 8   | 4    | 3   | 65  | 58  |
| 1983 |     |     |     |     |     |      |      |     |      | 98  | 154 | 119 |

Figures are monthly rainfall in mm.
*Source:* Agricultural Substation, Lanrang, South Sulawesi.

large area. Staggered harvests, by contrast, give rats, insects, and other pests the opportunity to feast first at one farmer's plot, then at another's.[6]

If the variations in and uncertainties of rainfall make difficult the planning and coordination of rice cultivation among farmers, the exigencies of reducing pest damage make such coordination imperative. This ecologically based tension between decentralized and centralized planning has given a particular shape to the local culture of agricultural time.

## Almanacs and Agriculture

Until very recently Panca Rijang farmers followed the lead of village calendrical experts in deciding when to begin their agricultural year. These experts derived their knowledge of the upcoming season from sacred books called *lontaraq*. These books derive their name from the palm-leaves *(lontar)* on which, until the 17th century, the books were written. Sacred books kept by Panca Rijang households today generally are commercially sold bound paper notebooks in which the Bugis script has been written by hand. Only a minority of Bugis speakers can read the Bugis script, and very few people understand the terms and references contained in these books. The sacred books deal with diverse topics, among them the rules of marriage, the proper conduct of government, and the characteristics of the seasons. The books I saw had been written in Panca Rijang, sometimes by men serving as village Islamic officials as well as calendrical experts.[7]

Two important systems of temporal information are contained in the books: the cycles of auspicious and inauspicious units of time in the Islamic calendar, and the characteristics of each day in the Gregorian calendar. I shall refer to the first system as the "permutational calendar," following Geertz (1973:392), and to the second as the "almanac." The two systems embody an identical attitude toward time—that particular dates or days carry particular qualities of good or bad fortune—but they deal with quite different kinds of time. The permutational calendars, based as they are on the Islamic lunar system of time-reckoning, regress approximately eleven days each year with respect to the solar calendar and its attendant seasonal patterns. These calendars are oriented primarily toward Islamic history and its implications for current choices and activities. The almanacs, by contrast, link current movements in the heavens to rainfall and success in diverse practical affairs. Both explain practical fortunes in terms of cosmology, but whereas the permutational calendars emphasize the lingering traces of the past in the present, the almanacs explain the consequences of observable movements in the heavens.

The permutational calendars *(kotika)* give predictive values to the years, days, and dates of the Islamic calendar.[8] They assign to each Islamic year an Arabic letter determined by the day of the week on which the year begins. There are eight such letters, and each predicts the rainfall pattern for the year. The Islamic year 1405, for example, began on Wednesday, September 26, 1984, and thus was a *ba* year in which one would expect, according to one book, "little dryness, a long rain."[9] Days of the week are assigned celestial objects that govern their characteristics. Friday, for example, is governed by the Pleiades and the quality of life that flows from God. All the major prophets were born on Fridays, and Friday is a good day for planting rice.

The dates of each Islamic month also carry particular characteristics. The fortune expected on the first day of the month is described in one book as follows:

> Anything that is done [on this day] turns out well, because on this day was born the Prophet Adam, who was given well-being and guidance from God. If sick, we heal rapidly. It is forbidden to weave, forbidden to sit in a floating boat, forbidden to cut one's hair or to engage in trade. It is good to serve the rulers, good to seek out experts in traditional norms, good to meet with rich people, good to set out on a journey, because we can succeed quickly. All this because of the will of God.

The first day of the month is thus on balance a propitious day for doing things. This positive quality is referred back to the birth of Adam, who is favored by God. Seven dates of the month are particularly unlucky because of disasters that befell major prophets on those dates in the past. These dates are widely known in Panca Rijang (see also Hamid n.d. [1978]). On the third of the month, for example, Adam and Eve were expelled from heaven; on the fifth Noah's ship was carried away and Cain slew Abel; on the sixteenth Joseph was thrown into the well by his brothers. The inauspicious qualities of the day are directly related to the events that mark them. A child born on the date of Adam and Eve's expulsion from heaven is likely to betray God, as they did; on the date that Cain slew Abel one should be suspicious of others.

This permutational knowledge, especially the seven inauspicious dates and the eight-year rainfall cycle, continues to guide the important annual actions of many villagers. One consults one's own knowledge or that of an expert before selecting a date for a ritual event such as a circumcision or a marriage, and before beginning the annual rice cultivation cycle. Because these systems are based on the lunar Islamic calendar, however, they do not correspond to seasonal changes, and for the determination of a planting time it is the almanac portion of a sacred book that is consulted.

The almanacs are organized according to the Gregorian ("Malay") months and dates. For most dates an entry combines one or more of the following statements: the position of a celestial object, a weather prediction, recommended agricultural activities, the characteristics of children born on that date, and a few scattered comments on other activities that one should or should not perform. On February 18, for example: "cold, dry. If there is rain or wind, it is a good sign for working the ricefields, but a trader will enjoy no profits." The entries thus link agricultural activities, the movement of the heavens, and general worldly fortune and misfortune.

The almanacs indicate three planting periods: an early period in late March, a second in early April, and a third later in April. Each of the three periods is identified by the name of one of the three stars in the master constellation called "The Chicken." The earliest season is "Body;" the second, "Right Wing;" the third, "Left Wing." The planting period begins when the star whose name it shares passes the center of the night sky. No fixed seasons are indicated for dry season planting, which, when it was practiced at all, usually began as soon as possible after the main-season harvest. The almanacs I inspected (including two that were compared date-by-date) and the calendrical experts I interviewed within the Panca Rijang area agreed on the approximate dates of these periods.[10]

## Decentralized Coordination

The dates and names for the three planting periods as given in the almanacs were known by many men and women in Panca Rijang. When village leaders in Rijang Panua village met to set planting times in 1983, for instance, they discussed the relative merits of each of the three almanac periods. But prior to rice intensification—and to some extent even in the mid-1980s—decisions as to the best moment to begin the rice cycle were arrived at and communicated in a decentralized and informal manner, outside the government sphere.

Any one village in Panca Rijang has a number of people who may be considered to be calendrical experts by some or most of the village residents. Aside from the government-designated expert (to be discussed below), no title or official recognition singles out any one of these experts and gives him precedence over the other. In the hamlet of Tellang-tellang, one of the two hamlets that make up Rijang Panua village, eight men were mentioned as calendrical experts, and addi-

tional men were acknowledged as having some knowledge in this
sphere. I did not encounter or hear of female experts.

The acknowledged experts tend to be of higher social rank than
others in the community. Bugis social stratification is marked by designations of rank, and persons of rank continue to carry authority in
everyday affairs.[11] Of the eight men of Tellang-tellang hamlet mentioned as experts, six claimed (and were generally referred to with) a
title. Three of the men, Pu [sometimes Andi] Wawi, Uwaq Jango, and
Pu Tiwiq, each farming in different parts of the hamlet, wielded the
greatest influence over farmers' timing decisions. Their authority
stemmed from their access to the knowledge contained in their sacred
books.[12]

Each man signals the beginning of the rice cycle by announcing a
date when he will stage the ground breaking (*mappalili*, lit. "to go
around") ritual on his own fields. Thus in the mid-1980s about twenty
farmers in Rijang Panua's western plots followed the lead of Pu Wawi
and would assemble at his fields for the ritual. An animal (ideally a
cow or buffalo, but in harder times a goat) would be killed and its
blood sprinkled on the plough. The blood was intended to replace any
blood that might otherwise be spilled from an accident during the rice
cycle. The ritual thus served to prevent accidents by giving blood in
advance.[13] After the sacrifice the expert or someone acting for him
would drive a pair of buffalo, male and female, three times around his
field in a counter-clockwise direction. (The three times stood for "Nur
[the Light of God or of Muhammad], God, and Muhammad," according to Pu Wawi.) Uwaq Jango and Pu Tiwiq performed their own
ground breaking rituals on their own fields, attended by the households who farmed near them. The other experts similarly initiated the
beginning of the rice cycle for smaller groups of farmers. In Panca Rijang, then, the authority to commence farming, like political authority
in general, has been relatively decentralized.[14]

In setting the time for the beginning of a season, the expert bal-
ances the need for a coordinated harvest with the need to stagger
planting so as to maximize the utility of the available water. In 1984 Pu
Wawi began the dry season cycle in mid-August so that farmers could
sow seed in mid-September. But in his directions to individual farmers
he staggered sowing times such that fields located on the upstream
half of the irrigation canal were planted about one month before those
located further downstream. This schedule allowed the available
water to be stretched. It also increased the amount of pest damage at
the time of the harvest, but Pu Wawi calculated the trade-off to be a
favorable one. In neighboring Baranti village, Petta Uda, whose high
rank gave him authority over a larger area, announced planting times

that began in mid-January for those who drew water from the up-stream portion of the nearby river, to mid-May for those whose water source was furthest downstream.

The coordination value of the expert's actions is appreciated whenever, in his absence, farmers plant in a haphazard fashion. In early 1984, at the beginning of the main season, Uwaq Jango was away visiting his son in Malaysia. There thus was no signal given for plant-ing in the northern part of the Tellang-tellang rice fields over which he normally governs. The result was that the farmers, deprived of their usual source of certainty regarding the rains, waited for the first rains and only then planted, making less effective use of the water than had those farmers who had followed the directions of Pu Wawi to under-take an earlier planting.

The several steps of the rice cycle are accompanied by rituals that remind the participants of the spiritual qualities of rice growing. At each ritual event a meal is held that involves the reading of petitionary prayers *(baca doa)*. Announcements of the upcoming cycle once were made from a spot favored by place spirits (there were three such spots in Tellang-tellang). The sprouting of the seeds and the transplanting of the seedlings are accompanied by an appeal to the spiritual guard-ians of the harvest for permission and by a reading, from a sacred book, of the story of the lord of rice, Sangiang Serri (Anwarmufied 1981:45–48; Messi et al. n.d.[1978]:34–35). The plough consecrated by blood for the ritual is momentarily sacred, and in other districts a rul-er's plough might be considered as part of his regalia (Anwarmufied 1981:45–48; 38–42); such regalia were material links between the ruler and the heavenly world from which his ancestors had come (Errington 1983).

The activities coordinated by the calendrical expert thus make of rice cultivation a cosmologically significant activity. Correctly timing the successive steps of rice cultivation ensures that the process of ma-turation and harvest will take place in accord with the movements of the heavens and the lot of fortune. The expert thus acts as broker be-tween agriculture and cosmology. But in doing so he also assumes the responsibility for correctly translating the dictates of one realm into the imperatives of the other, and he can be assessed blame if the results are wanting. Thus in 1984, when some experts predicted early rains, little rain fell until late in the season. The experts were criticized for this failure, and some farmers declared they would just await the rains in the following year. But the experts pointed to rainfall in neighboring districts and to short rainfalls early in the season as fulfillments of the prediction. As one village head complained of the calendrical experts:

"As long as it rains somewhere in western Sulawesi they say their predictions were confirmed."

Because harvest success is linked to the overall state of the cosmos, it depends on correct conduct by farmers, and especially by their rulers, as well as the correct timing of procedures. The sacred books contain numerous proverbs that linked immoral conduct to poor harvests. Petta Uda recounted the story of a man whose son used his neighbor's plough without asking permission. This breach of moral rules disturbed the relation of the father's crops to the world in general, and for seven years the crops failed. Finally the father discovered what his son had been doing and killed him. "Government knows neither fathers nor sons" he said, "only the law."

The permutational calendars and almanacs that ordered the ritual and technical steps of rice cultivation connected the practical, immediately observable exigencies of water, plants, and pests to the total cosmological order of good and bad fortune. A water supply that varied by year and by microenvironment required a decentralized and flexible system of timing; yet the need for simultaneous harvests required the coordination of timing. The institutions of agricultural almanacs and calendrical experts developed in response to these two imperatives. They also represented agricultural success as directly dependent on the predictive capabilities of the experts and on the morally correct behavior of all persons in society.

## The Ecological Fragility of Rice Intensification

The conditions of rice farming began to change in the mid-1960s when the Indonesian government instituted a series of programs designed to increase rice production and attain self-sufficiency. In 1967 the government introduced the high-yielding rice varieties (HYVs) developed at the International Rice Research Institute in the Philippines. These varieties had a shorter growing season and responded more dramatically to the application of chemical fertilizers than did traditional varieties. They thus made possible the growing of two (or even three) crops each year and the raising of yields from each harvest. The major push for use of the HYVs came between 1970 and the mid-1980s in the form of a national rice intensification program called Bimbingan Massal (lit. "mass guidance") or BIMAS. The BIMAS program was motivated by political as well as economic considerations: the Sukarno government had been weakened seriously by rice shortages in its final years and the new rulers had no wish to repeat that experience. BIMAS distributed packets of HYV seeds, fertilizer, pesticides, and cash to individual farmers on a credit basis. Many farmers who did not participate in the program nonetheless used the new varieties, and by the mid-1970s rice cultivation in Panca Rijang (and throughout South Sulawesi) had been transformed by the program.[15]

Yields under the program were higher under good conditions but lower, sometimes catastrophically lower, when fertilizer was not applied correctly, water supply was insufficient, or when pests flourished. New problems of water supply and pest control exacerbated the preexisting tensions between variation and coordination. Water problems worsened under BIMAS for several reasons. The new varieties required a better water supply to produce even adequate yields. On the poorly irrigated or rainfed fields worked by many farmers, HYV yields were markedly lower than those from traditional varieties.[16] Furthermore, the shorter growing season led more farmers to plant a second rice crop in the dry season and to demand more irrigation water. But during this time of increasing demand for water the irrigation facilities serving Panca Rijang experienced longer dry periods, a problem due primarily to the uncontrolled clearing of forests upstream and the consequent drop in the water table and greater incidence of erosion and flooding. Farmers fought over the use of water, and in the late 1970s one farmer, enraged over a diversion of water away from his plot, hacked to death the man, and his wife, whom he assumed to be responsible for the diversion.

The regency government responded to the water conflicts by establishing a rotation schedule for dry season irrigation water. Off-rotation areas were to plant vegetables and tubers, principally corn, beans, soy, and peanuts, which needed less water. Vegetable growing involved farmers in two further problems: drainage and marketing. If rains come during the dry season those farmers with poor drainage lost most or all of their crop to rot. Such was the fate of Rijang Panua farmers in 1980 and 1983. Farmers who grew vegetables depended on marketing the crops in order to purchase rice, and if floods of water did not rot the crop, floods of crops often lowered the prices. In some cases those farmers who defied the rotation order fared better than those who did not.[17]

Even those crops with sufficient water and fertilizer succumbed to an ever-changing array of insect pests and diseases. Farmers were more vulnerable to pest damage than before for three reasons. First, the HYVs, imported from the Philippines, lacked the resistance to local pests built over time by local varieties. Secondly, in order to harvest two crops, fields were barely cleared of the harvest before a new growing cycle began. In practice, each village was never completely in fallow. It became much easier for pests to reproduce from one year to the next because someone's field always was available to provide nourishment. And third, the pesticides used by farmers killed the natural predators of the pests more effectively than they did the pests themselves. In turn the natural processes of selection favored the development among the pests of biotypes that were unaffected by the chemicals and that found the new rice varieties attractive. (The availability of only a handful of HYVs rather than the wide array of traditional varieties made the evolutionary task easier.) As a result, by the mid-1970s newly mutated, pesticide-resistant, predator-free biotypes of two pests, the brown planthopper and the green leafhopper, had devastated crops across south Sulawesi and in much of the rest of Indonesia (Whitten et al. 1987:588–590).[18] And the tungro virus carried by the green leafhopper continued to plague all subsequently developed rice varieties into the mid-1980s.

The overall effect of the rice intensification program in much of South Sulawesi, including Panca Rijang, was thus to raise yields in good years on good fields but also to introduce new sources of disaster on poorer fields and in dry or plague-ridden years. Insufficient water became potentially more damaging than before, and to the old cycles of drought and rain were added new cycles of insect or viral infestation.[19] Furthermore, each type of problem compounded the others. Water shortages meant that farmers were more likely to wait until rains fell before sowing their seeds, a delay that led to staggered rather than coordinated harvests and that thereby exacerbated the problem of pest control.

The newly exposed fragility of the rice cultivation system led the government to attempt to exert greater control over rice cultivation throughout the Sidrap district. The district government created two new schemas for the centralized control of cultivation: a rotation schedule for the rice varieties, and a system of assemblies that would determine the timing of the rice cycle. The system for rotating rice varieties was designed to reduce the frequency with which virus-susceptible varieties were planted. The agricultural research station for South Sulawesi classified rice varieties into four groups according to their resistance to the virus, and ordered farmers to rotate seed choice among the groups. One variety in particular, the virus-sensitive but highly productive IR 42, was banned from use in alternate years. Farmers routinely violated the rotation orders, however.[20]

The second step involved the setting of planting schedules for the entire district. Rice timing, formerly carried out by individual calendrical experts within a village, now was to be placed in the hands of a districtwide assembly.

## Centralized Timing and Images of Consensus

The attempt to centralize rice timing began in 1974 when the rice intensification program had already exacerbated the tension between the need for coordination and the advantages of determining one's own best schedule. The program had added to the intensity with which this contradiction was felt through the crisis in water control and pest damage that it had produced. The crisis reached new seriousness with the widespread tungro virus damage in 1972 and 1973. Early in 1974 the district head responded by calling together village representatives and calendrical experts to receive, as a group, a districtwide schedule for rice planting and water rotation for the forthcoming year. The gathering was called by the Bugis term *Tudang Sipulung* (lit. "sit down together"). A similar gathering has taken place in each subsequent year.

In theory the Tudang Sipulung system consisted of deliberative assemblies on three levels of ascending scope. Each village was to decide on a schedule according to the findings of its own local experts and then send a representative from among those experts to a subdistrictwide assembly. Representatives from the subdistricts then were to report to the district Tudang Sipulung. At this final assembly their findings would be integrated into a schedule for the entire district.

The government represented the new system as the revival of a traditional Bugis institution. The government took a Bugis phrase *(tudang sipulung)* that referred to any local deliberative gathering and redefined it as the name of a formal institution. They then portrayed the creation of a new, and highly centralized, institution for the control of agriculture as if it were merely the coordination of an ongoing process of deliberation. Contrast the decentralized and divergent predictive practices of the calendrical experts with the official version of these same practices as carried in a 1981 story in Indonesia's major national newspaper:

> No one alive today knows when the first Tudang Sipulung was held in Sidrap. But possibly ever since the people began to practice settled agriculture rather than shifting cultivation . . . In past years the farmers, before working the earth, would gather under a shade tree and talk over problems they might face and how to overcome them. In those times they handled their problems in a traditional manner and by following custom and tradition.
>
> So, Tudang Sipulung comes from the bottom and is rooted in the agricultural population. The involvement of the district government in organizing the Tudang Sipulung into a permanent institution began in 1972. In that year Sidrap was hit by a long dry spell. In the planting season 1973–74 Sidrap was invaded by rats, which destroyed almost the en-

tire rice-growing area. The Sidrap district head at the time, Arifin Nu'mang, went into the fields to help rid the area of pests and received input from a farmer in Rijang Panua village, subdistrict Panca Rijang, that the year in question was really a "year of the rat." This farmer, a local notable, explained that rats had their own seasons.[21]

In this account, the district head discovered and revived a truly indigenous process of consultation. He did so by truly working with the people in the fields, and studying their own explanations and traditions. This story of the institution and its history meshed appropriately with the popularity of "bottom-up planning" in national development circles.

But then the article lets in a discordant note. A calendrical expert from Panca Rijang is quoted as criticizing the government for directing farmers to plant all at the same time, when staggered schedules would have been more appropriate. He then cites three conditions, stipulated by the sacred books of the Bugis, for a successful rice harvest: an honest government, a government capable of carrying out policy, and a firm but wise government. Without drawing conclusions from his statement, the author of the article affirms that the Tudang Sipulung is indeed a firm and wise policy, and thus is a proper "union of technology and traditions." But the potential assignment of blame for misfortune to poor government has been introduced.

In the ceremony of the assemblies as well as in the accounts of their origins and function, the district government has sought to underline the harmony between Bugis "tradition" and the requirements of the new rice "technology." The district assemblies have been rather gala affairs, with long lines of boys and girls in festive "traditional" dress greeting each arrival, the presence of calendrical experts, also in "traditional" dress, and the serving of sweets and coffee during lulls in the sessions. The 1981 assembly was attended by a former minister of agriculture for Indonesia and several provincial department heads.[22] Agricultural officials reported on the previous year's crops, calendrical experts for each subdistrict described the results of their own meetings, and, at the end, the regent read out the schedule for the coming year. Judging from the order of events, one would assume that the Tudang Sipulung did indeed ratify and coordinate the decisions taken on lower levels.

But in practice things worked very differently. Well before the villages held their assemblies, the district agricultural office had circulated the planting schedule they were to follow. Thus when the village head arrived at the Rijang Panua village assembly, held in January of each year, he brought the prescribed planting schedule for the coming year with him. Having been fixed in advance, the assemblies could proceed thereafter as if they were indeed processes of bottom-up planning.

Furthermore, the government (usually the subdistrict head) designated the individuals who were to represent the villages in the subdistrict assemblies. Many of the most influential calendrical experts understandably resisted the imposition of a planting schedule, and, their opinions known, were kept out of the process. Thus in Rijang Panua the three most influential calendrical experts were not involved at any stage of the Tudang Sipulung process. The village representative, chosen by the subdistrict head in consultation with the village headman, was a man strongly opposed to consulting almanacs. A modernist Muslim, he rejected the use of the almanacs on theological grounds that, by suggesting that stars control natural phenomena, they led people to the sin of polytheism *(shirk)*. "Those who have a religion do not believe in the books anymore," he told me. He based his own prediction of main-season rainfall on a simple test: if rain had begun by November 17 of the previous year, then rain was likely to occur early on in the main growing season. His opinions thus presented no difficulties to the government because he had rejected the only possible ideological basis of resistance to the Tudang Sipulung, namely, the traditional body of calendrical knowledge.

The Tudang Sipulung thus bypassed the local network of calendrical experts rather than coordinating it. It is perhaps for that reason that so much emphasis was placed on the presence of experts at the regency meeting. They were highly visible in their tall, cone-shaped hats and were featured in photographs of the meetings: in one they were captioned as "engaged in dialogue" with the district head, who, a broad smile painted across his face, is eagerly bending toward them to catch their words of wisdom.

## Technological and Political Tensions

Yet even with its top-down implementive practice and bottom-up consensual image, the Tudang Sipulung has faced extraordinary technical difficulties. The narrow window of time allowed by the district for each subdistrict contradicts the local practice of widely staggering planting times, sometimes by as much as four months. (Hence the criticism voiced by the calendrical expert in the newspaper article of simultaneous planting). The scheduled rotations between rice and dry crops often contradicts the predictions of particular calendrical experts as to the likelihood of rain. Furthermore, the government schedules have been set according to the needs of farmers who receive sufficient water through irrigation, and who can control drainage and thus prevent rot of their vegetables and tubers in the scheduled off-years.

The calendrical experts generally have continued to issue planting instructions based on their almanacs and their sense of local microecological needs, despite reminders of their obligations to support the government. Experts who are more visible because of their rank or position, such as Petta Uda, have been singled out for periodic scoldings. (Petta Uda, whose high-rank made him both feared and a bit contemptuous of bureaucrats, threatened to kill the official sent to reprimand him.) At first the district government threatened to fine those farmers who planted at the wrong times. But the noncompliance was too widespread to carry out this threat, and by the mid-1980s the government simply ignored the fact that planting took place with little regard to the Tudang Sipulung schedule.

On some occasions, and despite careful government screening, the official Tudang Sipulung experts voice their contrary predictions at the assemblies. At the 1984 assembly, for example, the official representatives stated that because the beginning of the Islamic year (1 Muharram) fell on a Wednesday the year would be a "year of chicken rain" *(taung busi manuq)* (referring to the constellation of the chicken), in which plentiful rain would fall in the main season and the dry season alike. They urged the government to let farmers throughout the region plant rice during the dry season. The subdistrict head for Rappang attended this meeting and was rather amused by the district head's quandary. "He could not oppose the experts because they were his own experts, after all," he said in a 1985 interview. Yet their request would have violated the principle of an alternation between rice and vegetable crops during dry seasons that the district government saw as the best solution to the water shortage. The district head also did not want to be blamed if the rains predicted by the experts did not come. In the end the government tolerated widespread disobedience of its rotation schedule. As it happened, the rains did arrive as the experts had predicted, and the farmers who had defied the government plan and planted rice enjoyed good crops. Some of those who planted vegetables saw their crops rot because of too much water.

Once granted the authority to speak by the government, the experts who attended the assemblies could not simply be silenced. The institution of Tudang Sipulung is based on the assumption that the bottom-up process produces consensus, and that this consensus becomes and law of the district. It becomes exceedingly difficult for the government to then oppose such a consensus when it contravenes the schedule that it has arrived at through independent, technical deliberations. Just as the general nature of an ideology constrains rulers and ruled alike (Scott 1985:335–340), so does the commitment to a certain process—even if originally designed to cover the true source of decisions—delimit the field of action enjoyed by the state.

But the district government's tolerance of noncompliance, and thus of widely varying planting times, has meant that the technical contradictions came to be felt as political tensions within the village. The struggle to obtain sufficient water and to control pests by coordinating planting was, after all, a real struggle, one intensified by the rice intensification program. The increased demands for water and the attempt to more strictly regulate farmers' planting decisions made the favored position of farmers with irrigation all the more apparent.

Thus in Rijang Panua farmers came to a meeting in December 1980 ready to accuse each other of causing setbacks in the rice cycle.[23] The district schedule had called for dry season planting to take place in late October, but those farmers whose fields were rainfed had waited until November rains fell before preparing their fields and were only then in the process of planting. In the previous year's dry season some of these farmers had followed the instructions of the Tudang Sipulung regarding the rotation of wet and dry crops and had planted corn instead of rice in the dry season, only to see rains and flooding ruin their crops. They were in no mood to follow planting orders: "rather than losing out twice; it's better that we use the water that comes to us, even if it is out of schedule," said one.

What once would have been simple, and appropriate, variation in planting times within the village now was a challenge to government authority. The village headman described the problem and warned that unless the farmers were brought into line quickly "they will just do as they please." Planting when one saw fit could lead a farmer to disobey orders on a broader scale. The wealthier farmers with well-irrigated land feared the greater pest damage that would result from uncoordinated harvests. They also remembered earlier bloody conflicts over water rights and feared the recrudescence of such strife unless water use was strictly regulated. The head of the local civil defense forces also stood up and castigated the farmers for planting without permission.

But another farmer shot back: "Not all farmers need permission; we only planted because there happened to be water running into out fields." This argument appeared to convince many of those present. The village leaders quickly moved to defuse the situation. The head of the village subdivision in whose area the forbidden planting had taken place publicly apologized to the headman for all those who had planted without asking permission. The headman then accepted his apologies, and accepted the convenient fiction that the farmers had simply reacted to the presence of water in their fields, rather than setting out to disobey the government. He then permitted (in technical violation of the Tudang Sipulung schedule) the farmers to continue to tend their crops.

The village assembly has continued to violate district Tudang Sipulung directives. In 1981, for example, the village began planting, with the headman's permission, one month before the time assigned to them, in order to take advantage of early rains. In 1985 planting took place four to six weeks after the prescribed dates. These acts of disobedience have been tolerated by the district government. But they have made what would have been local variations, sanctioned by the authority of the calendrical experts, into disobedience of the authority of the district head.

## Attributing Moral Responsibility

The Tudang Sipulung is an attempt to centralize the work of the calendrical experts and thereby to render it uniform. But the intensity of the contradictions between the need for centralized timing and the equal need to stagger timing and profit from water sources has not been surmounted by the Tudang Sipulung. In effect, the technological contradictions, that were also political contradictions, have merely been masked by the purportedly ground-up form of the assemblies.

But the state's appropriation of the functions performed by the local calendrical expert also has meant the appropriation of his responsibility. When it was the local expert who mispredicted rainfall, farmers could choose another expert or just grumble. To the extent that the state became the predictor of rain it also has focused potential blame onto itself. The possibility of blaming the state for agricultural failure was put clearly and repeatedly by the calendrical experts themselves at the 1981 district Tudang Sipulung assembly. Each of the seven experts, representing the seven subdistricts, cited Bugis proverbs regarding morality and responsibility. One expert began with the proverb:[24]

> *mallibu telo:* in Indonesian it means "round like an egg." An egg's characteristic *(sifat)* is that it is clean and whole, and that inside there is a pure element *(zat)*. [Please note: here religious terms, from Arabic, referring to the essence and characteristics of God.] The point of this Bugis proverb is aimed at government. Government must have the characteristics of the egg. Its leaders may not be evil or crooked; they must be balanced in their decisions.

Another calendrical expert mentioned the same proverb; others made similar comments. The last person to speak before the announcement of the agricultural schedule was the district religious official, who limited himself to quoting a Bugis proverb which he translated as

"If trickery has taken place, if the government has tricked the people or the rich tricked the poor, the prophet [Muhammad] said: 'God will hold back the rain'." Let us not let such a thing happen.

## Conclusions

Like other relatively marginal ecological regions in Indonesia's rice-growing zones, Panca Rijang is in a process of transition toward something like a Bali-type irrigation system, albeit one managed by the state rather than by a temple system. The transition has implicated the state in the control of agricultural time. In order to represent this expropriation as a benign coordination, the state has drawn on the preexisting categories of almanacs and calendrical experts. It also has invoked the locally effective combination of consensus democracy (hence bottom-up planning) with firm authority (hence a centralized assembly of experts).

The Tudang Sipulung resembles other pseudo-traditional categories and institutions that the Indonesian state has enlisted as cultural mediators of political-economic centralization. As I have argued elsewhere (Bowen 1986, 1988, 1989), the dialectic between local autonomy and central control in Indonesia often turns on the gradual transformation of certain key cultural categories from signs of local specificity into instances of a broader common culture.[25] These processes of cultural mediation aggregate local institutions into multiple pyramids of control and uniformization: of judicial control, of labor mobilization, or, as in the case studied here, of agricultural direction.

Yet the process is continuingly dialectical, and the capacity for challenge preserved. In Panca Rijang, the state's effort to cloak the technical basis of its timing schemes in traditional forms of knowledge and authority in turn has validated potential future claims against it. It has exposed itself to predictions by the experts that conflict with its own rotation schedule, and to their warnings that responsibility for a poor harvest is the result of its own failures of political nerve or moral fiber. At the close of the 1980s the state apparatus was strong, backed by the Indonesian military and by Bugis traditions of deference toward high-ranking rulers. But the contradictions remain and could reemerge in new circumstances.

## Notes

1. I make this argument at greater length in Bowen (1991).

2. As of 1983, 47% of Indonesian land area devoted to rice was rainfed or swamp, and an additional 22% was served by relatively simple village irrigation systems (Booth 1988:103).

3. Fieldwork in Panca Rijang was conducted by myself and a team of Indonesian social scientists throughout 1981 and over a total of about six months in 1983 and 1985. The fieldwork was part of a study of the local effects of development programs across Indonesia conducted by the Harvard Institute for International Development. A census and a survey were carried out in Rijang Panua village, and interviews conducted in the other villages of the subdistrict and in the other Sidrap subdistricts. Reports on the area include Bowen 1982 and Messi et al., n.d. [1988]. I would like to thank Greg Acciaioli, M. Nawir Messi, Yunus Riva, and Ilyas Saad for their partnership in the project, and M. Saad and family for their gracious hospitality and assistance throughout the fieldwork.

4. All figures are based on the 1981 survey and the 1985 resurvey. Other occupations included tending fruit trees and livestock, silk weaving, operating numerous commercial passenger automobiles, seven rice mills and a brick factory, and the civil service (principally the military and teaching). Here, as elsewhere in Bugis society, men often seek wealth, fame, and knowledge by spending months or years outside the homeland, usually elsewhere in Indonesia or Malaysia (Lineton 1975).

5. Ownership also was in the hands of a relative few: only 37% of the households owned any riceland in 1985, and only 21% owned more than one-half hectare (the area considered locally as the minimum required for subsistence).

6. Coordinated harvests also allow migrating harvest laborers from outside the area to time their arrival in Panca Rijang with the local harvest. In the mid-1980s poor harvests and a breakdown in coordination kept many of them away.

7. In the preamble to one book, the author reveals his qualms as to the theological appropriateness of predicting the future. He warns the reader that, because the book contains unconditional predictions, the reader ought to utter a prayer to God asking for forgiveness, "lest our hearts turn away from God."

8. These calendars have been described elsewhere (Matthes 1943; Pelras 1987). Similar bodies of knowledge are found throughout Indonesia: for example, in the Javanese *primbon* and the Balinese calendars described by Geertz (1973:391–398). Gayo ritual experts sometimes consulted the Taj u-Muluk, a printed Jawi (Malay in Arabic script) book that includes similar calendars. Snouck Hurgronje (1906 II:33) also mentions its use in late 19th-century Aceh.

9. This and the following excerpt are from the book owned by Petta Uda in Baranti. A similar cycle is reproduced in Sumhudi 1979:25.

10. I have not seen books from other districts, which, given the sharp climatic changes across the province, would be expected to differ markedly.

11. Respondents to the 1981 survey in Rijang Panua indicated five major rank categories. Datué and Petta were grouped in the category of "nobles" *(arung)*; Puang and Uwaq as "good people" *(tau dècèng)*, and the remainder as untitled commoners *(tau sama)*. Petta was the highest rank recognized in Panca Rijang in the mid-1980s, and persons so designated were given marked deference in speech and demeaner. Puang [address from Pu] marks a person's role and status to a lesser extent, and often the address form was used for persons whose rank was uncertain in the eyes of the speaker. The precise boundaries in the system depended on the respondent's own position: nobles gave more highly differentiated lists and considered Uwaq to be a commoner rank. Compare Errington (1989) on noble ranks and titles.

12. Some calendrical experts once consulted the movement of celestial bodies directly, what one expert called "the book of gazing up" *(lontaraq pacènga)* in contrast to "the book [that is] written down" *(lontaraq pecuku)*—an interesting rendering of the older stargazing science in terms of the more recent use of writing. The experts interviewed in the Rappang region all consulted the handwritten books, and only a few of them were able to describe the constellations named in those books.

13. Local Islamic modernists objected to the ritual on the grounds that it was a sacrifice to spirits. Others respond that it in fact reenacts the spilling of blood by the martyred grandson of the prophet Muhammad, Husain. The recitation of Arabic prayers by a religious official as part of the ritual may be a relatively recent addition designed to reinforce its Islamic quality.

14. In more politically centralized regions, the ground-breaking ritual was itself more centralized. In the area once governed by the ruler of Sidenreng, directly to the south of Panca Rijang, the ritual was held first on land belonging to the ruler before it could be held on the plots of other farmers (Messi et al. n.d.[1988]:31).

15. Thus although only about 20% of Rijang Papua farmers ever took out BIMAS loans, about 60'% were using the new varieties by 1981, and probably over 80% by 1985 (CPIS Survey Data). See Booth (1988:Chapter 5) for the overall context of Indonesian agricultural development. The demise of BIMAS in the mid-1980s was succeeded by a new packet program, "Supra-INSUS," in the last few years of the decade, and, as of mid-1989, an increasingly centralized control of seed distribution in Sidrap district (M. Nawir Messi, personal communication 1989).

16. I obtained rough estimates of changes in yields for Tellang-tellang farmers by comparing data for present and past (pre-HYV and pre-fertilizer) yields from our 1981 survey. Pre-HYV yields averaged 1.9 metric tons per hectare and rose to about 2.2 with the use of fertilizer and HYVs. But when HYVs were used without fertilizer the yields dropped from the earlier levels, to only 1.2 tons per hectare. Furthermore, the range of yields within the same village for any single year was from zero to eight tons per hectare, with the availability of irrigation the most important differentiating factor.

17. Thus in 1984, farmers who were not to receive irrigation water for the 1984-85 year were told to plant soy beans between late October and mid November. They waited for the rains before making up their own minds. When heavy rains arrived on December 1, many farmers planted rice despite the government order and enjoyed a good crop.

18. In Panca Rijang in 1973 all of the 1600 hectares that had been planted in high-yielding varieties were lost. Much of the area planted in the traditional varieties was destroyed as well by the large numbers of these insects.

19. Each drought and pest resurgence drove some households out of the village. Thus, between our initial survey of Rijang Panua village in 1981 and our second visit in 1983, 16 families had sold their land and left the village for Malaysia, where they hoped to earn a living as wage-laborers on oil palm estates.

20. Most farmers interviewed in Rijiang Panua in 1984 and 1985 said they used IR 42 in every season. For the 1983 main season 29% of the total planted area was found to be planted in prohibited varieties, and in 1984, a non-IR 42 year, agricultural inspectors found fifteen hectares planted in IR 42 that were already infected with tungro. The inspectors ordered them pulled up.

21. *Kompas,* March 2, 1981. p. 8.

22. Fieldnotes taken by Yunus Riva, February 17, 1981.

23. Fieldnotes by Yunus Riva.

24. Fieldnotes by Yunus Riva.

25. The Indonesian emphasis on continuities between agrarian traditions and development policies contrasts with the emphasis in the Western industrial revolution on temporal discontinuities. The shock of the abrupt shift from "nature's time" to "clock time" formed part of the social psychology of labor regimentation (Thompson 1967).

# References Cited

Anwarmufied, Sofyan
    1981    Ritus Tanah [Earth Ritual]. Ujung Pandang: Pusat Latihan Penelilitan
        Ilmu-Ilmu Sosial.
Bloch, Maurice
    1977    The Past and the Present in the Present. Man (N.S.) 12:278–292.
Booth, Anne
    1988    Agricultural Development in Indonesia. Sydney: Allen and Unwin.
Bowen, John
    1982    Rijang Panua. Jakarta: Center for Policy and Implementation Studies
        Manuscript.
    1986    On the Political Construction of Tradition: Gotong Royong in Indo-
        nesia. Journal of Asian Studies 45(3):545–561.
    1988    The Transformation of an Indonesian Property System: *Adat,* Islam,
        and Social Change in the Gayo Highlands. American Ethnologist 15:274–
        293.
    1989    Narrative Form and Political Incorporation: Changing Uses of His-
        tory in Aceh, Indonesia. Comparative Studies in Society and History
        31:669–691.
    1991    Sumatran Politics and Poetics: Gayo History, 1900–1989. New Ha-
        ven: Yale University Press.

Errington, Shelly
  1983   The Place of Regalia in Luwu. *In* Centers, Symbols, and Hierarchies: Essays on the Classical States of Southeast Asia. Lorraine Gesick, ed. Pp. 194–241. New Haven: Yale University Southeast Asia Studies, Monograph Series No. 26.
  1989   Meaning and Power in a Southeast Asian Realm. Princeton: Princeton University Press.
Geertz, Clifford
  1973   Person, Time, and Conduct in Bali. *In* The Interpretation of Cultures. Pp. 360–411. New York: Basic Books.
  1980   Negara. Princeton: Princeton University Press.
Hamid, Abu
  n.d. [1978]   Catatan-Catatan Tentang Beberapa Aspek Kebudayaan Sulawesi Selatan [Notes on Diverse Aspects of South Sulawesi Culture]. Manuscript.
Hobart, Mark
  1978   Padi, Puns and the Attribution of Responsibility. *In* Natural Symbols in Southeast Asia. G. B. Milner, ed. Pp. 55–87. London: SOAS.
Howe, Leopold E. A.
  1981   The Social Determination of Knowledge: Maurice Bloch and Balinese Time. Man (N.S.) 16:220–234.
Lansing, J. Stephen
  1987   Balinese "Water Temples" and the Management of Irrigation. American Anthropologist 89:326–341.
Lineton, Jacqueline Andrew
  1975   An Indonesian Society and its Universe. Ph.D. dissertation, SOAS, London.
Matthes, B. F.
  1943   De Makassaarsche en Boegineesche Kotika's. *In* H. van den Brink. Dr. Benjamin Frederik Matthes. Pp. 459–496. Amsterdam: Nederlandsch Bijbelgenootschap.
Messi, M. Nawir, Ilyas Saad, and Greg Acciaioli
  n.d. [1988]   Implementation of the Rice Intensification Program in South Sulawesi: The Case of Sidrap. Jakarta: Center for Policy and Implementation Studies (manuscript).
Pelras, Christian
  1987   Le Ciel et les Jours, Constellations et Calendriers Agraires chez les Bugis (Celebes, Indonesia). *In* De la Voute Celeste au Terroir, du Jardin au Foyer. Pp. 19–39. Paris: Editions de l'Ecole des Hautes Etudes en Sciences Sociales.
Scott, James C.
  1985   Weapons of the Weak: Everyday Forms of Peasant Resistance. New Haven: Yale University Press.
Snouck Hurgronje, C.
  1906   [Orig. 1893–94] The Achehnese. 2 vols. Leiden: E. J. Brill.
Sumhudi, Aslam
  1979   Konsekuensi Sosial dari Pembangunan Pertanian di Sidrap [Social Consequences of Agricultural Development in Sidrap]. Ujung Pandang: Pusat Latihan Penelilitan Ilmu-Ilmu Sosial.
Thompson, E. P.
  1967   Time, Work-discipline, and Industrial Capitalism. Past and Present 38:56–96.

Whitten, Anthony J., Muslimin Mustafa, and Gregory S. Henderson
  1987   The Ecology of Sulawesi. Yogyakarta, Indonesia: Gadjah Mada University Press.

# Bitter Money

## Cultural Economy and Some African Meanings of Forbidden Commodities

### by Parker Shipton

*Bitter Money* unites symbolic and economic analysis in exploring beliefs about forbidden exchanges among the Luo of Kenya and other African peoples. Luo classify money as good or evil ("bitter") according to its source. Selling certain commodities, including land, gold, and tobacco, connotes social injustice; and using the money for marriage payments, Luo believe, leads to family tragedy. Possessors of bitter money can be purified by blood sacrifice. Linked purchase and sale prohibitions reveal uncertainties and tensions about individualism and betrayal, involving gender, class, lineage, and religion. A comparative chapter draws parallels and contrasts between East African Christian and West African Muslim variants of "devil's money" beliefs, and between African and South American concepts. Shipton's multiparadigmatic theoretical explanation briefly summarizes a century of anthropological thought about African exchange, while integrating ways of understanding rural African economy, politics, and culture.

American Ethnological Society Monograph Series Number 1.
$7.50 to members, $10.00 to all others.
Please enclose payment in U.S. funds, with all orders.

**American Anthropological Association**
**1703 New Hampshire Avenue, N.W.**
**Washington, D.C. 20009**

# Nationalist Ideologies and the Production of National Cultures

## Richard G. Fox, Editor

Through case materials from Romania, Israel, India, Guatemala, Tanzania, and Guyana, this collection of essays investigates and analyzes the development of nationalist ideologies and the production of national culture. Nationalist ideologies, though responsive to material conditions, are nevertheless shown to be contingent and the outcome of historical processes. Each chapter investigates the relationship between nationalist ideology and national culture as contingent in two senses: the outcomes are predetermined neither by a universal form that nationalism must take nor by a compelling cultural tradition.

*American Ethnological Society Monograph Series Number 2.*
*$13.50 to members, $17.00 to all others.*
*Please enclose payment in U.S. funds, with all orders.*

**American Anthropological Association**
**1703 New Hampshire Avenue, N.W.**
**Washington, D.C. 20009**

# At Work in Homes:
# Household Workers in World Perspective

Roger Sanjek and Shellee Colen, Editors

*At Work in Homes* presents a global perspective on household work and those workers who perform it. This collection of case studies from around the world reexamines household work, exposing its distinctive transcultural features and questioning existing generalizations. Collectively, the chapters demonstrate that household work, linked to flows of capital and labor in a global economy, not only provides reproductive labor to employing households but simultaneously reinforces relations of power and inequality in each local society where it is found.

At Work in Homes I: Orientations
*Shellee Colen* and *Roger Sanjek*

Service and Status: Slaves and Concubines in Kano, Nigeria
*Beverly B. Mack*

Maid Servants and Market Women's Apprentices in Adabraka
*Roger Sanjek*

Household Workers in Nyishang, Nepal
*M. T. Cooke*

Ideology and Servitude
*Judith Rollins*

"Housekeeping for the Green Card: West Indian Household Workers, the State, and Stratified Reproduction in New York
*Shellee Colen*

Part of the Household Inventory: Men Servants in Zambia
*Karen Tranberg Hansen*

Female Household Workers in Industrializing Malaysia
*M. Jocelyn Armstrong*

Household Workers in Urban Martinique
*Michel S. Laguerre*

At Work in Homes II: Directions
*Shellee Colen* and *Roger Sanjek*

Household Workers in World Perspective
*Roger Sanjek* and *Shellee Colen*

*American Ethnological Society Monograph Series Number 3*
*$16.00 to members, $21.00 to all others.*
*Please enclose payment in U.S. funds with all orders.*

**American Anthropological Association**
**1703 New Hampshire Ave., N.W.**
**Washington, DC 20009**

# representations of Europe: transforming state, society, and identity

A collection of studies of contemporary Europe, the August 1991 issue of *American Ethnologist* investigates such critical theoretical questions as the relationships between national and local identities, institutional social science and local understandings, and state policy and private life. Issues of gender, class, and economic transformation provocatively shape the articles. Articles include:

Theorizing socialism: a prologue to the "transition"/*Katherine Verdery*

Bartók's funeral: representations of Europe in Hungarian political rhetoric/*Susan Gal*

Pigs, party secretaries, and private lives in Hungary/*Martha Lampland*

The transformation of the Norwegian notion of everyday life/*Marianne Gullestad*

Reweaving the fringe: localism, tradition, and representation in British ethnography/*Jane Nadel-Klein*

Ethnography, fiction, and the meanings of the past in Brittany/*Ellen Badone*

Backward countryside, troubled city: French teachers' images of rural and working-class families/*Deborah Reed-Danahay* and *Kathryn Anderson-Leavitt*

Unwed mothers and household reputation in a Spanish Galician community/*Heidi Kelley*

Constructing the sterile city: pronatalism and social sciences in interwar Italy/*David Horn*

Price: $18.00 ($22.50 nonmembers)
Send payment in U.S. funds with all orders

American Anthropological Association
1703 New Hampshire Ave., NW
Washington, DC 20009

american ethnologist

# New

# from

# the

# *American*

# *Anthropological*

# *Association*

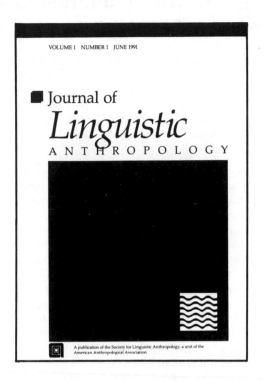

VOLUME 1  NUMBER 1  JUNE 1991

■ Journal of

## Linguistic
A N T H R O P O L O G Y

A publication of the Society for Linguistic Anthropology, a unit of the
American Anthropological Association

The *Journal of Linguistic Anthropology*, the semiannual journal of the Society for Linguistic Anthropology,

■ publishes articles concerned with the central role that language plays in the creation and re-creation of human societies and cultures

■ presents important perspectives on language and culture in an essay format

■ reviews current publications in linguistic anthropology

■ makes the scope and contribution of linguistic anthropology more visible and available to anthropology as a whole

■ is a valuable resource for *all* anthropologists

Editor: Ben Blount, *University of Georgia, Athens*

Subscription price is $30. Subscriptions are also available as a benefit of membership in the American Anthropological Association and the Society for Linguistic Anthropology. For more information, please contact:

American Anthropological Association
1703 New Hampshire Ave., N.W.
Washington, D.C. 20009

# American Anthropological Association
*invites you to join*

The American Anthropological Association, founded in 1902 to advance anthropology in all its aspects, is the world's largest organization of individuals interested in anthropology. Its purposes are to encourage scholarly and professional communication among anthropologists and to promote public understanding of anthropology and its use of anthropology to help address problems. The AAA carries on the tradition of holism. Anyone with a professional and/or scholarly interest in anthropology is invited to join.

Twenty-nine constituent units of the Association represent anthropology's many interests and fields: American Ethnological Society, Archeology Division, Association for Feminist Anthropology, Association for Political and Legal Anthropology, Association of Black Anthropologists, Association of Latina and Latino Anthropologists, Association of Senior Anthropologists, Biological Anthropology Section, Central States Anthropological Society, Council for Museum Anthropology, Council on Anthropology and Education, Council on Nutritional Anthropology, Culture and Agriculture, General Anthropology Division, National Association for the Practice of Anthropology, National Association of Student Anthropologists, Northeastern Anthropological Association, Society for Anthropology in Community Colleges, Society for the Anthropology of Consciousness, Society for the Anthropology of Europe, Society for the Anthropology of Work, Society for Cultural Anthropology, Society for Humanistic Anthropology, Society for Latin American Anthropology, Society for Linguistic Anthropology, Society for Medical Anthropology, Society for Psychological Anthropology, Society for Urban Anthropology, and Society for Visual Anthropology.

Past presidents of the Association include Ruth F. Benedict, Franz Boas, Joseph B. Casagrande, John P. Gillin, Ales Hrdlicka, A. V. Kidder, Clyde Kluckhohn, Alfred L. Kroeber, Ralph Linton, Robert H. Lowie, Margaret Mead, Elsie Clews Parsons, Robert Redfield, Edward Sapir, and Edward H. Spicer.

Every member receives the *Anthropology Newsletter,* published nine times a year, which reports current developments affecting the profession and Association news. Members select unit memberships that include subscriptions to the following journals: *American Anthropologist, American Ethnologist, Ethos, Anthropology and Education Quarterly, Anthropology and Humanism Quarterly, Cultural Anthropology, Medical Anthropology Quarterly,* the *Journal of Linguistic Anthropology,* and *City & Society.* Subscriptions to publications apart from membership are also available. Discounted dues are available to students, international members, and spouses of Members. Members also receive reduced rates for occasional publications, annual meeting registration, placement service, and other programs.

## Join today. You'll be in good company. Write to:

American Anthropological Association
1703 New Hampshire Avenue, N.W.
Washington, DC 20009
202/232-8800